African
Diasporic
Cinema

AFRICAN DIASPORIC CINEMA
AESTHETICS OF RECONSTRUCTION

Daniela Ricci
Translated from French by **Melissa Thackway**
Foreword by **Alexie Tcheuyap**

Michigan State University Press | *East Lansing*

♾ The paper used in this publication meets the minimum requirements of
ANSI/NISO Z39.48-1992 (R 1997) (Permanence of Paper).

Michigan State University Press
East Lansing, Michigan 48823-5245

LIBRARY OF CONGRESS CATALOGING-IN-PUBLICATION DATA
Names: Ricci, Daniela, 1970– author. | Thackway, Melissa, translator.
Title: African diasporic cinema : aesthetics of reconstruction / Daniela Ricci ;
translated from French by Melissa Thackway ; foreword by Alexie Tcheuyap.
Other titles: Cinémas des diaspora noires. English | African humanities and the arts.
Description: East Lansing : Michigan State University Press, 2020.
Series: African humanities and the arts | "Originally published in French under the title
Cinémas des diaspora noires: esthétiques de la reconstruction, Copyright © 2016 LHarmattan."
| Includes bibliographical references and index.
Identifiers: LCCN 2019037506 | ISBN 978-1-61186-364-2 (paperback)
| ISBN 978-1-60917-639-6 | ISBN 978-1-62895-401-2 | ISBN 978-1-62896-402-8
Subjects: LCSH: Blacks in the motion picture industry. | Blacks in motion pictures.
| Motion pictures—Africa. | Africa—In motion pictures.
Classification: LCC PN1995.9.N4 R5313 2020 | DDC 791.43/652996—dc23
LC record available at https://lccn.loc.gov/2019037506

Book design by Charlie Sharp, Sharp Deslgns, East Lansing, Michigan
Cover design by Shaun Allshouse, www.shaunallshouse.com

Visit Michigan State University Press at *www.msupress.org*

To my father

Contents

Foreword

Alexie Tcheuyap

What could Newton I. Aduaka, Balufu Bakupa-Kanyinda, Sarah Bouyain, Alain Gomis, and Haile Gerima possibly have in common? Anyone familiar with non-Hollywood cultural products would probably make use of a quick and easy shortcut and answer that they are all "African" filmmakers. And why not? For the most part, the directors in question have not been wildly successful at the box office in Northern countries and are mostly relegated to the "African" category. This is a useless, reductive, and imaginary place within which to deposit any film director with a distant African ancestor, and whose work includes the African continent as a category of representation. But how do we proceed when a director—for example Alain Gomis or Haile Gerima—is slightly better known, and when his biggest hits (or at least the ones he is most identified with) bear the label "made in Africa" at the Ouagadougou Pan-African Film and Television Festival? Is it time to take a closer look at forms of essentialism that reduce a number of "African" cultural workers to genealogical or racial considerations?

This is one of the questions Daniela Ricci invites us to consider in the reduction-free pages that follow. *African Diasporic Cinema: Aesthetics of Reconstruction* explores the films and trajectories of filmmakers who, because of their respective lives and careers, have found themselves far away from an African "origin." In several respects, that origin is merely umbilical for them. This book sets out to prove the urgent need for a theoretical and pragmatic reconsideration of that body of cinematic work. Daniela Ricci's methodical appraisal shows us that far from being a fixation or a fatality, origin is simply *a moment, a movement, one dot on a circle* that allows the filmmakers she examines to position themselves in a transnational space fertilized by different social, political, and cultural, individual and collective experiences. She wastes no time in pointing out that employing racial considerations as a category of analysis is a fragile and overwhelmingly ineffective practice. And how could it be otherwise?

To better situate these filmmakers in terms of attitude and position, *African Diasporic Cinema* begins with an intelligently brief picture of the cinematic concerns in various African worlds from the era of colonization. This focus on fundamentals then makes it possible for the author to better concentrate on the pertinence of a type of work that had never been explored till now, at least not from this perspective: the itinerary of *reconstruction,* such as *it is presented* in the films of the directors considered, through the use of a *specific cinematic grammar.*

What Daniela Ricci's book offers us is precisely what has been feebly or insufficiently illustrated by critics until now: the elaboration of new epistemologies in order to better understand films produced in different contexts, but which have in common at least two aspects—the diasporic dimension of becoming in the case of the new postcolonial subjects who are their directors, and the fruitful conjunction of these subjects' past, present, and process of becoming. This multiplicity of elements gives them what Daniela Ricci calls "complex identities"—new subjectivities that make it possible for them to overcome "misunderstandings" of several sorts: theoretical, political, and cultural. Again, how could it be otherwise?

Like anyone else with comparable experiences, black diaspora filmmakers are a walking illustration of historical movements that are felt and interpreted as personal and political experiences. But their specificity is due at least to one factor that cannot be underestimated when evaluating their work: their experience of the diaspora is *not* a forced one. In a world where the possibilities of circulating and meeting people are endless, the films of Newton I. Aduaka, Balufu Bakupa-Kanyinda, Sarah Bouyain, Alain Gomis, and Haile Gerima allow us to better measure the extent to which the postcolonial experience is no longer lived out in the ex-colony but beyond it, and often principally in mainland France, England, or the United States. When one is aware that these filmmakers have not lived under the weight of colonial violence and that their personal experience is often enriched by all manner of complexities, one can better understand—and Daniela Ricci shows us this—how their films give life to people who develop other, different subjectivities. This is all the more needed since in reality, the debate on Africa and its cultural production often leaves very little room for interventions venturing beyond the scope of the postcolonial exotic or a simplistic ethnographic digression.

As I noted above, these filmmakers' "diasporic situation" leads them to ask other types of questions and to explore other places where Africa may show itself to be simultaneously present and far away. This book articulates that quite clearly, for these filmmakers draw as much from their place of origin as they do from their new places of residence. It is the reciprocal fertilization between *yesterday and today,* between *elsewhere and here,* that makes it possible to develop new identities and a cinematic aesthetic freed of any genealogical anxiety or superannuated nationalist fervor. At the heart of Daniela Ricci's intellectual project is the exploration of "new syncretic identities," which allow a person to re-situate without necessarily having to give back "different territories, spaces, times, cultures, languages, histories, memories." In view of these challenges, by illustrating some cases of fertile "cultural contamination," this book shows us how the films it covers trace different migratory paths and diasporic experiences that deprioritize facile anthropological or cultural considerations. For Daniela Ricci, it thus becomes a question—and this is perhaps the high point as well as the hidden matrix of her project—of highlighting a community of artists that lives with the awareness of its own impossibility, that is, constantly aware/mindful of its own impossibility.

That is why, in the analysis that follows, there is no quest for an uncertain "African-ness." This option is reinforced by the choice of method at work: a detailed aesthetic analysis combined with an improved evaluation of production methods. This is an approach that allows for a better understanding of the central issues of the book. It also, finally, suggests that the real urgency lies in extracting the African cultural domain from the clutches of a sort of substantialist ontology in order to hand it back, in a burst of near sacrilege, to common usage, which in this case means that just like any other space, Africa may not be dealt with except in terms of what philosophers term a relation.

Outside any fixation on identity, the charm of the films Ricci considers, and of her analysis, is to finally show us how the world, just as the diasporas that constitute it, is in fact a place that houses a community of destiny—a community that is coming, to borrow Giorgio Agamben's term. In this world, subjects are no longer unique but fatally multiple; each of us carries the Other, and the Other carries each of us.

Ultimately, this somehow evokes the world of Rage, Newton Aduaka's character who lives inside all of us because the double, not to mention the multiple, resides in him. In this world, memory, poetry, and politics fertilize the imagination and reveal different cultural belongings (as in Balufu Bakupa-Kanyinda's *Juju Factory*). All in all, *African Diasporic Cinema: Aesthetics of Reconstruction* has the merit of showing us how filmmakers construct contemporary diasporic dynamics through films that teach us about *being* in the present tense, about *here,* without allowing ourselves to be immobilized (or trapped) by the dangers of a problematic essentialism or the risks of dwelling on the past. They represent the future of "African" film. They also represent the future of the contemporary worlds playing out around us, for the era of "authenticities" is past.

Acknowledgments

would like to express my immense gratitude to Jean-Pierre Esquenazi and Françoise Pfaff. I am also most grateful to Raphaëlle Moine and Martin Barnier.

My thanks also to the filmmakers Newton I. Aduaka, Balufu Bakupa-Kany-inda, Haile Gerima, Sarah Bouyain, and Alain Gomis.

Thanks also to Mille-et-Une Productions and to Sophie Salbot (Athénaïse Production).

It would be too long to mention here all the friends who have given me their support, but I particularly would like to thank Thomas Cepitelli and Thierno Ibrahima Dia.

For the richness of the both formal and informal discussions and exchanges that I have had with them, a special mention must also go to the colleagues at the African Federation of Film Critics (FAAC), and to Jean-Pierre Bekolo, Lizelle Bishop, the late Cheick Fantamady Camara, Odile Cazenave, Patrica Célérier, Claire Diao, Boris Boubacar Diop, Ken Harrow, Véronique Joo'Aisenberg, Zeka Laplaine, Stephan Oriach, Aicha Ouattara, Sheila Petty, Pedro Pimenta, Beatriz Leal Riesco, Catherine Ruelle, Nathalie Roncier, Gigi Saronni, Abeye Tedla, Jean-Marie Teno, Melissa Thackway, Jane Thorburn. Not forgetting Caroline Pochon, Mama Keita, Dani Kouyaté, and last but not least, Jean Odoutan.

My warmest thanks to Françoise Braud and Alexie Tcheuyap.

Finally, this book would not have been possible without the support of my family, of Paola Formenti, Jean-François Doussin, and Dominique Chauvin.

Introduction

Contemporary African Diasporic Films

African Diasporic Cinema: Aesthetics of Reconstruction proposes an analysis of the aesthetic strategies adopted in contemporary African diasporic films primarily to express the reconstructing of identity. It focuses on the constantly evolving and plural identities rebuilt after the traumas of history and the epistemic violence inflicted by hegemonic representations.[1] By inscribing these works in the context of their production and in the history of African cinema, this book highlights their specificities and their continuities and ruptures, similarities and differences with the pioneering films of the African continent. The aim, then, is not to limit the diaspora filmmakers' artistic works to a belonging to a continent that they have left for new horizons. Africa for them, as for many other artists, henceforth becomes a site of representation and cultural circulation. Even more so, Africa is perceived from abroad, from a diasporic elsewhere that shapes film practice.

Indeed, the diasporic experience transforms one's existence. It creates "a cut, in the psyche, between a past and a present, a here and a there."[2] It displaces the center and, forcing the self to realign, it forges syncretic new identities. Through migratory movement, people become foreigners, Other—and, in this instance, black. After the fractures of migration, self-reconstruction happens elsewhere, before the Other's gaze—one that is often full of prejudice and contempt.

Through its filmic analysis, the book will explore the African diasporic condition in the Western world. This is characterized by the intersectionality of different factors:[3] being African and bearing the historic memory of the continent; belonging to a black minority in majority white societies; and, finally, having historically been the object of negative, stereotyped representation. This is why questions of self-quest and self-reconstruction are so frequent in African diaspora film production. Its filmmakers nonetheless refuse to remain trapped in the confines of an assigned, rigid identity; they accord a considerable place to cultural blending as both a manifest reality of our times and a source of human and artistic wealth. It is for this reason that this book analyzes contemporary diaspora through the prism of cultural hybridization and the processes of recomposing fragmented identities, out of which new identities emerge.

Beyond their African belongings and their shared experience of displacement, these diasporic filmmakers are notable for the great diversity of their positions and paths. As Canadian academic Sheila Petty points out, "Black diasporic cinema demonstrates a breathtaking range of cultural critique from an amazing innovative array of identities, voices, and cultural influences, each interrogating the notion of identities within often hostile contexts."[4] Having left their respective countries, these filmmakers now reside in Paris, Brussels, Washington, or London, yet continue to travel the world. They can thus be qualified as transcontinental filmmakers,[5] for their lives and works are inhabited by several languages, territories, histories, and memories. They film from the interstices of society, from the cultural melting pots that are the border zones—or contact zones, to borrow Mary Louise Pratt's term[6]—in which cultures and peoples of different origins interact.

Lives, in their transcontinental dimension, draw on diverse cultural heritages and are enriched by passages, frictions, contaminations, and processes of cultural hybridization. The need to express this plurality and hybridity leads these filmmakers to invent composite film styles and innovative aesthetic forms. These are born out of the unpredictability that results from blending, and that enriches artistic creation in the culturally hybrid space of the diaspora. The films studied here place movement, becoming, and the construction and reconstruction of identity at their center. Through this movement, their filmmakers perform a perceptive and ontological decentering, which produces unique contemporary gazes that are both decentered and multifocal. It is my aim here to look through the prism of these gazes.

The Corpus of Works Analyzed

This book is centered on the aesthetic analysis of five emblematic feature-length fiction films from the early 2000s. While each is very different, they may all be defined as auteur films, both written and directed by their makers. These films thus express the filmmaker's own points of view and do so in highly personal cinematographic styles. As the Burkinabè director Gaston Kaboré describes, each filmmaker asserts his or her gaze and "makes films according to what they are" and from their position in the world.[7] But what kinds of films do these unstable positionings at the junction of cultures and memories produce? Each of these films portrays a specific universe, but all express a reconstructing of identity before the complexity of the contemporary world. They are rooted in the present, yet without neglecting the past. They have a multiplicity of characters who reconstruct themselves out of their versatile roots. They portray a plurality of subjectivities, histories, memories, perspectives, language, cultures, territories, and temporalities. They thus challenge a single mindset.

The force of these films also resides in approaches that stem from the convergence of personal experiences and theoretical thought. Indeed, the filmmakers in question address the themes of migration, of representation, and of reconstructing identity both as a social phenomenon and as an element of their own experiences.

In chronological order of production, the films studied here are *Rage* (Newton I. Aduaka, Nigeria/UK, 1999), *L'Afrance* (Alain Gomis, Senegal/France, 2001), *Juju Factory* (Balufu Bakupa-Kanyinda, Democratic Republic of Congo/Belgium/France, 2005), *Teza* (Haile Gerima, Ethiopia/Germany/USA, 2008), and *Notre étrangère* (*The Place in Between*) (Sarah Bouyain, Burkina Faso/France, 2010).

This corpus deliberately includes the films of Sarah Bouyain and Alain Gomis, both of whom were born in France respectively to Burkinabè and Senegalese fathers. They thus represent another diasporic experience. The subjects of their films, the countries in which they are set, and their narrative styles demonstrate the connection that these two filmmakers maintain with their fathers' homelands. Moreover, only one female filmmaker is present in this corpus: Sarah Bouyain. Other African women filmmakers exist, of course,[8] but they mainly work in documentary cinema (for example, Isabelle Boni-Claverie, Angèle Diabang Brener,[9] Anne-Laure Folly, Ramatou Keita, Oswalda Lewat, Katy Lena Ndiaye, Salem Mekuria, Monique Mbeka Phoba, Eléonore Yaméogo, or the late Khady Sylla, who passed away in 2013) and short film (notably Soussaba Cissé,[10] Wanuri Kahiu, Hiwot Admasu Getaneh, Rungano Nyoni, Ngozi Onwurah, Nadine Otsobogo, Asmara Beraki, Elisabeth Bello

Oseini, and Zalissa Zoungrana). As such, their films thus do not enter the present selection of feature-length fiction films. Nor can the works of Safi Faye or Sarah Maldoror, as their works are earlier than the present selection.[11] As for Regina Fanta Nacro, she currently works almost exclusively in Burkina Faso and is thus not a diasporic filmmaker as such, even if she did previously live for periods in Europe. The highly promising works of the (biracial) filmmakers Mati Diop and Dyana Gaye are not included either, as at the time when the research for this book was carried out, they were just preparing their first feature-length films.[12] Since, both are preparing their next films, which in both cases will be feature-length fictions. It must nonetheless be recognized that African and diaspora women filmmakers are still proportionally fewer in number—as women are in cinema in general. This reality is reflected in the present corpus of works, which were not selected on the basis of their auteur's gender.

The films examined here address the complex question of identities torn between a here and there, between belonging and exclusion, between past and future, between fractures and reconstruction. They offer a large array of points of view, both literally and figuratively, as well as geographically, culturally, and aesthetically speaking. The trajectories of their filmmakers, who hail either themselves, or through their parents, from five different African countries (Burkina Faso, Ethiopia, Nigeria, Democratic Republic of Congo, Senegal), are distinct and different, as are their highly contrasting artistic personalities. But all have taken on the risks of rupture, of uprooting, while also, from this distance, ceaselessly exploring their links with Africa. These experiences nourish the inventiveness of their fictional modes and cinematographic styles.

Fictional Worlds, Real Worlds

These fiction films have also been chosen because they are works that take their inspiration from the real world and evoke contemporary realities. Jean-Marie Schaeffer describes the fictional universe as "the real world in model form,"[13] in which the worlds of fiction and the real superpose and interpenetrate.[14] The following chapters will show the extent to which the real permeates the fictions selected here.

The approach I have adopted here draws considerably on the notion of *paraphrase,* as formulated by Jean-Pierre Esquenazi in his book *La Vérité de la fiction.*

Comment peut-on croire que les récits de fiction nous parlent sérieusement de la réalité?[15] This approach focuses on "the cohabitation between fictional universes and the real world."[16] Provided that the fictional text portrays certain fragments of the spectator's real world (what Jean-Pierre Esquenazi describes as *paraphrase*), the spectator may take the resulting fictional universe seriously and learn from it. Jean-Pierre Esquenazi adopts the point of view of the addressee (the spectator) who, depending on their particular *frame of interpretation,* and according to their perspective and experience, appropriates the narrative via the various characters presented. I shall borrow this concept, then, but shall apply it to the filmmakers and their films. In my analyses, I will indeed insist on the intimate relationship between these auteurs and their works—works created out of their experience of the real. Newton Aduaka confirms this: "I make films according to my vision of the world, in a mix of fiction and reality."[17] Similarly, Balufu Bakupa-Kanyinda asserts: "I also understand film as meditative, a sphere between reality and fiction."[18]

The paraphrastic hypothesis differs from what might be considered an autobiographical approach. It involves the invention of a complete fictional universe, the construction of a world within the world. In this sense, the fictions analyzed here can be read as *paraphrases* of part of their auteurs' trajectories and sociocultural realities. This is an almost unconscious process, through which the filmmakers transpose part of their real universes into the fictional world. The fictional worlds constructed are not simply inspired by individual paths; they entail a reorganization of lived realities, which are tested out, and find meaning, in an invented world. It is not a question of giving a sociological reflection of a world, but of shifting from the real world to a fictional one, from one language to another. I shall, more precisely still, show how the filmmakers in question *paraphrase* a segment of their realities and experiences. This process of "translation" gives rise to highly personal cinematic styles capable of illustrating each filmmaker's universe.

In this sense, the characters become "mediators," according to the definition of German philosopher Kate Hamburger[19]—or "intercessors," to use Gilles Deleuze's term[20]—between the fictional universe and the real world. Indeed, Alain Gomis accordingly describes why he chose the American slam artist Saul Williams to play his lead character, Satché, in *Tey* (*Today*), shot in Senegal—Satché, who, after a long period of absence, returns to Dakar, conscious that he will die that night: "In Dakar, he passed as Senegalese, but I also wanted to play on his position as a foreigner. The fact that he doesn't understand the language gives him a very specific way of listening and seeing. For me, he was a good mediator between the spectators and situations, between the places and people."[21] Irreal entities, fictional characters take on characteristics that often reflect "people's real properties and real situations stored in the auteur's memory."[22]

The film analyses will reveal the extent to which fictional characters embody situations, paths, and memories of the filmmakers and their worlds. The protagonists' processes of reconstructing identity call on the past to understand the present. These films thereby offer new perspectives on contemporary societies.

Methodology and Structure

African Diasporic Cinema: Aesthetics of Reconstruction focuses on creative processes in the diaspora and is based on the aesthetic analysis of films. It will also touch on certain questions that are as essential as they are complex, such as the distribution and reception of African films.

This work was first born out of a passion for, and a personal curiosity about, portrayals of the complexity and layered experiences that forge individuals whom we define as culturally mixed. The interdisciplinary and syncretic approach adopted reflects both the complexity and richness of the films studied, and my personal path. That being said, the very nature of the subject would have also imposed this. The works in question are analyzed simply as films, not as "African films." It is important to specify this as this reductive definition has often relegated African films to the margins of cinema and influenced how they are received by spectators and critics.

My methodological approach comprised several phases. First came bibliographical research into various subjects and disciplines: notably film theory, fiction theory, sociology, postcolonial studies, cultural studies, and studies specifically devoted to African and diaspora cinema. Specific references are given over the course of the following chapters. Readers will also find them in the bibliography. In order to select my corpus, I watched many old and recent films, and followed the new releases in festivals and cinemas. Once the corpus was defined, I studied an extract of each work that is representative of the whole film. My analyses operate a constant toing-and-froing between the filmmakers and their works as I have attempted to inscribe each film within the filmmaker's sociocultural milieu. I also interviewed a number of filmmakers, critics, institutional figures, and film professionals, all of whom were involved in one way or another in the making of the films chosen—and others, in order to be able to draw comparisons.[23]

African Diasporic Cinema: Aesthetics of Reconstruction comprises two parts. First, it contextualizes the work and establishes a theoretical framework for the issues that the film analyses then highlight. Next, it offers a detailed analysis of each film and of the aesthetic strategies that their directors devise to express hybridity and to represent the conditions of the African diaspora.

The first part explores the question of the construction of identity. This necessitates considering the question of representation and the place that individuals occupy within the collectivity. It looks into the filmic expression of these questionings and cinematic practices both in Africa and in the diasporic space.

This first section comprises three chapters. The first looks briefly at the question of the evolution of composite identities from a philosophical and sociological point of view, while also taking into account lived experiences through the testimonies of artists, filmmakers, or writers. Attention is always focused on what resonates with, and is the object of, my interest—namely, the African condition and the diasporic experience. The eclecticism of the bibliographic sources—from Amadou Hampâté Bâ to Norbert Elias, Jean-Pierre Esquenazi, Paul Gilroy, Edouard Glissant, Stuart Hall, Axel Honneth, Bernard Lahire, Amin Maalouf, Pierre Sorlin, Charles Taylor, and Gayatri Spivak, to cite but a few—reflects the cultural syncretism that the filmmakers studied here embody and express in their works.

The second chapter focuses on the media and cinematic representation of Africans. It analyzes their influence on the forging of people's personalities and on their daily lives. This chapter is very much inspired by the discourses of Chimamanda Ngozi Adichie, Homi K. Bhabha, Aimé Césaire, Frantz Fanon, Edward Saïd, Ella Shohat, and Robert Stam.

The effects of the Other's gaze and assignations to preconceived identities are a real issue. This terribly destructive exogenous gaze was also conveyed in colonial cinema. Its principal historical and aesthetic characteristics are recalled in this chapter, drawing on the writings of Jean Rouch, Jean-Claude Yrzoala Meda, Victor Bachy, Pierre Haffner, Guido Convents, Nicolas Bancel, Pascal Blanchard, and Femi Okiremuete Shaka. The chapter seeks to allow the reader to measure the ontological importance of the change of paradigm: namely, the new perspectives introduced by African filmmakers' first productions in the Independence era, explored in the following chapter.

The third chapter considers the history of African cinema, from its birth to the present, through the lens of the quest for identity. It seeks to highlight sociopolitical and aesthetic evolutions and their stakes, up until the explicit acknowledgment of hybridity by the diasporic filmmakers of today. The latter give form to the ruptures and reconstructions of identity that are the focus here. The works of Jude Akudinobi, Olivier Barlet, Férid Boughedir, Maria Coletti, Manthia Diawara, Giuseppe Gariazzo, David Murphy, Sheila Petty, Françoise Pfaff, Alexie Tcheuyap, and Franck Ukadike, among others, have nourished this reflection. The final pages focus on contemporary works and their contexts of production. They demonstrate the extent to which these works distance themselves from a certain "calabash cinema": a rural cinema that, while exploiting a certain humorous, naive vein, responded in the name of an original purity, of an immobile Africa, to certain audiences' expectations with archaic and simplistic representations. By highlighting plurality, displacement, and becoming as the structuring dimensions of individuals, the films of the new millennium portray all the contradictions and complexities of defining identities. Today's filmmakers do not renounce their cultural heritage; they adapt it, rather, to the new contexts that arise from permeable and porous cultural frontiers.

Part 2 of the book, which comprises six chapters, is notable for the originality of its approach. It contains shot-by-shot analyses of sequences from the five fiction films selected: *Rage, Juju Factory, Notre étrangère (The Place in Between), L'Afrance,* and *Teza.* The analytical method adopted, qualified here as socio-aesthetic, is outlined in the first chapter. Its originality lies in its being founded on a combination of internal and external analysis, of formal and historical analysis, that brings forth all the facets of the sequence concerned and highlights the *paraphrastic* dimension of these fictional worlds. The final five chapters are each devoted to the analysis of a representative extract of each film. Set in the context of its production, and within the director's oeuvre, each of these extracts is studied in terms of its specific content and formal characteristics.

In *Rage,* I have analyzed the sequence that takes place twenty-five minutes into the film, where the young protagonist, in the throes of an identity crisis, confronts his experiences with those of his elder. In *Juju Factory,* I have chosen the museum-visit sequence approximately an hour and eight minutes into the film. This is the moment when the spectator understands that the writer and publisher characters' different attitudes to the contemporary world lie in their approaches to the past and to history. The extract of *Notre étrangère* corresponds to the moment in which the protagonist is confronted again with her native land—the real and not the fantasized one. In *L'Afrance,* I study the opening sequence, which already in itself presents a certain number of the film's stylistic and narrative complexities. Finally, the extract of *Teza* is the one in which the spectator enters the protagonist's intimate world.

Identities, Representations, and Cinematographic Discourses

1

The Question of Identity

Each of us should be encouraged to accept his own diversity, to see his identity as the sum of all his various affiliations, instead of as only one of them raised to the status of the most important, made into an instrument of exclusion and sometimes into a weapon of war.

—Amin Maalouf, *In the Name of Identity*

Alterity nestles within identity.

—Francesco Remotti, *Contro l'identità*

Composite Identities

Humanity has undoubtedly always posed questions of the singular and the multiple, the same and the other. Tracing the history of this questioning would go well beyond the scope of this book. Looking to the recent period, there are two opposing concepts: for some theorists, identity suggests an essence. Others conceive of it as a constantly reconfigured movement of multiple components in a permanent (re) negotiation with others, society, and its representations.

The first understanding appears outmoded today. I only mention it here for memory's sake. The second constitutes the foundation of this work. It has been articulated in many forms by an array of academics, but also by writers and—as we shall see—by filmmakers. Each brings their own perspective to the common theme. Among the innumerable philosophers and theoreticians to have studied these questions, I shall, where needs require, refer to several more contemporary figures from diverse fields. This eclectic range of sources is justified by the realities of the films studied here.

The multidimensional nature of identity is a key factor. Sociologist Bernard Lahire suggests that the "self" is plural, comprising a multiplicity of aspects and variables, the onus shifting depending on the context and specific situation.[1] "The plural being" traverses diverse contexts and universes of socialization; it thus conveys multiple experiences. This does not produce fragmented personalities, however; it is the very path to constituting the person through an ensemble of "roles" that they are led to play in the "staging of daily life," to borrow a metaphor dear to Erving Goffman.

The Malian philosopher Amadou Hampâté Bâ also points to this plurality, using the Bambara saying "Maa ka Maaya ka sa a yere kono" (The persons of the person are many in a person).[2] In Fula and Bambara, there are indeed two words to define the person: for the Fulani, *Neddo* and *Neddaaku;* for the Bambara, *Maa* and *Maaya.* The first word signifies "the person." The second, "the persons of the person," evoking the multiple facets that constitute a human being.

Yet Amin Maalouf goes a step further, claiming, "the more ties I have the rarer and more particular my own identity becomes."[3] This strikes me as particularly pertinent in our times in which the question of identity has come strikingly to the fore, but is often reduced to a sectarian conception of identity—a reductive conception that tends, on the contrary, to crush the individual. Our specificity is determined by the combination of our diverse cultural belongings, our past experiences, and our current situation in society.

Identity, as it is understood here, is relational and perpetually evolving. Every individual must indeed constantly redefine himself in "interdependence" with society, to borrow the expression proposed by Norbert Elias.[4] The great Martinican writer Edouard Glissant spoke, for his part, of a rhizomic identity. The rhizome—a concept borrowed from Deleuze and Guattari—is a "root, but one set out to meet other roots, so what becomes important is not a so-called absolute of each root, but the mode, the manner in which it enters into contact with other roots: the Relation."[5] This image puts the accent on being confronted with others, and on a dialogue between cultures. It is, in the words of Sheila Petty, an "open, multidimensional, polyvalent conception of identity."[6]

For the American anthropologist Clifford Geertz, then, human beings are "incomplete or unfinished animals,"[7] who are socially constructed through specific cultures and milieus. If they cross the frontiers of diverse sociocultural spaces, it is the ensemble of these contexts that contribute to forming their specific identity. Everyone's uniqueness takes form in relation to the diversity of others.

Individual Specificity and Place in Today's Cultural Melting Pot

Everyone thus enacts their specificity within society, and artistic creation depends on the position of the artist. The film sociologist Pierre Sorlin notes that "the auteur speaks from the place that he or she occupies in the world."[8] Sorlin highlights the extent to which certain (personal and collective) experiences constitute what the auteur seeks to express. Before presenting the films selected here and their diegetic universes, let us pause an instant to consider the cultural and sociohistorical contexts in which their auteurs evolve.

The personalities and works of African diasporic filmmakers are marked by the memory of the traumatic collective experiences of slavery and colonization, and by the racial discriminations that continue to profoundly affect their existences. These directors occupy a specific place in the world, based on diverse factors. Beyond their individual characteristics (age, sex, gender, social status in their countries of origin and adoption, ideology, etc.), they are united by their being born and structured in an African country—and notably a former colony. They all grew up with the sentiment of belonging to a culture deemed inferior, with all the consequences that this implies in the structuring of one's personality. Similar issues apply, for that matter, to the filmmakers born in Europe to African parents, as John Akomfrah, a Ghanaian director living in London, describes:

> However much you become part of this place, you never quite forget that you have this double consciousness, in this sense of being both inside and outside of the society at the same time. Because even if you are part of this society you sense that

your parents are not, or your grandparents are not, or your uncles. . . . You know very early that there is a complicated way of belonging to this place if you are from a post-migrant community.[9]

Secondly, simply by virtue of crossing a border, migration (often to a former colonizing country) transforms an individual from national citizen into foreigner. This leads them not only to encounter other societies, cultures, languages, and traditions, but also other gazes. This displacement causes a change of both social status and self-perception. Furthermore, the African filmmakers who come to Europe or North American "become" black, perceiving themselves for the first time as such, with all the historical and social baggage that relates to this condition.

Let us now consider how these factors influence artistic creation.

Being African

I'm African, I come from that people who have been to a certain degree de-culturalized.

—Newton Aduaka, in *Imaginaires en exil* (documentary)

You can't be a filmmaker if you don't know history.

—Haile Gerima, *Imaginaires en exil* (documentary)

I make cinema for memory's sake.

—Mahamat Saleh Haroun, *Bye Bye Africa*

Being African, and what that might signify today, is indissociable from history. Slavery, the slave trade, and colonization have all left devastating scars on the populations victim to them. In collective history, slavery operated as a first denial of Africans' identity and humanity. The erasing of names and reduction of Africans to objects triggered self-contempt, as the Burkinabè historian Joseph Ki-Zerbo clearly writes:

It was from the moment that, taking advantage of their military superiority, [others] decided to make black people slaves, the contempt was born and black people entered this dynamic, this dialectic that consists of despising oneself. From that moment on, things went awry.[10]

Next, in the name of so-called Western superiority, colonization accomplished its "civilizing mission" by imposing its culture and language on indigenous populations, perceived as (good) savages, childlike, ignorant, backwards, situated "outside of history,"[11] naive, and emotive (reason being considered a Hellenic prerogative), as Senghor astonishingly claimed.[12]

It also introduced an emblematic hierarchy of different languages, cultures, values, symbols, and memories. Perpetrating widespread, extreme violence, colonial conquest profoundly perturbed collective representations and made the process of restoring self-confidence and personal and social dignity a necessity. Terribly damaging to the human spirit, this historical institutionalized violence still affects the artistic creation of Africa and its diasporas.

For all these reasons, the processes of reconstruction at the center of the films chosen here for analysis generally take the form of challenging dominant historical narratives. That is why history, memory, the colonial past, and diverse forms of resistance to these invasions are very present in a number of African and diaspora films. This shall be seen, for example, in *Juju Factory, Teza,* and *L'Afrance,* but is also the case in *Pièces d'identités,*[13] *Emitai,*[14] *Sarraounia,*[15] *Heritage Africa!,*[16] *Afrique, je te plumerai . . . ,*[17] *Sankofa,*[18] and *Keïta! L'héritage du griot.*[19] History's denial of African cultures has had such consequences that the key existential questions shared by all human beings are particularly pressingly posed here. Aimé Césaire's "most worthy question," "Who and what are we?"[20] is a matter of urgency.

The paths to reconstruction cannot operate amidst amnesia; they are rooted in a process of remembering, represented in narratives in which the past constantly returns through fragmented montages that disrupt chronology. The latter is at times completely jumbled (achronological, as in *L'Afrance*). But its construction may also be a spiral (*Teza*), or be split between reality and the imaginary/imagination (*Juju Factory*), between memory and amnesia (*Ezra,* N. Aduaka, 2007), or between personal histories and History (*Kinshasa Palace,* Zeka Laplaine, 2006). Finally, recourse to archive images may disrupt the linearity of the fiction.

Sheila Petty refers to these as "strategies of remembrance," a process of recovery and reconstruction that, surpassing the question of origins, is forged in an emerging space between the shifting notions of nation and identity.[21] The urgency of this strategy of remembrance is accentuated in the diasporic space, in which premigratory experiences further complexify the present.

Migrations and Diasporas

When you arrive in this new place, you can't quite forget where you came from.

—John Akomfrah

Even if I have chosen to live in France, I cannot forget the part of myself that is back there, those founding roots, that memory which remains very much alive despite exile.

—Mahamat Saleh Haroun

In the land of others, you are first and foremost confronted with yourself.

—Alain Gomis

Diasporic Africans must reconstruct themselves in new geographic, social, and cultural territories. They arrive with their cultural baggage, nourished by the layering of diverse experiences, histories, and memories. This at-times disorienting challenge to the self can stimulate artistic creativity.

If, generally speaking, the experience of exile is above all individual, it is not difficult to recognize the polycentric nature of the African diaspora's experiences, which are both collective and individual, as the American academic James Clifford demonstrates, each diasporic experience being lived by each person according to their personality and subjectivity.[22] Jean-Pierre Esquenazi also stresses this point, so as to avoid any misunderstanding: "The milieu's problems are not experienced in the same way by different individuals. Apprehending these milieus as the source of inventiveness does not mean ignoring human particularity."[23]

The notion of diaspora is a vast one, and different approaches to it exist according to various philosophical or ideological currents—hence the importance of specifying my own position. Following Christine Chivallon's analysis, one may observe the contrasting positions of French sociologist Alain Médam and the Jamaican-born British sociologist Stuart Hall.[24] Adopting an essentialist view, Alain Médam takes the Caribbean diaspora as an example of failure, describing it as "unstable, precarious, venturesome, fluid, amorphous,"[25] whereas Stuart Hall celebrates it for the very same reasons, positing cultural hybridity and mobility as positive values. It is interesting to note that Alain Médam is of Jewish origin (the archetypal diasporic people) and Stuart Hall West Indian. Beyond the complexity—and at times the violence—of cultural mixing, the West Indies can be considered as the site par excellence of multicultural richness, and the birthplace of *Créolité,* or, in other words, of "an interior attitude" that surpasses African, European, or Asian origins.[26]

I adhere principally to the concept of a hybrid and heterogeneous diaspora, in reference to the works of Stuart Hall and Paul Gilroy, the leading cultural studies and Black Diaspora thinkers. For Stuart Hall, the diaspora may be variable and changing, and in that respect echoes social mobility. It draws on a "necessary heterogeneity and diversity," thanks to "a conception of 'identity' which lives with and through, not despite, difference; by *hybridity.*"[27] A few years later, Paul Gilroy offered a new vision: that of a *Black Atlantic,* as his book was titled, in which he highlighted the plural, syncretic, and intercultural nature of the hybrid diaspora.[28] He defines the diaspora as stemming from the desire to transcend both the structures of the nation and the constraints of ethnicity and national particularism, thereby engendering a fluid identity.[29] The notions of plurality, syncretism, fluidity, and transcendence are particularly useful in the understanding of diasporic identity as complex and constantly shifting—a "process never completed."[30] Hall even conjures a warlike metaphor, referring to a "strategic and positional" concept.[31]

Cultural-studies approaches are particularly of interest here for their transdisciplinary nature and their ability to challenge the power of dominant cultural values. From a decentered perspective, cultural studies, like postcolonial studies, offer theories that can be applied to African diasporic filmmakers. These thinkers indeed adopt an approach that combines personal experience and theoretical reflection, enabling them to operate a perceptive decentering vis-à-vis a single Eurocentric vision, to change epistemological paradigms, and to propose new perspectives. They thereby deconstruct the truths that, eluding diverse subjectivities, claimed to be universal. Edward Said, Stuart Hall, Paul Gilroy, Avtar Brah, and Homi K. Bhabha, among others, base their theories on their own lives, migratory experiences, and the specific conditions that obliged them to constantly redefine themselves at the intersection of different cultural contexts. Moreover, just like the filmmakers in question here, having left their home countries to travel the world, these theoreticians are immersed in different languages, traditions, cultures, and heritages. The Palestinian American Edward W. Said felicitously illustrates the notion of "hyphenated citizens." The desire to hyphenate also inhabits the diasporic filmmakers studied in this book, who, caught between the diverse cultural belongings that they constantly traverse, find themselves perpetually faced with processes of transformation and reassembling of identities. The fact of being black, or nonwhite, places them in a specific symbolic position that is generally minoritarian in the host society, leading them to make this margin their privileged position of observation.

Being Black

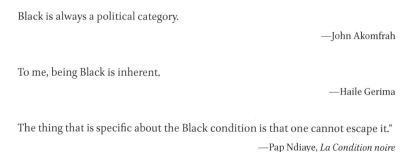

> Black is always a political category.
>
> —John Akomfrah

> To me, being Black is inherent.
>
> —Haile Gerima

> The thing that is specific about the Black condition is that one cannot escape it."
>
> —Pap Ndiaye, *La Condition noire*

Displacement causes transformations and new combinations of people's being. In emigrating to the West, Africans not only become foreigners; they also become black. In accounts of their personal paths, it is not unusual to hear that they only perceived of themselves as black once they left the African continent. Haile Gerima indeed describes this: "White people make me Black, I came [to America] as an Ethiopian, I became Black."[32] Dani Kouyaté also recounts: "I questioned myself what it meant to be Black as soon as I arrived in Europe."[33] The same goes for Abderrahmane Sissako: "In Russia, I felt Other, Foreign, Black for the first time."[34] A black person thus becomes black when others consider them so. Triggering an ensemble of stereotypes and clichés, the term "black" thus becomes a category of representation that bears the burden of the social imagination. Mixed-race people are also concerned by the "black question." While their questioning of identity is even more complex—they may not be able to completely recognize themselves in either of their parents or in both at the same time—they share the "nonwhite" identity that, in Western societies, appears as different from the "norm"—a "difference" that is marginalizing and a source of discrimination.

The "black condition"[35] is based on imaginaries, on prejudices that weigh heavily on self-perception, and on the place occupied in society. Indeed, among the different visible characteristics that found human identity, some—such as skin color—at times imperiously predominate and give rise to a considerable social connotation.

As Jean-Louis Sagot-Duvauroux writes: "Black is a color that is almost everywhere synonymous with subalternity."[36] A weighty symbolic frontier separates black and white people. This frontier—a taboo in discourses, but which does not change the state of things—can be surpassed but not erased. Although identities are not limited to ethnic origins, the "black question" occupies a prime place in many films precisely because it has a social and symbolic valency that is still deeply influential today.

This is clearly illustrated in Jean Odoutan's comedy *La Valse des gros derrières* (*The Waltz of Large Behinds,* 2004), in which Akwélé (Mata Gabin)—"a bootylicious black woman who goes by the nickname of Immeasurable Antelope—tells Rod (Jean Odoutan), who passes himself off as a lawyer: 'It's rare to meet a lawyer in Paris, in the Barbès hood, and a Black lawyer at that!'" The highly explicit response ("You know, Akwélé, you can be a Black lawyer in a country like France and not deny your roots") sounds more like an invitation to construct a future society than an observation. The surprise comes from that fact that it is rare to see an African lawyer on French screens, the roles attributed to black people still remaining rare and highly stereotypical.[37]

"When it doesn't specifically state "black" in a screenplay, the role is automatically for a white person," claims the Congolese director and actor Zeka Laplaine.[38] The few rare exceptions, such as Échappée belle (*Eva & Léon,* Émilie Cherpitel, France, 2015), in which the Nigerian musician Keziah Jones plays protagonist Clotilde Hesmes's lover without his (small) role being ethnically characterized, only confirm the rule. This absence on cinema screens reflects the marginal place assigned to black people in white-majority society. It is against this invisibility that Alain Gomis started making films: "I wanted to tell stories that were not told, to portray people who were not seen."[39]

Black people's social position in Europe is at the heart of a series of films, whether set in London (*Rage,* or *Coffee Colored Children*), Brussels (*Juju Factory*), Paris (*L'Afrance*), or its suburbs (*Djib*).

To take one example, *Djib* (Jean Odoutan, 2000) is a social comedy set in Asnières-sur-Seine, in a neighborhood where Odoutan lived at the time of making the film. It portrays the eponymous protagonist's struggles to exist. A black teen living in the working-class suburbs, in search of himself and wanting to lead an honest life, finds himself confronted with the vision and prejudices of others (his friends, the imam, his grandmother, his girlfriend, the local youth workers, and so on), who all try to shape him as they see fit. *Djib* also includes animated discussion about Negritude, the group of adults' subject of predilection. Odoutan explores these questions in upbeat dialogues, in a half-burlesque, half-eloquent style. In almost all of his comedies, in which he films himself to better subvert the clichés, his sociological gaze goes hand-in-hand with a subtle irony and at times bitter humor. In his short film *Le Réalisateur nègre* (*The Negro Director,* 1997), whom he plays with his typical comic verve, he pokes fun at the recurrent conflicts between Africans and West Indians. The embracing of both black *and* French identity is at the heart of all his films.

Dani Kouyaté films similar reflections in his documentary *Souvenirs encombrants d'une femme de ménage* (*Burdening Memories of a Cleaning Lady*), which tells the story of Thérèse Bernis, a ninety-year-old Guadeloupean woman. Beyond the suffering of Thérèse, who never felt "French like everyone else," this film also reveals her strength and hopes. The synopsis begins: "French *but* Black, free but the descendant of slaves . . ."[40] The importance of this "but" resides in the fact that French society does not yet appear ready to embrace its multiple identities, as is shown in the question posed by Isabelle Boni-Clavérie in her documentary *Trop Noire pour être Française?* (*Too Black to Be French?*).

The same problems, cultural specificities notwithstanding, can be found in other European countries with black minority populations. In her short film *Coffee Colored Children* (1988), filmmaker Ngozi Onwurah drew on her own experience (born in 1964 in Nigeria to a Scottish mother and a Nigerian father, she then moved to England) to portray the difficulties of biracial children growing up in white London neighborhoods.

In the Eyes of Others

It is often the way we look at other people that imprisons them within their own narrowest allegiances.

—Amin Maalouf, *In the Name of Identity*

The first encounter with a white man oppresses [the Negro] with the whole weight of his blackness.

—Frantz Fanon, *Black Skin, White Masks*

Constructing oneself is strongly linked to the perception and knowledge of Others, as Edward W. Said stressed in his founding postcolonial studies work,[41] and V. Y. Mudimbe in *The Invention of Africa.*[42] The indissoluble link between identity and social recognition has notably been theorized by Axel Honneth,[43] who reactualized the theories of the Frankfurt School. He notably demonstrates that a society's well-being and justice depend on its ability to guarantee the "conditions of mutual recognition in which the construction of personal identity and, in the process, individual fulfillment, can take place."[44] Moreover, as the Canadian philosopher Charles Taylor states:

> our identity is partly shaped by recognition or its absence, often by the *mis*recognition of others, and so a person or a group of people can suffer real damage, real distortion, if the people or society around them mirror back to them a confining or demeaning or contemptible picture of themselves.[45]

Lack of recognition can become a form of violence and social oppression. Stuart Hall describes how dominant regimes of representation have operated so that black people too perceive themselves as Other.[46] It is this question of the representations that the Other projects, with all their psychological and social consequences, that I shall now focus on through the highly influential prism of cinema.

CHAPTER 2

Cinematographic Representations

Representations and Their Consequences

By resolving the problem of images, we resolve the rest.

—Jean-Pierre Bekolo, interview with Olivier Barlet

elieving, as Stuart Hall does, that identities "are constituted within, not outside, representation,"[1] it is useful to pause for a moment to consider the question of the cinematographic representation of Africans. Africa and its peoples were first represented by Others in stereotypical, reductive, and distorted images. The "symbolic" violence described by Pierre Bourdieu, and at the heart of Eurocentric discourse, has had devastating consequences on the construction of imaginaries, on relations of social domination, and on people's daily lives. Similarly, the lack of valorizing images and the erasure operated by the dominant media have nourished the collective unconscious and forged social constructions.

By historical necessity, Africa's filmmakers are highly aware of this. One of the pioneers, Mauritania's Med Hondo, stated that "You cannot defend your dignity if you don't see yourself on the screen. . . . If Africans don't see images of themselves, they remain dominated, alienated."[2] Burkinabè director Gaston Kaboré echoed this: "All individuals have a vital need for their own reflection, for their own image, for a major part of the equation of existence lies in the ability to establish a dialogue with this image in order to question it, to measure oneself against it."[3]

Indeed, the all too rare presence of black and African people on the screen and the deformation of this image when it does exist have created a void, an impossibility of recognizing oneself. A certain identification with Western heroes thus occurs. In his seminal work *Black Skin, White Masks*, Frantz Fanon analyzes the degree to which black West Indians, like Africans, were confronted with "an all-white truth."[4] This generated an interiorization of a sense of inferiority and a lack of self-esteem, which nourished a mimetic dream of a "white mask." More than a kind of "schizophrenia," this provokes a triple fragmentation: between what one is, what one dreams of being, and the image of the self projected by the Other. This cultural domination begins right from childhood. Fanon took the example of the many Tarzan-inspired stories, "put together by white men for little white men,"[5] but eagerly consumed by children in the colonies:

> The Wolf, the Devil, the Evil Spirit, the Bad Man, the Savage are always symbolized by Negroes or Indians; since there is always identification with the victor, the little Negro, quite as easily as the little white boy, becomes an explorer, an adventurer, a missionary "who faces the danger of being eaten by the wicked Negroes.[6]

Taking *Tarzan* as a metonym for stereotyped imaginaries, Robert Stam and Ella Shohat reference not only Fanon, but also Edward Said and the director Haile Gerima, all of whom "have . . . registered the impact of Tarzan on their impressionable young selves."[7] Haile Gerima recounts that as children, he and his friends reproduced what they saw at the cinema:

> We used to play cowboys and Indians . . . whenever Africans sneaked up behind Tarzan, we would scream our heads off, trying to warn him that "they" were coming! It was the politically and psychologically damaging exploitation of my very being.[8]

These are not isolated instances. Before the rarity of black heroes to identify with, African American director Melvin Van Peebles also recounts the shame felt when he caught himself wanting to identify with Tarzan.[9] This mimetic desire is also remarkably illustrated in *Le Retour d'un aventurier* (*Return of an Adventurer*, Moustapha Alassane, 1966), in which the hero, Jimmy, returning to his village in Niger after a trip to the United States, brings his friends back cowboy outfits.

It was precisely to fight against this interiorization of the Other's exoticizing and objectifying gaze that Haile Gerima made a short film when he was a student, emblematically entitled *The Death of Tarzan*. He states: "When I did the film, I thought that was only my problem. Now I find a Native American who has a problem with Tarzan . . . , I found a Mexican who has a problem with Tarzan, I found women who have problems with Tarzan. I said: "Hey, I think I'm [going] in the right direction!"[10] The problem lies less in the existence of this type of Tarzanesque image in which Africa and Africans were nothing more than an exotic backdrop, but rather in the lack of other references. Writer Chimamanda Ngozi Adichie's "The Danger of a Single Story" TED talk demonstrates this well.[11] Also basing her reflections on her personal experience as a young Nigerian brought up on Western stories and references, she describes the danger of wallowing in ignorance when one contents oneself with a single story about other countries or peoples. She insists: "The single story creates stereotypes, and the problem with stereotypes is not that they are untrue, but that they are incomplete." The effects of the unchanging stereotyped media representations that persist today are all the more damaging considering that they come after the films, exhibitions, and shows of the colonial era. Let us not forget that those were times of "human zoos," the clown Chocolate, and "Banania" images.

To better understand the remarkable change of viewpoint that African and diasporic filmmakers have brought, it is useful to briefly recontextualize colonial cinema.

Colonial Cinema

As Nwachukwu Frank Ukadike remarked, colonial discourse (cinema included) forged a skewered perspective through which to observe the African continent.[12] Colonizers used the cinema, like all forms of power, to influence consciences and minds. Colonial cinema constantly translated into images the ideology of a Europe whose mission it was to come to "civilize" a continent of "savages" and "barbarians." Colonial films reflected racist and paternalistic mentalities, "always in glory of the colonizers and their enterprises."[13] This perspective clearly highlights the traumatic nature of colonization in its exercising of a normative cultural power. The colonial films made by Europeans fulfilled a dual function: educating the "natives," on the one hand, and showing European audiences the childlike, "savage" populations who needed to be "civilized" by "white saviors" on the other. Secondarily, they countered the negative image of Europeans conveyed in certain Western films.[14] Finally, these films responded to fantasies of possessing far-flung territories and to the desire for exoticism.

Without wanting to generalize, and even though each colonizing nation had its own modes of cinematographic production, a recurrent aesthetic approach can be found in colonial films. The "natives" are often filmed as anonymous entities, in indistinct group shots from behind or in profile, in figurations that are reminiscent of anthropometric images. They are often shown naked to insist on their "primitive" status, or in torn clothes. Often, they are positioned to seem smaller than the colonizers, framed on the ground (in a state of nature and animality) or in high-angle shots (low-angle shots, which accentuate humanity and noblesse, being reserved for colonizers). When a "native" is filmed in close-up, facial shots generally accentuate physical racial stereotypes. The opening of *L'Homme du Niger* (*Forbidden Love,* Jacques de Baroncelli, 1940) is a perfect example. The film starts with a short image of an empty expanse of an arid, deserted terrain when suddenly colonizers ride into the frame on horseback. The following excerpt shows a local woman sitting on the ground, bare-breasted, an expression of suffering on her face, crushed by a high-angle shot that speaks realms about the spirit of the film. Then we see other locals, still shot in high-angle, shown as an anonymous mass of individuals waiting for the foreigners' help.

Belgian Colonial Cinema

In the Belgian colonies, cinema was produced by the Bureau du film et de la photo (Film and Photo Office)—which shut in 1960 with the advent of Independence—and by the Centre congolais pour l'action catholique au cinéma (CCACC, Congolese Center for Catholic Action Cinema).[15] The latter was placed under the direction of Father Alexandre Van den Heuvel, producer of educational films and newsreels. In Congo, Rwanda, and Burundi, the educational and religious were closely connected. The force of Catholic action in Congo is also explained by the existence of a concordat between the Congo Free State (under the sovereignty of Leopold II of Belgium, from 1885 to 1908) and the Vatican, which entrusted Catholic missions with the task of educating the local populations.

A form of apartheid existed in Congo. Citing Van Bever, Manthia Diawara recounts that in 1945, the Belgian government promulgated a law reserving cinema access to Europeans and Asians only.[16] Furthermore, a 1936 decree authorized only films approved by the colonial government in Congo, Rwanda, and Burundi.[17] According to Jean Rouch, the Film and Photo Office's governmental films were "of a confounding naiveté and paternalism. The African is always represented as an overgrown child who must be taught everything."[18] Many colonial films produced in Congo (today's DRC), Rwanda, and Burundi celebrated Leopold II and the courage of the Belgian colonizers and their antislavery crusades. Attempts at local resistance were portrayed as acts of violence and insubordination. It will later be seen how Balufu Bakupa-Kanyinda offers an iconic counterpoint to the figure of Leopold II in *Juju Factory,* as does Mweze Ngangura in *Pièces d'identités (Identity Papers).*

Portuguese Colonial Cinema

Film history in the Portuguese colonies was different. The Portuguese limited their action to producing monthly news programs relaying colonial propaganda, and to shooting pornographic films produced directly in the colonies by the Portuguese and South Africans. In the 1960s and 1970s, the Seventh Art was used above all by the liberation movements. They—and notably the Partido Africano de Indêpendencia da Guinea Bissau e do Cabo Verde (PAIGC) in Guinea Bissau and Cape Verde, Frente de Libertação do Moçambique (FRELIMO) in Mozambique, and the Movimento Popular de Libertação de Angola (MPLA) in Angola—called on foreign militant filmmakers. French, Dutch, Swedish, Yugoslavian, Cuban, Brazilian, Italian, and American filmmakers were invited by the liberation movements to film the revolution. Films such as *Venceremos,* shot in 1965 by the Yugoslav Dragutin Popovic; *Dez dias com os guerrilheiros de Moçambique,* shot in 1967 by the Italian Franco Cigarini; *Viva Frelimo!,* shot in 1971 by the Russians Leonid Maksimov and Yuri Yegorov; or *A luta continua,* shot in 1972 by the African American Robert Van Lierop, backed the liberation struggles. The aim of these documentaries was to inform the rest of the world about what was happening and raise the population's awareness of the importance of education—until then neglected by the Portuguese. Often, the revolutionary leaders were interviewed in the films directly, which thus served as an echo chamber for their actions. These first productions made in the Portuguese colonies were thus "guerrilla" films, in the spirit of Fernando Solanas and Octavio Getino's Third Cinema.[19]

After Independence, and despite their lack of means, these governments continued to believe in the importance of cinema. As producer-director Pedro Pimenta rightly indicates, Mozambicans, who were predominantly rural, were less alienated than others by dominant imperialist cinema, primarily because they had no access to screenings.[20]

Nineteen seventy-five, the year of Independence, marked the golden age of Angolan cinema. Film production also continued in Mozambique, thanks mainly to the National Institute of Cinema (INC), set up in 1976. This illustrates the importance that the Mozambican leaders accorded cinema in their country's development, to fight against capitalist imperialism and to help decolonize minds. Pedro Pimenta stresses that one of the objectives of the INC was to set up a national distribution system to stop the country depending on foreign distributors.[21] Mozambique was a leading force among the former Portuguese colonies, however. In Guinea Bissau, it was not until *Mortu nega* (Flora Gomes, 1987) that an African made a film.

While not all Western filmmakers relayed exoticizing or colonial representations of Africans—the exceptions of René Vautier and Chris Marker come to mind, for example—cinema in general fixed stereotypical images. Hierarchical relations between black and white people were represented as natural.

Italian Colonial Cinema

Italian colonial cinema,[22] which was limited in terms of production and not very influential,[23] was aimed primarily at entertaining audiences, even if it is easy to detect its racist, Catholic, patriotic propaganda. Silent films already played on the exotic imaginary. Later, cinema was put at the service of fascism, especially from the 1920s onwards when the young Italian nation sought to redeem itself after defeat in the First World War. In the 1930s, films served the colonial empire with the aim of spreading the ideology of the regime and demonstrating the supremacy of Italian culture over the colonized populations. One must not forget the role played from 1922 to 1930 by the Luce Institute (the regime's educational body, before it became an autonomous organization). One must remember too that the fascist regime invested in cinema—above all as a means of distraction, in both senses of the word (entertainment, and a diversion from more pressing questions). At the time of the Italo-Ethiopian War (1935–1936), various crews were sent with equipment to screen newsreels and documentaries. From the 1930s onwards, the aim—particularly in Ethiopia—was to propagate the ideology of the fascist regime, which portrayed itself as the descendant of the great Roman Empire. Films such as *Scipione l'Africano* (*Scipio Africanus: The Defeat of Hannibal,* Carmine Gallone, 1937) testify to this.

Maria Coletti indeed claims that, in Italian colonial films, indigenous men were often (re)presented as dangerous rebels, or as submissive, willing to serve, and self-sacrificing.[24] Certain films have been lost. Among those that have survived, *Lo squadrone bianco* (*White Squadron,* Augusto Genina, 1936) portrays virile and macho heroes who sacrifice themselves for their colonial ideals. Others, such as *Sotto la Croce del Sud* (*Under the Southern Cross,* Guido Brignone, 1938), portrayed the Italian colonialist as benevolent and loved by the Africans (*Italiani brava gente* was the message). Women, perceived as seductresses, were either seen as objects to satisfy the colonialists' desire or, on the contrary, as a source of temptation to be resisted, in the name of racial purity. To all intents and purposes, the portraits of "Black Venuses" can also be read as a metaphor for the African territories, desired and there to be taken. In the colonial era, Italian filmmakers also saw Africa as a mythical, folkloric place, the ideal setting for their adventure and travel films, thereby satisfying their appetite for primitive exoticism.

The films of the colonial era also embodied the spirit of revenge that inhabited Italy, which was less culturally and politically influential than other European powers. The Italians did not develop an industry that left a notable trace in its former colonies.

British Colonial Cinema

The British colonial government used films firstly for educational purposes, and this as early as the 1920s.[25] Productions focusing on health education were made under the direction of the British doctor William Sellers. Next, films sought to demonstrate the benefits of colonization and to combat the influence that damaging images of Europeans in Hollywood movies might have on colonial subjects. Later still, the Bantu Educational Cinema Experiment (active from 1935 to 1937, under the direction of Leslie Allen Notcutt) and the Colonial Film Unit (active from 1939 to 1955) were set up. During the Second World War, the Colonial Film Unit above all produced war propaganda films, backing the intervention of the British army. After the war, the aim was to celebrate European interventions in the conflict. Manthia Diawara states: "The Bantu Cinema Experiment and the Colonial Film Unit were in many ways paternalistic and racist. They wanted to turn back film history and develop a different type of cinema for Africans because they considered the African mind too primitive to follow the sophisticated narrative techniques of mainstream cinema."[26] Traces of such racist principles can also be found in Notcutt's book *The African and the Cinema.*[27] The Colonial Film Unit's mission was above all to censor the films believed to discredit the British army or to encourage possible reactions against white people.

While British productions ended with Independence, French intervention in the production of African films instead became more active, in the form of the provision of equipment, funding, postproduction (often carried out in France), and via the direct intervention of French technicians on film shoots.

French Colonial Cinema

In the French colonies, production was left to private initiative, which saw it as a source of revenue, and which also explains why Africans were permitted into movie theaters. Locals went both to screenings of (predominantly French) auteur films in French cultural centers and to essentially European and American commercial shows: thrillers, Westerns, or adventure movies. French directors also shot films in Africa. As Jean-Claude Meda remarks, these films essentially conveyed a series of clichés, in which indigenous populations were "presented as savage hordes who killed and ate one another. Colonial conquests were thus portrayed as humanistic; they were presented as efforts to pacify these populations."[28] Meda illustrates his analysis with several eloquent titles: *Au pays des sorciers et de la mort* (*In the Land of Witch Doctors and Death,* Marquis de Wavrin, 1933), *Chez les cannibales* (*In the Land of Cannibals,* Martin and Osa Johnson, 192–), *Chez les chasseurs de têtes des mers du Sud* (*In the Land of South Sea Head-Hunters,* Martin and Osa Johnson, 1923), *Chez les mangeurs d'hommes* (*In the Land of Man-Eaters,* André-Paul Antoine and Robert Lugeon, 1927–1928), *Chez les buveurs de sang: le vrai visage de l'Afrique* (*In the Land of Blood-Drinkers: Africa's True Face,* Baron Gourgaud, 1930–1931).

Moreover, there was no place for local reflection in the French colonies, where the Laval Decree (11 March 1934) prevented any non-authorized film shoots. Named after the then minister of colonies, this decree meant that any filming in French West Africa had to be approved by the governor. Films had to follow a pre-agreed scenario and be shot in the presence of a representative of the colonial authorities. According to Paulin Soumanou Vieyra, the purpose of the Laval Decree was to control the content of films shot in Africa and to minimize the role of Africans in them. Jean Rouch adds: "This ruling, which was practically never applied to French filmmakers, served as a pretext to refuse authorization to shoot to young Africans considered too unruly by the colonial administration."[29] Africans did not have access to production systems and resources.

In addition to colonial cinema, Africa was also swamped with foreign films from Europe, India, and Hollywood, which in turn conveyed distorted images of Africans who were almost always relegated—when they were actually represented—to passive, secondary roles. For a long time, Africans—the Other of dominant discourse—thus only saw themselves through exogenous and ideologically charged images.

CHAPTER 3

African Cinema

New Perspectives

Until lions have their own storytellers, hunting tales will continue to glorify the hunter.

—Bantu Proverb

If I take up a camera to contribute my own vision to film language, then I become interesting for my people and for the world.

—Dani Kouyaté, in *Imaginaires en exil* (documentary)

Beginnings and Evolutions

I do not aim here to examine the entire history of African cinema, which has already been addressed in works cited in the bibliography. Works by Olivier Barlet, Ferid Boughedir, Mbye Cham, Thierno Ibrahima Dia, Manthia Diawara, André Gardies, Giuseppe Gariazzo, Pierre Haffner, Kenneth Harrow, Françoise Pfaff, Melissa Thackway, Alexie Tcheuyap, Catherine Ruelle, Alessandra Speciale, Frank Ukadike, and Paulin Soumanou Vieyra offer the foundations for such an exploration. The Internet sites *www.africultures.com* and *www.africine.org* are also key references.

It is important, however, to examine the change in perspectives and new cine-matographic representations formulated by African filmmakers after Independence.

Burkinabè director Gaston Kaboré indeed insisted on the need for new perspectives:

> During my master's degree in history [in France], I noticed that Africa was always recounted almost exclusively by non-African anthropologists, ethnologists or sociologists. Where was Africa's research into itself? I decided to analyze the way in which Africa was depicted beyond words, in images. . . . Africans, and I as a historian, had to change this vision of Africa because it created misunderstandings. . . . It was a unilateral point of view.[1]

"Longtime consumers of overseas images,"[2] and long rendered folkloric by an exterior gaze, Africans thus needed to reappropriate their perspectives and stories. The pioneers' films did not completely replace the other films, which continued to be screened, however. "Imported cinema [remained] dominant still," Victor Bachy comments.[3]

Films made by Africans necessarily offer a change of perspective. That is of interest here, given that it offers us a chance to change our own, to see differently, to broaden our perspectives beyond the often terribly destructive clichés and stereotypes. It is important to analyze this crucial reversal of viewpoint, the position of the filmmakers, and the perspectives from which they film. It does not suffice to be African, to boast about the prerogative of an "authentic" gaze uniquely because of one's origins, or to proclaim oneself a spokesperson for the continent, denying this legitimacy to others. As Dani Kouyaté states, one cannot speak of cinema "in terms of geography, but in terms of gaze, of viewpoint."[4] I categorically want to avoid an essentializing approach that risks falling into binary oppositions, based on a cultural belonging, as Ella Shohat and Robert Stam explain well.[5] They warn of a double trap: that, on the one hand, of believing that only the Yoruba can speak in the name of the Yoruba, for example, or, on the other, that of facile appropriation by which a tourist who has spent two weeks in the Yoruba region believes they have understood everything.

African filmmakers took up the camera to portray their points of view, to convey their versions of history. They filmed in response to the initial erasures and deformed representations, feeling the urgency to express their visions and for these to be recognized. Melissa Thackway's title *Africa Shoots Back*[6] (inspired by

Bill Ashcroft[7]) speaks to that. Paradoxically, they took up the camera and spoke out, giving other images of their continent while remaining dependent on foreign funding, predominantly from the former colonial powers, and notably France. It must nonetheless be stressed that African films surpass the binary schema of a "counter-cinema," a form of resistance to colonial representations. Contemporary films are born from a "manifested desire not to reverse things as such, but to show another reality," states Zeka Laplaine of his film *Le Jardin de papa* (*The Garden,* 2004).[8] While unquestionably rooted in their sociohistorical contexts of production, then, these artistic creations are not limited to an automatic, and to a certain extent predetermined, response.

The 1960s

It may be said that the sub-Saharan filmmakers' first works go back to the time of political independence, in the sociocultural and cinematographic effervescence of the 1960s.[9] This sociohistorical period spanning the 1950s and 1960s coincided with the emergence of the Nouvelle Vague in France and movements of cinematographic rupture and innovation in other countries. It coincided too with the liberation movements and struggles against Western cultural imperialism, such as Third Cinema in Latin America. After the Cuban Revolution (1959), the Vietnam War (1955–1975), and the Algerian War of Independence (1962), the sociopolitical climate in the recently decolonized countries of the South became a ferment of change on sociocultural, political, and artistic levels. It was a precious moment of collective struggle, marked by a certain solidarity: "Every time one of us wrapped up a film, it was a victory for us all," Sembène Ousmane said.[10] Supposing that this was true, it can unfortunately be said that such fraternity has become a rarity nowadays. Today, the scarcity of funding, the difficulties encountered, and production and distribution policies more frequently provoke fierce competition than collaboration among filmmakers.

In the 1960s, Africa's directors were also in contact with their Latin American counterparts in the fight for cultural liberation, such as Fernando Solanas, Octavio Getino, Jorge Sanjinés, Tomas Gutiérrez Alea, Humberto Solàs, and Glauber Rocha.[11] In the late 1960s and the 1970s, Pan-African and Tricontinental (Africa, Asia, Latin America) events were held and associations were set up. Among these, for example, were the first Festival mondial des arts nègres (World Festival of Black Arts) in Dakar in 1966; the 1968 Cultural Congress of Havana on the liberation struggles of Third

World peoples; the creation of the Pan-African Federation of Filmmakers (FEPACI) in 1969; the 1966 creation of the Carthage Film Festival (JCC) by Pan-Africanist Tahar Cheriaa. Or, again, in 1968, the initiative of the Pan-African Cinema Meeting in Ouagadougou, the first stirrings of what would shortly afterwards become the Ouagadougou Pan-African Festival of Cinema, or FESPACO.

At the same time in the United States, civil rights and black liberation movements were developing. Thanks to his dual African American and African belongings, U.S.-based Ethiopian director Haile Gerima was involved both in the struggles in the United States (as shown in his films *Hour Glass, Bush Mama,* and *Child of Resistance,* inspired by the story of Angela Davis) and in the cultural liberation movements of the South (*Sankofa* and *Mirt Sost Shi Amit—Harvest: 3000 Years*).

The camera became an instrument of struggle, destined to help the masses liberate their colonized minds. The act of filming thus acquired sociopolitical signification. As Olivier Barlet writes, the cinema of the pioneers "aimed to decolonize the gaze and mindset, to reconquer its own space and images, but was also a cultural affirmation."[12] The pioneers' works responded to the artistic need to create in order to exist, but also to the urgency of throwing off a foreign cultural domination that sought to standardize visions. This was a crucial stance if one considers that cinema was born in Europe at the time of colonial expansion and had always been associated with the West. It is indeed significant to recall that one of the first films in the history of cinema, *Le musulman rigolo* (*A Funny Mahometan,* Georges Méliès, 1897) already mocked North African culinary habits.

Nonetheless, many of these filmmakers were also based outside of the continent, and their relation to migration and Europe was ambivalent. The ambiguity and complexity of this Africa that found its self-expression in France was present starting with *Afrique-sur-Seine* (Vieyra, Sarr, Kane, Caristan, 1955), produced under the auspices of the Comité du film ethnographique (Ethnographic Film Committee).[13] Alexie Tcheuyap rightly remarks that this film reproduced the colonial idea of Africans as "Others."[14] Many historians situate the birth of "African Cinema" in 1955 with this film. This was not its director, Paulin Soumanou Vieyra's first short film, however. In 1954, he had already shot his graduation film *C'était il y a quatre ans* (*Four Years Ago*) in Paris. Giuseppe Gariazzo also cites earlier works, such as *La leçon du cinéma* (*Cinema Lesson*), made by Albert Mongita of Congo in 1951.[15] Mention is also made of other films, such as *Les pneus gonflés* (*Pumped-up Tires*) by Lubalu (Congo, 1953), or *Mouramani,* said to have been shot by the Guinean Mamadou Touré in France the same year. According to the website *www.africultures.*

com, "Raberono appears to have been the director of the first sub-Saharan African film: *Rasalama* (1937)." Among the first works shot by Africans a few years later, one may also mention the short film *Aventure en France* (*French Adventure*), by Cameroonian Jean-Paul N'Gassa (1962); and in 1963, Cameroon's Thérèse Sita Bella (the only woman director at the time according to Alessandra Speciale and to Frank Ukadike, cited by Gariázzo) made the 30-minute documentary *Tam-tam à Paris* (*Drums in Paris*). The same year, Timité Bassori began his career in Ivory Coast and the Guinean Alpha Adama started out in France. A certain confusion thus exists over the origins of sub-Saharan African cinema. What is certain is their late emergence in relation to other world cinemas.

As concerns the quest for the self and the complexity of belonging, it is significant that much of Sembène Ousmane's *La Noire de . . .* (*Black Girl,* 1966), which is considered sub-Saharan Africa's first feature-length film (60 minutes), was shot in France. Here, Sembène adapted one of his short stories, itself inspired by a true news report. Right from its title, with its enigmatic three suspension points, this fiction foregrounds the obsession of any migrant: self-awareness, rooting, and belonging. The emblematic annihilation of the Other is condensed in the humiliated existence of Diouana, a young Senegalese maid taken to Antibes by her French employers, and who ends up committing suicide. Sembène Ousmane had already achieved international recognition at this point, his short film *Borom Sarret* (1963) having won the top award at the Tours Film Festival in 1963.

For that matter, numerous first films bore titles that were emblematic of identity quests and in-betweenness—notably, *Concerto pour un exil* (*Concerto for an Exile,* Désiré Ecaré, 1968); *À nous deux, France* (*To Us Both, France,* Désiré Ecaré, 1970); *Bou-bou-cravate* (*Boubou and Tie,* Daniel Kamwa, 1972); *Identité* (*Identity,* Pierre-Marie Dong, 1972); *Les Princes noirs de Saint-Germain-des-Prés* (*Black Princes of Saint-Germain-des-Prés,* Ben Diogaye Bèye, 1975); *Nationalité immigré* (*Nationality: Immigrant,* Sidney Sokhona, 1975); *L'Exilé* (*The Exile,* Oumarou Ganda, 1980); *Comédie exotique* (*Exotic Comedy,* Kitia Touré, 1984); or more recently, *Immatriculation temporaire* (*Temporary Registration,* Gahité Fofana, 2001). Representations of the ambiguities of identity remain topical in both fiction (for example, *Identité malsaine/Toxic Identity,* by Amog Lemra, 2010), and documentary (*Noire ici, Blanche là-bas/Footprints of My Other,* by Claude Haffner, 2012, or *Trop Noire pour être Française? / Too Black to be French?* by Isabelle Boni-Claverie, 2015). From the very start of African cinema, the complex question of constructing one's identity vis-à-vis the Other, the European, has thus been central.

The 1970s

In the 1970s, women began making films. After a first short film, *Monangambé* in 1969, Guadeloupean Sarah Maldoror—widely "adopted" as an African filmmaker—finished her feature film *Sambizanga* in 1972. The same year, Senegal's Safi Faye made *La Passante* (*The Passerby*), historically considered the first fiction short made by an African woman. Her first feature film, *Kaddu Beykat* (*Letter from My Village,* 1975), reached spectators around the world, even though it was initially banned in Senegal.[16]

This was also the decade that *Touki Bouki* (1973) was released, a film that Olivier Barlet describes as a "surrealist, prophetic manifesto."[17] The film indeed reflects the artistic intuitions and aesthetic rupture of the Senegalese avant-garde visionary Djibril Diop Mambéty, who had already made a name for himself with his short films *Badou Boy* (1965) and *Contras City* (1969).[18] Mambéty is often described as an exception in the African film world as he eschewed the social realism that was so prevalent in early works. I personally would argue, however, that his filmmaking is totally representative of the stylistic variety of cinema on the African continent and its artistic vitality.

It was also in the 1970s that filmmakers from the former British colonies began to emerge. In Nigeria, Ola Balogun's *Amadi* (1975), which followed *Alpha,* his 1972 Paris-based film about the cultural alienation of an artist in exile, marked an important step forward. In Ghana, Kwaw Ansah shot *Love Brewed in the African Pot* (1980) with private funding, the film becoming a huge hit in many African countries. Kwaw Ansah later won international acclaim with *Heritage Africa!* (1989). Nigeria and Ghana remained the two "Anglophone" countries to produce the most films.

Year after year, the number of international events multiplied. In 1973, directors from the African continent and Latin America gathered in Algiers for the Third World Film-Makers Meeting to discuss their common problems and to fight against the repercussions of imperialism and neocolonialism. It was in Algeria again that on 18 January 1975, during the second FEPACI congress, the Algiers Charter was unanimously adopted. It translated the militant filmmakers' commitment to their anti-imperialist combat. The charter, whose foundations were above all ideological, specified that "the question of commercial profit can be no yardstick for African filmmakers."[19] Yet, it is well known that cinema is an industry that, to exist, must be financially viable. Filmmakers' freedom of expression was recognized by the charter, but it was also stipulated that African filmmakers must "see themselves as creative artisans at the service of their people," tending to shut them in a rigid schema of militant, didactic duty that put artistic considerations second. The text also specified that cinema must express "the needs and aspirations of the people," implying that it be should be destined for Africa's mass audiences. This has not always proven to be the case, especially when it comes to auteur cinema, which, like it or not, is often more widely seen and better appreciated outside of Africa, and more often than not by international niche audiences. At its outset, the FEPACI as a filmmakers' organization was animated by political, rather than aesthetic preoccupations: namely, the cultural liberation of the African continent and other oppressed countries. This cinema was thus intended to raise consciousness given that African societies were "still objectively undergoing an experience of domination exerted on a number of levels: political, economic and cultural."[20] Driven by preoccupations that were more political than cinematic, the Federation thus adopted a directive and authoritarian role. Alexie Tcheuyap indeed stresses that, while undoubtedly necessary in the historical and sociopolitical context of the time, these ideological and peremptory manifestos nonetheless influenced the films and discourses about Africa's cinema for some fifty years.[21] He rightly points out just how directive the Algiers Charter is. In under two pages, the verb "must" is repeated eight times.[22] According to him, this document defined the nature of most early African films, which adopted a "semi-documentary" form.[23] This perspective also conditioned critical perspectives and marked the analyses of film historians. This is not to deny the artistic quality of certain pioneering films, but rather to remark that critics celebrated their sociopolitical engagement, rather than their aesthetic characteristics. It may be noted that this was not the case for Latin American filmmakers, who were also initially animated by a militant spirit. They equally rejected making just entertainment works, but for them, the aesthetic dimension remained primordial. From the outset, then, specific criteria were applied to African films.

Meanwhile, audiences on the African continent continued to watch Westerns, Bollywood, and Hollywood films, screened in cinemas run by foreign companies (SECMA and COMACICO, notably in the "Francophone" countries). That is perfectly illustrated in the documentary *Afrique je te plumerai . . .* (Jean-Marie Teno, 1992), in which the children are captivated by the Indian dancers they see on the screen. The sub-Saharan filmmakers were thus heir to a foreign film culture. Not only did they have to fight an exogenous, distorted representation of Africans; they also entered a market dominated by foreigners, and it was too late to change the rules of the game. In the 1970s, the question of distribution was crucial. In 1977, after the Conferência Africana de Cooperação Cinematográfica in Maputo in the freshly independent Mozambique, various countries came together in the African Association of Cinematographic Cooperation (AACC) in an attempt to challenge the foreign monopoly of distribution. This goal was never achieved due to the limited political commitment of most of the participating countries.[24] In 1979, the Inter-African Film Distribution Consortium (CIDC) was set up, which bought the distribution rights of UAC (African Film Union) films in fourteen African countries.[25] The CIDC, whose headquarters were based in Paris—which might at first seem paradoxical, although, given the history of African cinema, was not really—only lasted five years.[26] According to Olivier Barlet's analysis, the failure of the CIDC reflects the disillusionment that followed people's post-Independence hopes and their disappointment vis-à-vis the attitudes of the ruling elites.[27]

The 1980s

In the spirit of Pan-Africanism, relations between filmmakers from the different African regions continued to strengthen in their shared struggle against standardization and cultural domination. In Niamey in 1981, Med Hondo of Mauritania, Ousmane Sembène of Senegal, Tahar Cheriaa of Tunisia, Lionel N'Gakane of South Africa, Haile Gerima of Ethiopia, and others formed the Comité africain des cinéastes (African Committee of Filmmakers) to fight for new film practices. This was a collective undertaking on their part to share their resources and to work together, as was also advocated continent-wide by the L'Œil Vert collective created the same year in Ouagadougou. According to the Senegalese director Ousmane William Mbaye, L'Œil Vert was set up to contest a certain "static, political cinema [of the] predecessors," was animated by aesthetic ambitions, and was conscious of the urgency of "saying things differently."[28] This collective also insisted that it was vital to filmmakers to free themselves from their financial dependence on European countries, for African cinema's true liberation would only be possible with a change in production strategies.

In 1982, the Niamey Manifesto was drawn up. Contrary to the Algiers Charter, it focused on the need to create a film industry, rather than on the ideology of anti-imperialist struggle. This manifesto was written by filmmakers, film critics, and those in charge of film and television institutions in Africa and elsewhere, who came together in Niger for the first international seminar on film production in Africa. The text defines four main axes of development: the exploitation of cinema theaters; the importing and distribution of films; technical infrastructures; and professional training. It concluded on the imperative involvement of the state and of television. Unfortunately, however, over thirty-five years later, the situation has not significantly improved.

Filmmakers have also consistently interacted in the different spaces of the diaspora. In 1988, diasporic filmmakers joined together in the Paris-based association, the Guilde africaine des réalisateurs et producteurs (African Guild of Filmmakers and Producers).

Two decades after the emergence of the first overtly political films, filmmakers sought to reappropriate the gaze. Their films were marked by the need to rewrite both individual and collective history and memory. The filmmakers' subjectivity was liberated, the intimate foregrounded, and the personal and political intertwined. With films predominantly backed by Western, and predominantly French, funders, the 1980s represented a golden age of African cinema that some now accused of falling into a kind of folklore destined to seduce an international audience in search of exoticism. International recognition reached its zenith when Malian Souleymane Cissé's *Yeelen* won the Jury Award at Cannes in 1987. Two years later in Cannes, Burkinabè Idrissa Ouédraogo won the International Critics Award for *Yaaba,* then the Jury Award for *Tilai* in 1990. After this moment of glory, the following years saw a decline in international success. In the 1990s, funding from the French Ministry of Cooperation, the European Development Fund, and the European Union suffered what Elisabeth Lequeret qualifies as "draconian cuts."[29] It was not until twenty years later that a Cannes jury gave an award to an African film again. The film in question was *Un homme qui crie (A Screaming Man)*, by Mahamat Saleh Haroun (2010), but this time around, the film was not a box-office hit in France. In 2013, Mahamat Saleh Haroun's film *Grigris* was again selected in official competition at Cannes but was not favorably received by the critics. Conversely, Abderrahmane Sissako's *Timbuktu,* selected in the official competition at Cannes in 2014, won no awards, but was a major commercial success in France (over a million tickets sold).[30] Nominated for the Oscars, it won seven César awards in France.[31] In terms of international acclaim, the passing of the baton between the Cissé/Ouédraogo and the Haroun/Sissako pairs marked the transition between the millenniums in France.

The 1990s and the New Millennium

To escape the "straitjacket" of difference and categorization, filmmakers in the early 1990s sought to free themselves from the label of "African filmmaker" that trapped them into a kind of exotic folklore. The watchword became: "I'm not an African filmmaker, I'm a filmmaker who is African."[32] Idrissa Ouédraogo was the first to insist that he was "a filmmaker, period," just as the Canadian filmmaker Xavier Dolan refuses the epithet "young." Dolan indeed asked that we see his films as just films, not as films by a young filmmaker:

> I simply hope that I will be judged mercilessly, without my age being an excuse for any awkwardness. I hope that the epithet "young" added to "filmmaker" will not confine my films to a restricted category of "courageous" first works. I want my cinema to be as little labeled as possible, that my films are described as good or bad, never as "good for a 20-year-old director."[33]

It is this infantilizing, paternalistic, and ghettoizing vision that African filmmakers also refuse.

As of the 1990s, a major role was also granted to video, which became a more economic and simpler way of telling stories. Balufu Bakupa-Kanyinda devoted the documentary *Afr@digital* (2002) to the possibilities that new technologies offered African countries. It was indeed at the start of this decade that the Nollywood phenomenon emerged.

In 1992, the popular success in Nigeria of *Living in Bondage*,[34] produced by Kenneth Nnebue and directed by Chris Obi-Rapu, can be considered the starting point of the Nollywood industry. These are films produced in national languages, often made with small budgets, and which, while dealing with social themes, are primarily entertainment films. They are nonetheless very well distributed on the (legal and illegal) VHS and, nowadays, DVD markets. They can be picked up for next to nothing in the street and watched at home, not at the cinema.[35] Nollywood has evolved today towards a greater opening into the international market. Today, academics acclaim a New Nollywood.[36] The "Nollywood phenomenon" is in full evolution, as attested at the Nollywood Week festival that has been held at the Arlequin Cinema in Paris since 2013. Here, the films are subtitled in French and the (private) funding is almost entirely Nigerian. Young video filmmakers have also emerged all over the African continent, but their work struggles to circulate beyond their national borders.

In the 1990s, film production slowed, but most notably, a new group of filmmakers emerged towards the end of the decade. During this period, certain filmmakers, such as Mweze Ngangura or Jean-Pierre Bekolo, distanced themselves from the more didactic, social-realist cinema of the pioneers, such as Sembène Ousmane, whose work they nonetheless appreciate. The artistic sensibility of Cameroon's Jean-Pierre Bekolo emerged in *Quartier Mozart* (1992). Bekolo defends his right to the imaginary and explains how cultural oppression also took the form of making Africans believe that their imaginations could not surpass reality.[37] Bekolo later brought his questioning of cinema, its production and reception in Africa to the screen in *Le complot d'Aristote* (*Aristotle's Plot*, 1996),[38] which contested the images of a wretched, unchanging Africa. *Le complot d'Aristote* is of a highly demanding aesthetic standard. Its style parodies different genres, from Hollywood action movies to Westerns, comedies, and detective movies, thereby deconstructing certain clichés. A filmmaker deliberately looking to the future, Bekolo chose the following subtitle for his blog: "Can cinema help us give birth to a new world?"[39] *Les Saignantes* (*The Bloodletters* 2007) is an avant-garde film that oscillates between eroticism, satire, and sci-fi, its plot set in 2025. Always "between the light and the serious," as the director himself puts it, this film proposes a sociopolitical critique of Cameroon, and more broadly Africa's corrupt systems. It is interesting to note that Bekolo drew his inspiration from the Beti women's ritual *mevungu,* which is used to transform unacceptable situations. The director, who is Beti himself, nonetheless discovered this myth in books.[40] Having studied in France and taught in the United States before returning to Cameroon, Bekolo—an extremely interesting polyvalent artist—is emblematic of cultural hybridity, which he translates in the syncretic styles of his films.

Many films in the 1990s and 2000s have increasingly explicitly portrayed the hybridity that their filmmakers experienced in their daily lives. The works of Newton Aduaka, Jean-Pierre Bekolo, Sarah Bouyain, Andrew Dosumno, Dyana Gaye, Alain Gomis, Mahamat Saleh Haroun, Balufu Bakupa-Kanyinda, Mama Keita, Wanjiru Kinyanjui, Dani Kouyaté, Zeka Laplaine, Jean Odoutan, Kivu Ruhorahoza, and Abderrahmane Sissako (to cite just a few) demonstrate this well. Alexie Tcheuyap,[41] following Jude Akudinobi,[42] dates the emergence of films that break away from the "ideologically oriented" aesthetics of the pioneers to the 1990s. New, heterogeneous aesthetics drawing on both Western and African cultures and artistic expressions were born. Mbye Cham, for example, describes the films of the 1990s as "taking racial and cultural hybridity into account as a direction for the future (as opposed to a narcissistic and essentialist, racial, ethnic and cultural nationalism."[43] Or, as Olivier Barlet writes:

> A new cinema emerged at the dawn of the century, announced by films such as Mauritanian Abderrahmane Sissako's *La Vie sur terre* (*Life on Earth,* 1998) or *Bye Bye Africa* by Chadian Mahamat Saleh Haroun (1999), emblematic of a new style capable of taking risks in terms of form and content, of asking questions without responses, of uncompromisingly exploring humankind.[44]

In *La vie sur terre,* it is the filmmaker himself who returns to Sokolo, Mali, to visit his father. In this film about exile that is midway between documentary and fiction, the director portrays life in the village, which he himself rediscovers after having lived abroad. The film is the fruit of a gaze that returns from abroad and focuses on the problems of village life. In contrast, the young Malian Abdallah, the lead character of the fiction *Heremakono* (*Waiting for Happiness*), comes to visit his mother in Mauritania, where he is an outsider; his gaze remains turned towards an overseas world. The loop is looped in *Bamako,* which questions the circumstances that force people to leave and to seek the means of their existence elsewhere. *Bye Bye Africa*—Mahamat Saleh Haroun's first feature film and the first made in his country, Chad—is a fiction that draws on the documentary register. The filmmaker returns home when his mother dies. This brings him to question the state of cinema in his war-torn country. His reflections become a personal film about the Seventh Art on the African continent.

At times, these directors revisited old themes, apprehending them in the light of the experience of the contemporary world. Films such as *La Vie sur terre* and *Bye Bye Africa* (like *L'Afrance* and *Teza* too) deal with the question of "return" to the African continent, as did in their day Senegal's Abbacar Samb Makharam in *Et la neige n'était plus* (*There Was No Longer Snow,* 1965) and Amadou Saalum Seck in *Saaraba* (1988). The difference here is that in *La Vie sur terre* and *Bye Bye Africa,* it is the directors who perform themselves, exposing their subjectivity all the more as they position their focus on their own countries as that of an "outsider."[45]

Contemporary Films: Reconstructions

The journey is home.

—John Akomfrah, *Nine Muses* (documentary)

For me in the twenty-first century I fight using the camera to have the right to remember.

—Haile Gerima, in *Imaginaires en exil* (documentary)

Contemporary filmmakers of the sub-Saharan diaspora are united by their plural identities, belongings, and their feelings about bearing diverse cultural heritages and memories, which merge in their composite narrative styles. They have positioned themselves in the interstices of cultures, which affords them a specific view of contemporary societies. They are in constant (physical and metaphoric) movement.

Accordingly, "the resulting rhythm [is] bluesy, in keeping with the themes of errantry," as Olivier Barlet comments.[46] As in the blues—a "delocalized" music that stems from a fusion of different styles and experiences—these filmmakers seek to harmonize dissonant notes and features that appear contradictory, but that can be combined in an inclusive, rather than exclusionary, logic.

These new cinematographic approaches illustrate each filmmaker's aesthetic plurality and specificity in highly personal styles, notably Jean Odoutan's acerbic humor, Henri Duparc's comedy, Flora Gomes's adopting of the musical, Mama Keita's expression of social violence, Abderrahmane Sissako's "aesthetic of silence," Mahamat Saleh Haroun's cinema of memory, Wanuri Kahiu's science fiction, and Dyana Gaye's fables.

These polyphonic filmic narratives are born from errantry, movement, transit, and transitions, transformations, and the crossing of diverse borders. It is in this respect that Olivier Barlet prefers to talk of a "nomadic" rather than ethnically or culturally mixed cinema.[47] He writes: "Films in the 2000s often use journeys across the world as a form of questioning. Their nomadism is a philosophy—that of understanding that the Other is enriching."[48] In his famous article "Thoughts on Nomadic Aesthetics and the Black Independent Cinema: Traces of a Journey,"[49] Teshome H. Gabriel already evoked "nomadic aesthetics," which went hand in hand with what he called Black Cinema's nomadic thought. The latter is defined as "travelling cinema," which goes forth to meet others and the unknown, and in which the imaginative and symbolic dimension is very powerful. The similarities that Teshome Gabriel identifies between nomadic thought and certain black and/or African filmmakers come from their belonging to several cultures and their constant crossing of both real and symbolic borders. But above all, Gabriel indicates that, for nomads, the art of storytelling draws on memory, and that, more than official history, collective memory occupies a crucial place in these directors' works.

The diasporic experience necessarily involves a questioning of origins. These filmmakers thus reconfigure themselves in the light of various elements, including their African roots, their migratory trajectories, their diasporic experiences, and cultural contaminations. In this respect, many films urge self-(re)discovery, shunning mimesis in order to go forth, to encounter others, and to assert one's own specificity and composite identity.

"The future comes from the past," says the griot in *Niaye* (Sembène Ousmane, 1964). The same phrase, almost word for word—"The future is *born* from the past"—is spoken by the griot in *Keïta! L'h*éritage du griot (*Keita! Voice of the Griot,* Dani Kouyaté, 1995). In *Taafe Fanga* (Adama Drabo, 1997), the griot Sidiki Diabaté expresses the same idea when he states that his "duty is to capture the past to nourish the present and prepare the future."[50] In the diasporic space, filmmakers may initiate a process of recovering their roots—roots that are supple enough to plant themselves elsewhere. Memory plays a key role in this process, and diverse histories, memories, and trajectories converge. It is precisely the awareness of these new syncretic identities, which are forged elsewhere but draw on roots, that constitutes the richness of the films in question. I shall come back to the role of memory in the films analyzed.

For some, uprooting has become the basis of their existence and their work. Indeed, diasporic identities are also structured by displacements, by journeys that "[acquire] the form of a restless interrogation."[51] As Sheila Petty states: "Perhaps it is the travel that defines identity, and we exist in some (not-here/not-there) state oscillating between arrival and departure, global and local, nation and (non) nation"[52]—between private and political, I might add.

Thus, the integration of diverse visions and cultural, social, and historic references generates new mentalities capable of surpassing single modes of thought. The concepts of "mestizo thought,"[53] of "intrinsically multi-dimensional thinking" are useful here.[54]

It is vital to surpass single thought, to fight the uniformization latent in the construction of the Other via logics of binary opposition: Orient/Occident; you/

us; black/white. The Negritude and Black Power movements were founded on this dualistic vision, which does not truly transform ideologies, but contents itself with reversing points of view. These movements at times fell into the trap of embracing the very binary logics they claimed to be fighting and focused their attention on a single aspect of the person—namely, the color of their skin. They left no place for a third path—that of something new born out of encounters, out of hybrid blending. The ideas of the Negritude and Black Power movements conveyed fundamental demands, but nonetheless had to be surpassed to achieve a world in which tigers no longer need to proclaim their "tigritude" (Wole Soyinka), in which each and every human has the same right to exist, to express themselves, to occupy their place. To cite Jean-Paul Sartre: "Thus Negritude is for destroying itself, it is a 'crossing to' and not an 'arrival at,' a means and not an end."[55] Today, the concept of Negritude is increasingly contested, both on a theoretical level and in literature, music, and cinema. Many cultural productions now explore notions of complex identities that include several variables.

"Multi-dimensional thinking" is in keeping with what Homi K. Bhabha defines as "third space," or a new and hybrid space, "which enables other positions to emerge,"[56] interstices, nuances, new terrains of negotiations and new representations. The "third space" is thus a site of cultural hybridization. The mixing of two or more elements that, as in a chemical reaction, transform as they reassemble differently produces something completely different from the original elements. The result of cultural blending is unpredictable. Sheila Petty demonstrates the degree to which these films pay the same acute attention to the complexities of reconstructed identities in transnational contexts as Black Diaspora theories do.[57]

But, as they incorporate different territories, spaces, temporalities, cultures, languages, histories, and memories, these films move even further from spectators' expectations of a so-called "African authenticity."

Cinema, Africa, Misconceptions, and New Paradigms

Why don't we make films like others do?

—Jean-Pierre Bekolo, interview, Paris, August 2011

I'm Beninese, but the films I make are French.

—Jean Odoutan, interview with David Cadasse

Indeed, there have very often been ambiguities in the reception of African film, often perceived as a rigid category, distinct from the rest of world cinema. When the adjective "African" is added to a film, it changes spectator expectations, as Sarah Bouyain attests:

> What is sometimes difficult when you are a filmmaker and African—my own case—is that when the public comes to see a film that has been described to them as African, people seek a sociological truth, an example. They don't look at the work of the filmmaker and that is pretty annoying.

She continues: "I don't think anyone makes African cinema; people are what they are and make the films that they make. It is others who then go and classify the films as *African cinema*."[58] David Murphy and Patrick Williams describe this situation as "a form of exceptionalism, which views and classifies African cinema in very different terms from those we might find in film studies more generally."[59] Today still, African films are not well known due to their poor, unprofitable distribution and their limited access to classic commercial circuits. Olivier Barlet notes the absence of most of these films in film journals, and the few reviews that are available tend to give an impoverished vision.[60] Often, moreover, theoreticians and critics specializing in African film, in dedicated spaces, have also perpetuated misconceptions by focusing less on their aesthetic forms than on their "African" aspects. Often, spectators who do have access to these films discover them in highly specific conditions (unconventional cinemas, niche contexts, and so on). They are mainly screened in specialist festivals or in special sections of major festivals. Spectators may come away with a skewed impression based on the expectation of discovering a mythical elsewhere, an ancient world that is primitive and set in its immobility, confirming a certain idea of pure, original *Africanity*—an expectation that risks hindering the simple pleasure of discovering a work of art.

As Olivier Barlet comments, audience expectations are shaped by two trends: on the one hand, a "demand for exoticism" on the part of those seeking a rural, mythical, legendary Africa; on the other, a "demand for reality" on the part of those who are more interested in the description of the problems of Africa's modern cities. Come what may, "films by directors of African descent have intrinsically to prove their Africanity. They can then receive the holy unction: in general the recognition of their 'authenticity.'"[61]

Perceived and legitimated as "African films" and not simply as films, these works are thereby reduced to a "genre unto themselves." The Congolese filmmaker Bakupa-Kanyinda recounts that he did indeed, at one time, consider "African film" as a *genre,* just "like a western or a porno. The rules of this genre say these films must deal with poverty—otherwise people in Europe will say it's not a genuinely African film."[62] This anecdote illustrates well the existence of a specific "horizon of expectations,"[63] or of "generic expectations"[64] relating to folklore, exoticism, or being limited to alterity. Among my own experiences, during a conversation on a train, for example, my neighbor, on learning that I was on my way to an African film festival, exclaimed: "Oh, I love animal documentaries!" But surprise can also be encountered in the academic world: after the screening of the film *Daratt* (Mahmat Saleh Haroun, 2006), an African studies scholar present commented: "Now that was a *real film!*" When I asked him what he was expecting when he came to see a *film,* he replied: "An African film, a film set in the village, with a shaky camera and women pounding millet."

Filmmaker Imunga Ivanga states: "When new proposals emerge, it is not uncommon to hear: 'It's not African!'" One thus sees "the South being transposed into the North, which adds to the confusion of those who call for authenticity." What, then, "to think of an Alain Gomis who made *L'Afrance?* Or a Zeka Laplaine with his *Paris XY?*" Manifestly, "initial definitions are soon surpassed by creators' desires; their status cannot be straightjacketed."[65]

One might also question the different ways in which figures such as Alain Gomis, Fabrice Eboué, Dyana Gaye, and Thomas Ngijol are perceived in France. Similarly, when films like *Handsworth Songs* or *The Nine Muses* (John Akomfrah, 1987 and 2010) are at times perceived as "strange" or "weird"—comments that can be heard after screenings—to which codes and to what normality are spectators referring? It is precisely against such expectations, which assigned African films to a homogeneous cinematographic genre of its own, that filmmakers spoke out in the early 1990s.

I am perfectly aware that it is difficult to define and classify certain films. Alexie Tcheuyap stresses how challenging attempts to define can be, especially today.[66] Asmara Beraki is emblematic of this difficulty. How to define her, given that she was born in the United States to an Eritrean father and an American mother, and currently lives in the Czech Republic? She has made films in both the United States and her current country of residence. Her 2012 film, *Anywhere Else,* addresses the Black Diaspora's identity issues. She has also made Czech short films, in the sense that they were shot in Prague, in Czech, with a Czech crew, Czech actors, and Czech musicians. Ultimately, the question is why we feel the need to define at all costs? When it can be freely expressed, artistic freedom has, by ricochet, an emancipating effect on the auteur's personality—a plural, composite personality in the making, which is likely not to fit into rigid, predetermined slots.

Is it possible to evoke an "African authenticity" today?[67] Or do we rather need "new answers to the question of knowing 'who is African' and who is not?,'" Achille Mbembe inquires.[68] Following Iain Chambers, I believe that authenticity is constituted today of a syncretic and dynamic present, forged by cultural transfigurations that must be constantly renegotiated.[69]

"Are my films African?" asks Ivoirian Isabelle Boni-Claverie. "At any rate, I am. But from a contemporary, cosmopolitan, complex-free Africa that remembers its traditions, but that no longer needs to hide in them to define an identity."[70]

The filmmakers studied here do not deny their Africanity; they question and enrich it. "They thus testify to new, blended, fluid, evolving forms of Africanity, expressed by each person through their own experiences and perceptions, refusing to let themselves be trapped in fixed conceptions of identity or authenticity, thereby refusing sectarian, culturalist, or essentialist discourses idealizing cultural values."[71] Inhabited by cultural blending, constantly calling themselves into question, they in general refuse all Manichean opposition between Africa and the West, in the name of innovative syncretism. Their specificity precisely appears to lie in the expression of a reconstruction, of a recomposed identity that is plural and "beyond territorial belongings,"[72] in shifting and changing spaces—spaces of transformation. Far from being fixated on identity, their films call for a renewal and seek an appropriate language for their questionings. They naturally slip into "contact zones,"[73] cross flexible and permeable boundaries, escaping all rigid classification. It is in this respect that Africa's cinema(s) must be repositioned in light of these multiple incidences and in light of the global cultural exchanges that characterize our times.

These films are postnationalist, in the sense that Alexie Tcheuyap employs.[74] That is, they are situated beyond the forms of resistance that accompanied the pioneering films at the time when the young African nations were founded. The "post" thus suggests a process in the making rather than a temporal designation. Tcheuyap clearly illustrates the way in which the new postnationalist cinemas question protean identities and new, unstable social constructions, characterized by dynamics of cultural hybridization.[75] He proposes an interesting analytical rupture, deconstructing readings of African films as a genre.

Indeed, as Kenneth Harrow also insists,[76] it is urgent today to renew critical paradigms, to reconsider the analytical approach to these films in the light of contemporary praxis.[77] This new approach aims to firstly take into account artistic and aesthetic aspects, nonetheless without forgetting the specificities that arise from the historical, political, economic, and sociocultural milieus of production. The *socio-aesthetic* approach adopted here, which shall be illustrated in more detail in the second part of this book, follows this direction.

Production Contexts: Milieus, Institutions, and Subjectivities

Film productions reflect not only each filmmaker's aspirations to freedom of artistic expression, but also specific sociocultural and historical milieus, and constraints arising from the mode of production. Before studying the chosen corpus of films, and in order to better understand the complexities, ambiguities, and stakes, I propose to look first at the conditions of production. A brief analysis of the film institutions and economic frameworks of production will help contextualize the films studied.

Films are made within "organized communities" that the film sociologist Pierre Sorlin calls the "milieus of cinema."[78] They are influenced by diverse components, including the economic context, but also historic and sociocultural circumstances. As cinema is also an industry, one cannot analyze film works without taking production "directives" and "constraints" into account.[79] Jean-Pierre Esquenazi demonstrates how directives from film institutions—that is, the places where films are made—define genres and formats.[80] Highly specific situations generate works and may determine their filmic grammar. The directives that presided over the making of certain African films—or, above all, "Francophone" African films—were founded on the expectation of a "calabash cinema," or, in other words, a timeless, exotic rural cinema, from which transnational filmmakers seek to distance themselves.

Filmmakers' artistic projects do not always find financial backing. So, to preserve a certain artistic freedom, they are obliged to fulfill several roles, as Sembène Ousmane's pioneering work demonstrated. Françoise Pfaff accordingly described "the tradition of one-man-band filmmakers who exhaust themselves writing, producing, and distributing their films."[81] More recently, the example of Jean Odoutan, who produces, distributes, acts in, and composes the music of his own films, is emblematic. Likewise, Jean-Marie Teno produces, writes, films, edits, and records the sound of many of his documentaries, which he narrates himself in voice-over. He too distributes them via his company, Les Films du Raphia (*www. raphia.fr*). Even though Jean-Pierre Bekolo's films can be found on sale in France's FNAC cultural retail chain, or on Amazon (which is quite exceptional), he, who is also a "one man band," sells his DVDs himself via his blog (*www.jeanpierrebekolo. com*). If these filmmakers become the producers or coproducers of their films, it is often out of necessity. As Haile Gerima states: "I would have preferred that there were people who identify with my philosophy, who would have been distributors, the business people. I should have been only the filmmaker. But the world is not like that. I said, 'OK, as I haven't found such people, I should control my intellectual property.'"[82]

The situation of African filmmakers is complex because there are many directives to consider. Diasporic filmmakers draw on both their milieu of origin and their milieu of residence. While it is widely understood that a film is always a collective work, these filmmakers, who are forced to shoulder several roles during the making of their films, are a living link between their different communities of belonging. Their films traverse different social spaces, milieus of production, and film organizations, which do not always share the same communication codes. Financial constraints obviously are a major influence in the sense that, of all art forms, the Seventh Art is the most expensive. One of the specificities of the films in question's production comes from the fact that their funding—and thus the tastes of the selection committees—is foreign, and predominantly European, and mostly comes from the former colonial powers, a unique phenomenon in the world. Elisabeth Lequeret describes this as "economic censorship":

> While filmmakers do not like using the term censorship, the fact is that they are more dependent than ever on the verdict of a few screenplay readers. One thus hears mention here and there of such-and-such a screenplay being rewritten to "flesh out the role of the colonialists," or of diverse recommendations to "tone down" a political screenplay to make it more comic or to dilute a burning subject. . . . This is proof that censorship remains. Only it is internalized and often anticipated by the filmmakers themselves: no longer political, but economic.[83]

Production constraints also influence a film's aesthetic. The Cameroonian filmmaker Bassek Ba Kobhio, founder of the Ecrans Noirs Festival in Yaoundé, states that, contrary to what certain critics advance in their analyses, certain films use traditional music not out of artistic choice, but due to financial limitations.[84] Another particularity of films from Africa resides in the fact that, at festivals, the nationality of the film given is that of the director, when it is normally determined by the nationality of a film's production. In this respect, the title of the *Africultures* issue *Cinéma: l'exception africaine* (*Cinema: The African Exception*) is emblematic of a situation that is unique in the world when it comes to film production.[85] While it is true that diasporic filmmakers can look for funding on both continents, one must not forget that there is a dearth of film institutions in most countries on the African continent. Certain countries' (such as Morocco, Gabon, South Africa, and Senegal) commitment to funding remain an exception. That is why many filmmakers are forced to seek funding elsewhere.

Funding

One may note a tendency today for "Francophone" directors to seek institutional funding, whereas the "Anglophones" prefer a form of cinematic independence. In Britain in the 1980s, the Greater London Council and British Film Institute (BFI) favored the emergence of film workshops in immigrant communities. In their wake, various black film collectives were founded in Britain, including the Sankofa Film and Video Collective and the Black Audio Film Collective, of which John Akomfrah was a founding member. These reflected a growing awareness of identity issues. Among the emblematic black British filmmakers were Isaac Julien (born in London to Saint-Lucian parents), cofounder of the Sankofa Film and Video Collective, and Trinidadian Horace Ové, director of *Pressure* (1975). The first black British feature film, it became a source of inspiration for many other filmmakers, including Barbados-born Menelik Shabazz, director of *Burning an Illusion* (1981). Unfortunately, these modes of production remained isolated in the community-based system characteristic of British multiculturalism. In France, conversely, while a tradition of *Beur* cinema did emerge, there remains a lack of black filmmaking. Olivier Barlet attributes this to France's assimilationist tradition:

> Backing the creative expression of minority communities amounts to acknowledging their existence, and thus their right to be different. That would imply accepting a mutation of our own identity, enriched with the experiences of Others and the confrontation of cultures. That is what Black Cinema notably invites us to do.[86]

Nonetheless, this state of affairs is also related to the conditions stipulated by the funding bodies specifically devoted to "African" films. In France, African diasporic filmmakers can apply to standard film funds—the National Centre for Cinematography and Moving Images (CNC), the noncommercial Company of Film and Television Producers (PROCIREP), the noncommercial Company for the Administration of Artists and Musicians' Royalties (ADAMI)—or, on a European-level, benefit from various ad hoc regional or television funds. In many respects, they take steps similar to French filmmakers: they propose a screenplay, look for a producer, and make institutional funding applications. Filmmakers may thereby obtain CNC funding—writing funds, rewriting funds, the *avance sur recettes* (advance on takings, before or after shooting), development funds, production funds, postproduction funds, completion funds, distribution funds—and funding from French regional and other bodies. However, it must be said that not many obtain CNC backing. Among the films in this corpus, only *L'Afrance* and *Notre étrangère* did, made by Alain Gomis and Sarah Bouyain respectively, both of whom are French-born.

Otherwise, as Africans, they can apply for the very limited funding devoted to cinema of the South. In this case, their films must obligatorily be shot in countries of the South. This explains why few films are made in France by African diasporic filmmakers. Among the rare exceptions, one may cite *Ragazzi* and *Le onzième commandement* (*Eleventh Hour,* Mama Keïta, 1991 and 1997); *Une Couleur café* (*Coffee Color,* Henri Duparc, 1997); *Sexe, gombo et beurre salé* (*Sex, Okra and Salted Butter,* Mahamat Saleh Haroun, TV film, 2007); *Paris XY* (Zeka Laplaine, 2001); *Paris selon Moussa* (Paris According to Moussa, Cheick Doukouré, 2003); and several of Jean Odoutan's films, notably *Djib* (2000), *Mama Aloko* (2002), and *La Valse des gros derrières* (*The Waltz of the Big Behinds,* 2004). Another example is Newton Aduaka's latest independent film, *One Man's Show.* The commercial release of *Rengaine* (*Hold Back*) in November 2012 (after screening during the Directors' Fortnight at Cannes in 2012) perhaps marked a new trend in this respect. It must be pointed out, however, that, like the film *Donoma* by Haitian Djinn Carrenard (2011), *Rengaine* is an independent film, shot with a tiny budget, which was later bought by French television. Its director, Rachid Djaïdani, who was born in France to a Sudanese mother and an Algerian father, was ignored by the French producers and fought nine years to complete this first feature-length film. *Rengaine* portrays today's multicultural, complex Paris. These recent independent productions pose the question of the cinematographic institutions, film classification, and production contexts.

Sometimes—and still today—funding commissions' choices are motivated more by sociologic or paternalistic arguments than by artistic criteria. "These commissions give out of pity, with arguments that have nothing to do with cinema," Jean-Pierre Bekolo complains.[87] Films that do not meet funders' "generic expectations" often struggle to obtain funding. Ivoirian Alex Ogou, for example, published the following phone conversation about his crime film project on his Facebook page:[88]

MR. X: We have a problem. Your film isn't very African.

ME: Um, maybe . . . It's a crime movie . . .

MR. X: Yes, but it doesn't deal with African issues.

ME: What are African issues?

MR. X: You know . . . I mean, we can't feel the African touch . . .

ME: Are you interested or not?

MR. X: Oh yes . . . But how can we pitch it?

ME: . . . Like you would any other crime film.

Among the other funding sources available to African filmmakers, the Fonds Images d'Afrique was funded by the French Ministry of Foreign Affairs from 2004 to 2009 in order to back the production and distribution of African films. Of the films in this corpus, only *Teza* received funding from it.

In 1988, the International Organization of Francophonie (OIF) set up the Fonds francophone de production audiovisuelle du Sud. Commonly known as "the Fonds," this multilateral Francophone funding mechanism is placed under the joint responsibility of the OIF and the International Council of French-Language Radio and Television (CIRTEF). The Fonds is administratively managed by the OIF's Department of the French Language and Cultural and Linguistic Diversity.[89] It is open to OIF member countries of the South. Film projects are selected "according to their artistic potential and their universal character, their accessibility to both national and international markets, thereby widening their audience." They have to include a significant number of elements from the South: content, themes, screenplays, producers, directors, actors. It is clear the extent to which such production directives can influence the fabrication of works, which thereby result from a compromise between filmmakers' intentions and desires, and the practical conditions of production. The extent of this compromise varies according to each filmmaker's determination and ideological position.

Another major source of funding was the Fonds Sud Cinéma, set up in 1984 and conjointly funded by the French Ministry of Culture and Communications (via the CNC) and by the Ministry of Foreign Affairs. *Teza* received this funding. Coproductions between a French company and a company from the South could also benefit, but in this case, 75 percent of the film had to be shot in a country of the South.[90] Speaking in 2003, Zeka Laplaine complained of this:

> My next film project is about the African minority in Paris, a comedy showing that this presence and cohabitation, which some may find frightening, is not as bad as all that. The difficulty will be convincing the Fonds Sud and other funders of the need for such a film when their official criteria is that most of the film be shot in Africa.[91]

However, 50 percent of this funding from the CNC had to be spent in France. Likewise, the postproduction had to be done in France, even though 75 percent of the film had to be shot in a country of the South. Ultimately, then, provisions like these clearly do not contribute to developing film industries in the countries in question.

In 2012, the Fonds Sud Cinéma was replaced by the Aide aux Cinémas du Monde, which also subsumed the AFLE foreign language film fund. Only films coproduced by a French and a foreign company, directed by a foreigner—or exceptionally a French person, the brochure stipulates—and shot outside of France can apply, before or after shooting. African filmmakers wanting to apply thus remain dependent on France but are obliged to shoot elsewhere. Funding for cinema of the South, and notably African cinema, also exists in various European countries. Each has its own rules and selection committees. Other funds are linked to festivals, such as those in Rotterdam (the Hubert Bals Fund), Amsterdam (the Jan Vrijman Fund), or Amiens (a screenplay development fund). The Flemish Audiovisual Fund set up in 2002 backs international coproductions with Flanders. Today, the European Union also plays a key funding role with its triannual ACP Films program (Africa, the Caribbean, the Pacific). It is in this framework that *Teza* received funding from the European Development Fund.

A significant proportion of film funding also comes from television channels, such as Canal Plus (*Notre étrangère*), Canal Horizon (*Juju Factory*), TV5 Monde, Arte, TF1, France 2, France 3, and France 5 in France; WDF, ZDF, and ARTE in Germany, which also helped fund *Teza;* Channel Four and the BBC in Britain; or Vidéo-Tiers Monde in Canada. Television channels sometimes buy films once they have been made and broadcast them, as was the case with *Rage* (ARTE). Funding attributed by regional institutions in France is another possibility. The Ile-de-France region thus contributed to the postproduction of *L'Afrance* via its Thécif program (Theater and Cinema in Ile de France), and to the production of *Notre étrangère. Teza* received funding from the Alsace region (the Urban Community of Strasbourg), and *Juju Factory* from the Brussels Region in Belgium. In the United States, filmmakers can apply for funding from private foundations, company donations, and sponsorship.

Otherwise, there remains the option of making and producing a film with one's own funds, with no public funding. Of those to have done this, one may cite Newton Aduaka's films *Rage* and *One Man's Show,* the first shot in London (1999) and the latter in Paris (2012). "After finishing a film, we are usually financially ruined," confirms Mama Keïta.[92]

More recently, new means have emerged. Filmmakers are turning to audience-funded coproductions, via Internet crowdfunding campaigns. The late Guinean filmmaker Cheick Fantamady Camara, for example, raised part of the funding for his final film *Morbayassa* (2014) this way.

Generally speaking, the fact that funding sources exist specifically for films from Africa or the Global South, even if they are highly limited, constitutes one of this cinema's specificities and reinforces their image of productions that struggle to establish themselves in the mainstream.

Who Do These Films Address? Distribution, Reception, and Interpretation

When films do end up getting made, the question of distribution arises. This is a crucial question in the sense that "the life of a film does not stop at its production. Its 'real life,' as one might be tempted to put it—that which makes it a film work—begins with its appropriation by the audience."[93]

The question of distribution is a highly delicate one and involves that of reception and audiences, which is an increasingly urgent one. It is one that constantly animates the debates among filmmakers, researchers, and all film professionals. It was echoed in the title of Jean-Marie Teno's paper at a conference in London in November 2010: "Who Do You Make Your Films For?"[94] In it, the Cameroonian filmmaker described how this question, which he has been asked all his life, ended up inspiring his documentary *Lieux saints* (*Sacred Places*).[95] At the same time, he challenged the very question. Do people ask Ken Loach, for example, for whom he makes his films? Jean-Marie Teno thereby highlighted another anomaly. Indeed,

African filmmakers more often than not find themselves face to face with foreign audiences, who expect them to behave like ambassadors of their countries. Beyond the festivals, these films are rarely seen on the African continent. In Mama Keita's words:

> Until now, African cinema has been made by African filmmakers, but not for Africans. I'm not saying it's an obligation for an African filmmaker to make films "for his or her people"; that's not how I function. But I note, on the other hand, that cinema has been made for a certain public, for certain commissions, for certain festivals or certain selections, and that it has thus been a reductive cinema.[96]

The stakes are clear, for as Tahar Cheriaa put it, "whoever controls distribution controls cinema."[97] The question of distribution is beyond the scope of this work, however, which focuses rather on the analysis of films and on the context of their production.

Film
Analyses

2

CHAPTER 4

Introduction to the Socio-Aesthetic Analysis of African Diasporic Film

Unlike classical studies of African cinema that have often sought to identify "African authenticity" rather than seeing these works as artistic productions first and foremost, I propose an aesthetic and artistic analysis here, as I would for any other film. This analytical approach is one of film studies, then. While recognizing the social and political commitment of the filmmakers selected, I wish to distance myself from the idea that art and cinema be purely educational (which would sadly echo colonial film). I have, therefore, adopted an approach that moves away from this perception of African cinema as *a genre unto itself*. I shall focus instead on the variety of narrative and aesthetic styles.

I will therefore carry out what I call a "socio-aesthetic" analysis: one that takes into account both a film's aesthetics and its context of production. These are films that cannot be limited to a culture or confined within the borders of one nation. Indeed, the filmmakers in question are heir to a process of identification that goes beyond a unique, monolithic culture, giving rise to composite cinematic styles.

I will focus on camera positions and movements, and on the aesthetic approaches that reflect the filmmakers' becoming and cultural plurality. I am referring here to Edward Branigan's notion of the "camera."[1] According to him, the camera is not a concrete object, but a perception, a "semantic label." He argues that we can speak of "Hitchcock's camera," for example, not in reference to the physical equipment itself, but to the vision, the aesthetics—that is, a mental attitude. The notion of camera and its movements is thus related to signification and the production of meaning. Branigan develops this understanding of the camera—which is not to be seen as a profilmic material object, but as a hypothetic reading of the film space—in his book *Point of View in Cinema: A Theory of Narration and Subjectivity in Classical Films.*[2] Through the analysis of perspectives adopted, of what the camera does or does not show, and the way in which it does this, I shall thus examine the *mind* of each film.[3] According to Branigan, it is the *mind* that constitutes the unity of a representation and gives it its meaning. The *mind* of the film defines the angle from which we watch the story told—a kind of articulation between the narrative and the fictional world. What is interesting in his analysis of viewpoint is thus the recognition of the relation between the *frame* and the camera position (*origin*). I will focus on the different characters' points of view. By this, I mean their "viewpoint," but also their "vision" in the practical and abstract senses. The point of view adopted (the place from which we look, or Branigan's *origin*) indeed produces a vision effect that is both physical and metaphoric: what we see, but also the way of seeing and representing it. I shall also question vision as the idea one has of a situation, as a hermeneutic function of understanding and interpretation.

I was at first tempted to carry out textual readings based purely on the internal filmic diegesis, analyzing the points of view adopted by the camera, and its movements. In this respect, Laurent Jullier's position is invaluable: in his book *L'analyse des séquences,* he limits his study to an internal textual analysis, independent of and disconnected from the context.[4] Defending this approach, he cites Roger Odin, asserting that film analysts must "close their eyes to the *external pointers* (outside the film) and concentrate on the *internal pointers* (provided by the 'film text' alone)."[5] To support his argument, Laurent Jullier insists on the limits of certain external "thematic" analyses, which focus only on what a film says without considering it as an oeuvre with its own specific language. In avoiding the risk of a thematic analysis, however, one might easily fall into the structuralist formalism that only takes a film's textual structure into account. Laurent Jullier also demonstrates that "pure internal analysis itself is a chimera,"[6] which "misses a certain degree of a film's richness."[7] This being so, he proposes a "prudent mix of the internal/ external."[8] In my opinion, several variables must be considered when analyzing a film, including the historical, sociocultural, and economic context of production on the one hand, and the filmmaker's sensibility and personal artistic path on the other. A purely internal approach would thus not suffice.

To demonstrate the complexity of the fictions' universes studied here, I thus also adopt an external analytical approach. The works of Noël Burch and Geneviève Sellier (notably *La Drôle de Guerre des sexes du cinéma français: 1930–1956*) were very useful in this respect.[9] One particularly interesting aspect of their study is that they take into account systems of representation and their impact on collective imagination. To do so, they draw on gender studies and cultural studies, which offer new analytical perspectives. They thus go beyond habitual analytical norms to also reflect on symbolic productions. This approach is particularly pertinent in analyzing the films selected here, which, as they perform a perceptive and cognitive decentering, open up other points of view. The authors also highlight how films' (hi)stories are intimately linked to general history—an interrelation that is found in the works of this corpus. A purely external analysis that ignores the film language chosen and overlooks aesthetic and cinematographic specificities would not suffice here, however, for it would risk becoming a purely thematic approach again.

Questioning the "what" without the "how" would be to neglect important semantic and semiotic elements that belong to the artistic expression that is cinema. I am indeed convinced that beyond the plot itself, the way in which the story is told—that is, the narrative—has its importance; it is an element of comprehension unto itself. It is important, then, not to separate form and content. As Gianni Rondolino and Dario Tomasi also describe: "In cinema, as in all productions of signifiers, no content exists independently from the form in which it is expressed."[10]

If exclusively textual readings do not allow us to grasp a film's context of production and sociocultural milieu, exclusively contextual readings rob us of the points of view and perspectives that films express in their specific diegetic universes. For these reasons, my methodological approach conjointly draws on both analytical approaches, in a study that is both textual and contextualizing. This mixed analytical approach echoes the composite character of the chosen filmmakers' realities and of their fictional worlds. This internal/external, formalist/historical, textual/contextual intersection helps grasp the films' aesthetics, but also the filmmakers' position in the sociocultural contexts in which they find themselves.

The diversity of factors that influence each filmmaker's style—context of production, sociocultural environment, historical events, personal trajectories—justify opting for this approach.

To carry out these "socio-aesthetic" analyses, I have chosen a sequence or an extract from each film that I consider representative of its *mind*—an extract that I have also contextualized within the filmmaker's entire work. Furthermore, I have adapted the analysis of each film to the different imperatives relating to its nature and structure.

CHAPTER 5

To Each Their Own Truth

Rage, by Newton I. Aduaka

T his chapter analyzes the different narrative and aesthetic approaches that depict the evolution of the film characters and their interior journeys. It also examines the portrayal of the subjectivity of the truths and visions in which each must find their own path. It explores the ways in which Newton I. Aduaka's reflections are embodied in the heuristic path of *Rage*'s young protagonist, whose biological mixedness represents the director's cultural hybridity.[1] *Rage* is set in the context of late-1990s Britain, where Aduaka lived at the time of shooting. Three teenage London friends—Jamie (nicknamed Rage), Thomas ("T"), and Godwin ("G") seek self-fulfillment by recording a hip-hop album. Jamie (Fraser Ayres) is a working-class mixed-race youth. Prone to angry outbursts (hence his nickname, Rage), he lives with his white British mother (Alison Rose) and his little sister. He works as a shelf stacker in a supermarket and regularly buys weed for his friend Marcus (Shango Baku), a black Rastafarian adult who becomes indebted to Pin (Wale Ojo), a dangerous drug dealer. T (Shaun Parkes) is the only child of a wealthy white family, although he cannot access his money until he turns twenty-one. G (John Pickard), from a middle-class black family, is a promising pianist who loves jazz and gets on well with his parents. Searching for their own identities, the three youths struggle to find their place in society. They are at odds with the system, talk of their dreams, their identities, and what it means to be black. As one after the other of the record labels turn down their project, they need money. Rage and T decide to burgle T's parents' house (where he still lives). G reluctantly goes along with the plan, but something irremediably breaks between them. Rage and G get arrested. In prison, they are mistreated by the police. After this experience, the three friends drift apart. Despite a few attempted reunions initiated by T, who needs to complete their album to assert himself and gain some distance from his parents' plans for him (notably to go away to university in Scotland), they go their separate ways. We do not learn what path G takes, whereas T goes on to work in a record shop. Rage manages to find his path and records his album on his own.

Rage and Black British Cinema

Rage was the first completely independent film made by a black director to be released in cinemas all over the UK. With this film, Newton Aduaka established himself in the lineage of Trinidadian Horace Ové (*Pressure,* 1975), Barbadian Menelik Shabazz (*Burning an Illusion,* 1981), and British (of Saint Lucian descent) Isaac Julien (*Young Soul Rebels,* 1991). It is indeed interesting to note that while in France, where Aduaka now lives, he is seen as belonging to the group of African filmmakers; in Britain, his films were assimilated into Black Cinema. Nicolas Dambre qualifies him as "British,"[2] and Th. M. D. as "a Nigerian Londoner."[3] Aduaka defines himself as follows:

> So, for a while now, I have no longer considered myself just a Nigerian, but a Nigerian who lives in London. I would even say that I am a Londoner. Not English, which is not something I deeply feel. But the term "Londoner" suits me because it suggests an idea of mixedness. It's a place where different cultures mix.[4]

He adds: "I'm a filmmaker living in Britain, who happens to be black. I also come from Nigeria, and beyond that I come from a little village and a family within that."[5]

On its release in the UK, *Rage* won critical acclaim and was declared one of the best British films of the year.[6] It won several awards at the London Film Festival,[7] where Aduaka was acclaimed and celebrated as a new British talent.[8] It was at this point that Metrodome Distribution (in the person of Rupert Preston) and Feature Film Company (David Shear) offered to distribute the film on the condition that twenty-five minutes of the initially two-hour work be cut and that certain sequences be removed (including one showing two of the male protagonists kissing). Aduaka claims to have thus sadly learned that you cannot be truly independent unless you are in charge not only of the production, but also of the distribution of your own films.[9] Despite these concessions, distribution did not meet up to expectations, due mainly to a poor promotions campaign. According to Aduaka, Metrodome did not really believe in the film and pitched it as a subculture hip-hop product, which thereby limited its potential audience.[10] Certain fans launched an Internet campaign that elicited a considerable mobilization. *Rage* was thus given a second release in UK cinemas, the advertising funded this time by the British Film Council. In France, the film rights were bought by ARTE.

Rage explores the place allocated to young people of diverse cultural belongings in British society. It thereby highlights the consequences that the country's multicultural policy concretely has on peoples' lives. Dealing with his sentiment of exclusion—that of belonging to neither of his two cultures—Rage discovers his dual identity. This was unusual in British cinema of the time, placing *Rage* in a novel position in relation to the films that came before it (*Pressure, Burning an Illusion . . .*). *Young Soul Rebels* already had a mixed-race protagonist, Chris (Valentine Nonyela). However, he is not especially searching for his identity as, in this feature film, Isaac Julien above all focuses on racial differences and sexual orientation. The common denominator between these two films is, rather, the social role that music plays.

The three-friend formula is not new in cinema. It is found in *La Haine* (Mathieu Kassovitz, 1995),[11] *Mean Streets* (Martin Scorsese, 1973), *Husbands* (John Cassavetes, 1970), but above all in *Shadows* (Cassavetes, 1959). However, here the trio has a symbolic function: Jamie's two friends—one of whom is black, the other white—embody his conflict between his dual identities. In this maieutic path in search of the self, it is no accident that the epilogue presents a now fulfilled Rage. Thanks to the production of his album, alone, without his friends, he has found his path. It is as if he has metaphorically incorporated and reconciled both colors and cultures that compose his being. Not only does *Rage*'s trio recall Cassavetes's triads, but Charles Mingus's improvisations constitute another commonality with *Rage*, in which music plays a central role. But it is above all by virtue of their independent, experimental approaches, and the racial questions that both films evoke that a comparison may be made. *Shadows* was, of course, shot in the United States in the days of racial segregation. Both films invite the defining of one's own identity. But in addition to this heuristic path by which the characters end up dropping their masks and finding themselves, the two films are also aesthetically similar. Like *Shadows*, *Rage* was shot with a small crew and a low budget, a condition that allowed both to preserve their sought-after energy.[12] However, unlike *Shadows*, which was shot with amateur technicians, *Rage* had a professional crew, many of whom, like Aduaka, had graduated from the London Film School. *Rage* was a collective effort, realized under the direction of Newton I. Aduaka, who often expresses himself in the plural when speaking about this film, thereby highlighting everyone's contribution to it.[13] The film's transnational spirit was already present in its crew too: the director of photography, Carlos Arango De Montis (who later worked with Aduaka on *Ezra*), and the editor, Marcela Cuneo (who had already edited *On the Edge*), are South American. Aduaka shared certain aesthetic and stylistic choices with them. They also had shared references: "Carlos [Arango Montis] and I are major admirers of the films of the Italian Neo-Realists, Cassavetes, the French New Wave and recently Dogma 95."[14]

The complicity between Newton Aduaka and his director of photography, who also works as a documentary cameraman, in part explains the aesthetic of this fiction. Coming from the world of music,[15] Aduaka adopts the aesthetics of a "hip-hop urban movie" here. *Rage*'s style, Newton Aduaka adds, comes from his way of always shooting under pressure, from his relationship to hip-hop culture, and from the priority given to his actor's performance.[16] It bears the mark of urgency. The hand-held camera is immersed in the real, following the characters without judgment and capturing the souls of the protagonists, who do not represent invincible heroes, but human beings, with their contradictions and weaknesses. The narrative structure of *Rage* is not linear; it begins with a flash-forward that comes to an end just after halfway through the film. After this, the narration continues in a linear manner. With a rapid and fragmented rhythm, a style and a montage resembling music videos, the film and camera are constantly moving. The camera is "nervous, jerky, street-level," as Julien David describes it.[17] This mobility conveys the characters' instability and their difficulty in finding a steady base. The camera indeed enters the protagonists' turbulent psychological universe. From time to time, it marks a pause, as if to signify that they will sooner or later have to stop their flight and face the world. The camera frequently pitches as the characters walk a slippery slope in this game of masks that they appear to wear before society, behind which they try to hide, until they find their own identities.

This energetic mise-en-scène, which captures the intimate turbulence of the protagonists well, also echoes the filmmaker's questionings as he constantly seeks a balance and his place as an artist before society's injustices and complexities. Aduaka's artistic sensibility also stems from his own path. Coming to London from Nigeria in the 1980s to study at the London Film School, he found himself confronted with racism and with Britain's multicultural politics, which have often led to an essentialization of difference and to shutting cultural groups in on themselves, like islands. As his screenplays were not selected by the British institutions or television channels, Newton Aduaka made his first short film, *On the Edge* (28 min., 35 mm, 1998), with his own money, following the British and American independent filmmaking models.[18] While all of Aduaka's films are in one way or another highly personal, *On the Edge* can, by its title alone, be considered a paraphrase of his life. The director defined his film as a diaspora director's cry—a cathartic one. *On the Edge* is the story of Lorna (Susan Warren), who is struggling with drug addiction, and Court (*Maynard Eziashi*), her boyfriend—two Nigerians living on the edge of London life. Ironically, they dream melancholically of returning home under the regime of Abacha, one of the harshest in Nigeria's postcolonial history.

This position "on the edge" was also that of the filmmaker. He was born in 1966 in South-East Nigeria, a region that would become Biafra after a war that ravaged his country and saw the massacre of his ethnic group, the Ibo.[19] Ever since, migration has marked Aduaka's entire life. His family moved to Lagos when he was only three, and he lived on the edges of society to escape the hatred that reigned there against the Ibo. As a child, he had to learn to live discreetly. Later, he went to study in London, where he experienced racism firsthand, before finally moving to Paris. Even if this marginal position has not always been a choice, Newton Aduaka embraces it (or rather accepts it, adapting to the place that it allows him). This perspective from the margins affords him a specific point of view that differs from that one may have from the center.

This complexity and the portrayal of different viewpoints is also found in *Ezra* (2007, 102 min., 35 mm).[20] While it was a television film (commissioned by ARTE), Newton Aduaka, who is particularly sensitive to scarred childhoods and adolescence, drew on his own memories of having been born in a time of war. Retracing the path of a child soldier who is both a victim and a perpetrator, *Ezra* challenges the logic of the international system. The film depicts a trial held under the auspices of a "Truth and Reconciliation" operation, in which the judges must determine whether the child, conscripted by force, is guilty or victim. At first amnesiac, Ezra gradually remembers the terrible crimes he committed under the effects of drugs and recklessness. The fragmented montage, in which memories resurface in an unchronological fashion, reflects the complexity of the question, which cannot be understood if one only considers one part of it. Ezra is ultimately in part saved by his amnesia. This feature film also denounces the foreign and commercial interests that fuel wars and the enlistment of children in various countries in the world.

Between *Rage* and *Ezra,* Aduaka made other shorts, including *Funeral* (2003, 12 min.).[21] The film is an improvised discussion between filmmaker friends about cinema, its value and its force, following the suicide of a friend. Newton Aduaka later returned to independent cinema, again exploring exile and the quest for identity in *One Man's Show* (2012), shot in France, where he now lives. This feature film was produced by Granit Films, the production company that Newton Aduaka set up in Paris in 2009 with filmmakers Valérie Osouf and Alain Gomis, actress Delphine Zingg, and with producer Eric Idriss Kanago. Granit Films "defends multicultural, independent creation that places individuals and the universal plurality of their cultural influences at the heart of the stakes of globalization."[22]

This time, the film centers on the interrogations of a Paris-based Cameroonian actor (played by Emile Abossolo-Mbo, who is himself a Paris-based Cameroonian actor), who, as he turns fifty, discovers he has an incurable illness. "Emile is fifty years old, the same age as his native country, Cameroon. Born at the time of independence, he must now achieve his own intimate and psychological decolonization," the brief synopsis states.[23]

It is clear, then, the extent to which *Rage* bears the seeds of Aduaka's entire oeuvre to date, which portrays humans, their contradictions and difficulties, in diverse contexts and situations. The sequence that I have chosen clearly represents this complexity in its portrayal of interraciality and cultural blending and the plurality of points of view.

Confrontations and Doubles: Rage and Marcus (Extract)

The sequence analyzed begins twenty-five minutes into the film and lasts approximately three minutes. It is isochronic and takes place in the afternoon in a unity of place, in the interior in Marcus's house. The characters are Jamie, nicknamed Rage, the film's eponymous young biracial protagonist, and Marcus, an older black Rastafarian. The sequence comprises thirteen shots. The rare cuts serve the continuity (of axes and gazes) in the sequence shots. At first sight, the entire scene may be mistaken for a sequence shot. A gentle, pleasant, diegetic piece of jazz plays in Marcus's apartment.

Shot 1: 25' 05"

Marcus is sitting on a red sofa. The camera films him in a medium 45° profile shot that also reveals part of the room. He is center-frame, dressed in a short-sleeved Hawaiian shirt, with graying dreadlocks. He is surrounded by disorderly stacks of books, some of which are on the sofa. To his right, on the nearby dresser, a yellow lamp stands above him, shining a soft light. The shadows of the curtains and an (offscreen) window form bars on the wall behind him. Rage's knee is visible to the right of the screen. A slight tracking movement follows Marcus's gesture (he affectionately hits Rage with his newspaper to get him to take his foot off the coffee table) and the young man thus comes into view on the screen. Head shaved, dressed in a blue hoodie and baggy beige rapper pants, he is sitting on a chair looking downwards next to Marcus, but slightly elevated. The contrast between the two protagonists is thus established from the start, through their looks and attitudes. We later indeed discover that their looks (their choices of hairstyle, for example) signify their more or less formed and accepted identities.

25' 08": Both sit facing the camera as they discuss Marcus's debts. The medium-long shot offers a glimpse of the dimly lit kitchen area behind Rage.

25' 36": The young man stands up, the camera panning to follow him. He takes an apple in the corner kitchen and crosses the room to the window, and from one side of the frame to the other. Midway, he is lit both by the exterior natural light and by the artificial interior light, as if he were neither with Marcus nor outside. This accentuates his search, his identity that is midway between his not yet entirely embraced dual cultural belonging. Engrossed in his reading, Marcus tells the young mixed-race rapper that he lives on "fruit, vegetables, and water." "And spliff," Rage adds ironically.

25' 50": Alone, in profile in medium-shot, his face now lit only by the natural white exterior light, Rage questions the now offscreen elder man: "What d'you do all day?"

Shot 2: 25' 51"

Rage's movement thus provokes a change in the camera's focus point and thus of perspective. The older man in the foreground is absorbed in his newspaper. The young man watches him from by the window. The camera pulls back with a jerk to almost fully reveal the young man, his back to the window. He thus stands near to the opening to the world (and the future), but looks in the opposite direction, as if to show that his future is still uncertain. Contrary to Marcus, who is sitting comfortably, Rage is standing, his weight on one leg, a position that may be seen to

represent his turbulence and the precariousness of his condition (or the fact that, for the time being, he can only root himself in one of his two cultures, because he has not yet embraced his composite identity?).

Through the play of light (the camera framing them frontally), Rage's shadow is projected doubly on both walls. One of the shadows is just behind Marcus's head, which is framed in the bottom right-hand quarter of the image. This shadow appears to be veiled by that of the net curtain, which is superposed on it. This almost erased silhouette is another clear sign of the incomplete identity construction of a person who has not yet fully discovered himself.

There is a thick black edge to the frame, and the window divides it in two, as if the two spaces—Rage's and Marcus's—for the moment remain separate, as if the two do not really enter into a dialogue. Without raising his eyes from his paper, the older man answers Rage's question: "Read," going on to explain that he is retired. Having "done [his] bit for Queen and country," he can now do what he likes. Several times, his eyes flick up from the paper to the young man. The camera jerkily approaches Rage again, who retorts: "Reading don't feed no one." The moving camera indicates that, despite the affected certitude of his words, Rage's position is still unstable. He has no clear references yet, nor a solid support base.

26' 23": Just when Rage no longer seems willing to talk ("Arguing with you is a waste of time, Marcus," he states), Marcus puts down his paper and turns to him. Marcus is right next to the camera and looks in the same direction as it. The point of view has changed: the older man was being watched by the young man in the background, but now the viewpoint is associated with the older man's gaze from the focus point of the camera. He now leads the conversation. That is what the camera insisted upon in moving closer to him.

26' 33": As Marcus begins to question Rage about his music and what he is writing about, the camera now singles out the older man, again insisting on the turn that the conversation has taken. When the camera advances until it reframes the Rasta from the same point of view as at the beginning of the shot, Rage's shadow can be seen on the wall just behind his head.

At this point, Rage is only present in the shot via his shadow. This image evokes his uncompleted rap. This presence/absence on the screen as Marcus questions him about his music illustrates that the young man cannot yet manage to express himself. His rap is still stuck in his head; he is just a voiceless shadow.

Shots 3–8: 2' 36"

Although still pointing in the same direction, the camera is now further away. From different positions, Marcus and the camera observe Rage, who goes to sit back down on his chair, now in slightly low-angle. Walking towards the camera without looking at the older man, he tells him what his songs are about: reality—or rather, "my fucking reality," he retorts when Marcus asks him, "Whose reality?" That stresses the multiple (and subjective) facets of reality. Rage's shadow on the wall moves with him, as if his double being were manifesting itself and pursuing him, without him necessarily realizing it. A second shadow appears and disappears just as the first is right behind Marcus's head. Although still unstable (he moves continually), Rage pretends to be sure of himself. His shadow is no longer there; center-frame, the real Rage looms large. Our eye is drawn to his head, lit by the natural light. As he passes in front of the camera before exiting the frame to go back to his initial position sitting on the chair, he fleetingly masks Marcus (who appears tiny, in the bottom right-hand quarter of the frame).

Asked to describe what his reality consists of, he begins in voice-over: "Racism, oppression, people like me not getting a break in life . . ." All is now clear: we understand Rage's anger and his need to express himself. The older man listens to him, sitting comfortably between his books and the lamp. The scene continues in shot/reverse shot (shots 3 to 8), an alternation that suggests that a true dialogue and real reflection are now established between the protagonists. Rage can finally manage to confide, and they enter a discussion about the different weapons available to combat racism.

26' 45": The camera is almost equidistant from both characters. The framing divides the space into two zones of light. Rage is in the middle between the warm artificial light that envelops Marcus and the cold white natural light coming in from outside and dimly lighting the corner kitchen. Once again, he is thus placed in an in-betweenness that echoes his still uncertain biracial identity. The two cultural components of his personality are still divided. Straddling both, Rage has not yet managed to blend them and find his own equilibrium. At one point, he is lost for words. When Marcus asks him: "How many soldiers have you recruited to fight this war with you?," he is only able to swear back. His solitude and despair are visually translated by an incensed Rage, who, in the half-light (he is now far from that warm light illuminating Marcus), plays nervously with his apple, his eyes lowered, trapped in the right-hand side of the frame.

Throughout this exchange, the shot/reverse shot operates either by the camera panning, or by a change of shot. Thanks to slight changes in the camera's focus point, changes of scale, or reframing, the director subtly conveys a multiplicity of points of view.

Shot 9: 27' 08"

A return to a long shot of the young man getting up and walking off, not able to stand Marcus "taking the piss out of [him]."

27' 12": Once again, Rage's movements induce a change of point of view. Marcus again looks in the same direction as the camera, which has the effect of highlighting this moment, as if to indicate the great importance of the lesson he is about to give Rage, offering him the foundations on which to possibly build his own future.

Their points of view on the Black Panthers and on the different possible attitudes to adopt in the face of racism diverge.[24] Their spaces thus remain separated: Marcus is lit by the warm artificial light, whereas Rage, on his feet, is almost in the shadows, as if to insist on the fact that he has not yet reached the illumination of wisdom. The older man's stability contrasts with Rage's nervous movements. He defends the action of the Panthers, who "were fed up with all that white supremacist pile of bullshit" and who "just went in there and kicked everybody's ass." Although his position remains unstable and uncertain, he attempts to stare Marcus down.

Je n'ai rien contre le film,

27' 24": At this moment, the older man turns around laughing, backing off and encouraging Rage to forge his own opinion and to not blindly believe what he has seen in a film. As the older man moves back, he is bathed in exterior light. Does that mean that he is closer to reality (this seems to me a possible hypothesis)?

"Nothing wrong with the movie, but always do your own research. Formulate your own ideas," Marcus insists. The filmmaker thus relativizes the story he is telling, positioning it as specific and as one that can not necessarily be generalized.

Marcus sinks back into the sofa, as if to demonstrate that people are more at ease when they rest on their own ideas and values. The mise-en-scène is highly evocative of the battle that Aduaka wages against dominant representations and single mindsets.

Shot 10: 27' 39"

A close-up of Marcus, who explains to the young man that culture can be an even more powerful weapon than arms. This close-up accentuates these wise words, which invite the young man to carry out an internal revolution, and to discover the potentialities of his own mind and the power of rap in order to combat social injustice.

C'est beaucoup plus subtil.

Shot 11: 27' 50"

A low-angle zoom in on the youth, who, almost still for once, looks up and listens to the older man in silence. We can see that he has understood: the framing, in which his head looks as if it is touching the ceiling, gives him an impression of grandeur.

Panning slightly, the camera, which was filming him frontally in the last close-up, now films him in profile. He is at last completely in the warm light, which gives the room a pink hue. Here again, the change of point of view accentuates the change of perspective that the lesson has given Rage.

Shot 12: 27' 58"

Back to a close-up of Marcus. He advises Rage to learn from the errors of the previous generations. As the camera continues to film Marcus in close-up, Rage says he should be a preacher.

Shot 13: 28' 08"

Return to a medium long shot. The sequence ends with the same frame and with the characters almost in the same positions as at the outset: Marcus on his red sofa,

his nose in his newspaper, and Rage on the chair facing him. His foot is back on the coffee table in front of him.

However, Rage is a little more in the foreground than the first time round, as if he has grown, thanks to what he has just learned. When he sits back down on his chair, he has changed his ideological position on the weapons of combat. Initially convinced that an AK-47 machine gun is the best means of overcoming one's enemy, he will follow the wise opinion of Marcus, who teaches him that the mind, art, and culture are arms in the struggle.[25] The conversation turns to the same subject as at the start: money. Beyond the two men's dreams and need for self-expression, they are aware of the necessity of meeting one's daily economic needs.

Following the Characters: Camera and Becoming

The camera's various focus points and the array of perspectives they offer invite us to reflect on the film's different forms of duality: that of its places, roles, character positions, and finally that of the young protagonist.

First, place. The choice of Marcus's home brings to mind Cassavetes-type independent cinema, and in particular *A Woman Under the Influence* (1976), which *Rage* is also reminiscent of in the way that the camera follows the character. Cassavetes experimented with this "method" of the camera following the character in *Shadows,* facilitating the actors' improvisation and free movements.[26] I have already highlighted the space's dichotomy, symbolically divided into two via various procedures. At times the edge of the window delineates the two spaces; at others the sitting area contrasts with the corner kitchen. At others again, the zone lit by the warm lamplight contrasts with that lit by the outdoor light that shines in through the window. Moreover, Marcus's apartment also takes on a double semiotic value, appearing as both a refuge and a prison. It is here that Marcus withdraws to enjoy his passions, such as reading. Comfortably installed in his home on his sofa, the light warm, the image is not one of confinement. The apartment appears cut off (we hear no outdoor sounds and see nothing through the window). The bar-like shadows that the window projects on the wall are very visible, accentuating this universe's closed-in and static character, which contrasts with the movement that the young man brings. Throughout the narrative, Marcus is filmed in this place, apart from at the end of the film when Rage spreads his wings. This reinforces the image of a symbolic prison that the two characters free themselves from in the epilogue. Towards the end of the film (1 h 22' 25"), Rage and Marcus are seen on the balcony of Marcus's new apartment; facing them, the fixed camera is far away. This long sequence shot (3' 30") is a kind of epilogue and denouement. It is during this scene that Race receives the confirmation of his father's suicide (which the spectator discovers). It is here that Rage, lit by a bright natural light, expresses the importance of being and accepting oneself, with all of one's fragilities and one's errors committed out of desperation.

In contrast, in a scene at the start of the film (4' 30"), Rage is framed behind bars: that is, the banister of the staircase up to Marcus's place. In this sequence, the static camera in the street waits as Rage's car pulls into the frame. In a long, approximately one-minute shot, it observes the young man as he gets out and walks down the street, firstly from the front, then from behind. The camera follows him until he turns to enter the building. It lets him disappear from view, awaiting him when he enters on the other side. In between, a pan and forward track reveal the bars in front of an empty, dark space. This is where Rage appears and waits a moment in the background for the elevator. The camera moves to reframe him so that he clearly appears to be behind the bars; his feeling of claustrophobia and anxiety is reinforced by the fact that he impatiently, and as if fleeing, decides to take the stairs and runs towards the camera. His frustration at not managing to express himself becomes his metaphorical prison. Once again, in a moment of strong emotional force, the director does not resort to fast cutting, but rather to long takes as if to capture all the dramatic intensity of the scene. (Here, a particular use of the music can be noted too, which appears to be extradiegetic, but which in reality comes from Marcus's radio, as we discover later). In Marcus's home, in this space that is both comfortable and uncomfortable, the biracial youth in search of his own identity comes to measure himself up to a black adult who has found his equilibrium and who represents a substitute father figure.

Their relationship is not just one-way, however, which brings us to the second type of duality: that of the two characters' roles. Circulating in both spaces, Rage connects Marcus's remote world to the outside one. He receives and he gives. He learns from the older man's experience, but at the same time is protective towards him. He takes care of him, does his shopping, gets his joints, while at the same time advising him to stop smoking. Moreover, he is the guarantor of Marcus's debts, while also encouraging him to find solutions to escape the debt that curtails his freedom.

The dual relationship between Marcus and Rage and the reversal of their roles is reflected in the placement of the camera, which allows us to discover the relationship that unfolds between them. The respective positionings vary throughout the film. In the sequence analyzed, their places are inverted compared to a previous scene, also set in Marcus's apartment, in which he was sitting on the chair and Rage on the sofa. This was the moment when Rage brought Marcus food and joints. In this scene, while providing the foodstuff and drugs, Rage says he does not want to share the joint because he does not want to become blind like Marcus. Marcus retorts: "on the contrary, this might help you see better." This passage illustrates other interesting aspects. First, contrary to cliché, the young rapper does not smoke or take drugs. Even though he is in contact with this shady underworld, he is "clean." He sets himself certain moral standards, refusing to sell drugs. However, he is willing to steal to make his album. This feature film counters dominant representations, avoiding certain stereotypes found in other films about hip-hop, which, as Aduaka describes, often deform reality and rob this culture of its dignity.[27] He also restores the real complexity, going beyond the prejudices found in representations of black people: G, the young black character, is not from the projects, his parents take good care of him, we do not know if he has siblings, he loves jazz, plays piano, and appears set to go to music school. Aduaka does not offer a partial or rose-tinted vision, however; the real is fictionalized in its diverse facets, as he also portrays delinquent black youth.

In the above extract, the camera isolates Rage at this point as he sits on the sofa next to the lamp, but lit by the outside light, whereas Marcus is in the dark corner of the apartment. The filmmaker thereby noticeably brings a plurality of truths and viewpoints to the screen; what Rage calls being "blind" physically speaking is, for Marcus, a way of "seeing better" philosophically and metaphorically. The question of viewpoints and perspectives is thus subverted. When Rage goes to sit on the sofa, for example, he is completely lit, whereas Marcus is in the dark. Then, thanks to a shot/reverse shot, the play of light changes, Marcus being more lit, Rage less, and the contrast between the two men diminishes, as if to express the fact that reason is never in one camp alone, nor is it always in the same one.

Coming back to the sequence analyzed, Marcus remains sitting calmly and comfortably on his sofa. He is stable, while the on-edge Rage is constantly moving, echoing his instability. At most, Marcus leans backwards or forwards, his eyes following Jamie/Rage, who, in contrast, is constantly agitated and never stops pacing from the chair to the window and the kitchen. He passes from one side of the frame to the other, as if he were trying to follow the different parts of his still divided, fragmented being. He seeks his place, without really finding it.

The camera follows the two characters, accompanying Rage's physical coming and going and Marcus's slight movements or change in the direction of his gaze. It is often Rage's movements that cause the camera to move, triggering a change in point of view, as if to show that before choosing and finding his equilibrium, Rage must explore reality from different angles, without restricting his gaze to a single perspective. This is the only way he will be able to free himself from the masks he wears and be himself, instead of complying with what others expect of him. The two characters Rage/Jamie and Marcus are (re)presented thus, respectively symbolizing a still disjointed and torn composite identity, and assumed identarian and cultural complexity. The youth questions his identity-in-the-making and his future. Marcus, who has already reached a certain age and is retired, has at last found harmony by accepting his cultural identity. For example, when he says, "I've done my bit for Queen and country," Marcus demonstrates his belonging in Britain; he is thus black *and* British, which is not a contradiction, but the reflection of an inclusive identity. The jigsaw of his being has been assembled out of the different pieces of his being. At this point in the narrative, the two figures thus represent two different attitudes towards cultural blending; they illustrate the fact that it may leave one torn, or be a source of enrichment.

Throughout the sequence, the remarkable play of the two sources of light represents these two ways of being. The blue—a primary color—gives a cold light, typical of the early morning, which well illustrates the incompleteness of Rage's personality, whereas the composed soft, warm, orange artificial light exemplifies the unity that Marcus has reached. Moreover, this warm orange light comes from indoors, from an intimate world. It is evocative of the sunset, suggesting that the character has reached maturity. What is more, the light/knowledge dichotomy is clear. The diverse light sources that occupy the scene also represent the different forms of knowledge and multiple truths, subjected to the eternal question of viewpoint. We are confronted with two different attitudes before the same difficulties. The camera adopts their two visions of the world, their two universes and their two truths, both of which are legitimate. Nonetheless, the older man, based on his experience and the equilibrium he has reached, has things to teach the younger man. These moments of transmission are accentuated by the close-up shots of Marcus and one close-up of Rage, listening. The words that the wise Rastafari says to Rage bring to mind the scene in *Djib* (Odoutan, 2000) in which the grandmother encourages the young black man whom the film is named after to take his destiny in hand. Djib is struggling to find his place and path in the Paris suburbs. Visible to the spectator (and to the fixed camera) in profile, his grandmother occupies the screen and berates the youth, offscreen:

> Djibi, when will you understand that you must take yourself in hand? When will you understand that if you want to be someone, you must be yourself and not imitate others? Not blindly follow the bad boys, who go "Yo! Yo!" in the street, "I'm a rapper and fuck your mother"?

In *Djib,* Odoutan, who has a past as a musician and rapper himself, caricatures the grandmother's prejudices about hip-hop culture. It is, for that matter, interesting to note that the two films are almost contemporaneous. In both cases, it is the elders who speak to the youth, just like in *Keïta! L'h*éritage du griot (Kouyaté, 1995), in which the old griot teaches the young Mabo Keita to explore the history of his past and his ancestors. Marcus encourages Rage to learn from the past: "The tactics and efforts of my generation and those past are there for yours to analyze and learn from." This affirmation is accentuated by a close-up of Marcus, which follows a close-up low-angle shot of Rage, an exemplary method to show that the young man has learned, and thus that his point of view has changed. However, Marcus is also disposed to learn and change, in keeping with the evolution of the social context. After having given his highly persuasive speech, he picks his paper up again (a symbol of the constant flow of current news), sits back to read it, and, for a moment, is lit again by the outside light—in other words, he is open to today's world, not trapped in his past ideas. That echoes the understanding here of identity as a constantly evolving process, which Aduaka depicts on the screen.

Despite their differences, the connection between Marcus and Rage is strong. Contrary to Rage's mother, who is English and white and who does not seem to completely understand her son's angst, Marcus knows what Rage is going through because, as a black man, he has experienced similar difficulties due to the racism and social oppression that exist in today's societies. During one of their previous exchanges, Rage, isolated in the shot, sitting on the sofa looking at all the books in Marcus's place, lit by the exterior light, spits out: "You got all these books, right? And you've got it all so figured out. Then tell me this: how come you're in a shithole just like the rest of us?" In an earlier scene, we have seen the daily psychological violence black people are subjected to. When the police stop the three friends' car and threaten to arrest them on the false pretense that they were smoking joints, one of the policemen says to Rage: "It's your word against mine," making it clear that he will have the final word before a judge. This scene illustrates the context; it explains too that the rage that inspires Jamie's moniker also stems from these difficult social conditions. Social recognition is also questioned here: the authority of a white English government employee versus the impossibility for a young black man to speak *his* truth. We thus understand that Rage's anger comes from the fact that his words are not listened to (metaphorically, but also literally when it comes to his songs, his rap, his self-expression). The film thus concretely explores what happens when people are desperate, when they live in humiliation. "When a man resorts to profanities, it's a sure sign of his inability to express himself," says Marcus, while at the same time recognizing the need to express oneself as primordial. This fiction demonstrates how violence is fueled by suffering and social exclusion.

The mother's difficulty in understanding her son's malaise is portrayed towards the end of the film in one crucial sequence. Finding Rage prostrate in his room, she attempts to reassure him of the sincere love that she and her husband shared. "What are we, black or white?," he asks, referring to himself and his sister. "Neither. Both," his mother replies. He thus explains where his anger is coming from: "I'm black. It's not even down to me. It's black people who decide whether I am or not. I always fucking have to prove myself." It is not only his full-blown identity crisis that is manifested here ("What the fuck am I?," Rage asks in tears); other key themes transpire too: self-image, assigned or chosen identities, and the place people occupy in the public space.

This sequence shot marks the culminating point of this identity-based questioning. As is often the case in Aduaka's cinema, this key scene is a sequence shot filmed with a fixed camera. It follows the shot in which Rage descends the stairs in slow motion, with no music, to his room (and metaphorically, into himself), and the high-angle shot of Rage sitting on his bed, all alone. These images—which start and end with a black frame and silence—flag the gravity of the sequence. Here, Rage liberates himself from his inner questions that disrupt his existence, for he cannot say these words in public until he has said them to his mother and to himself.

That seems to me to be all the more true if one thinks of the theater sequence that comes shortly after the extract discussed here, and which so perturbed Rage. A black actor removes a black veil from his face, as if to rid himself of a mask, while a biracial actress sits on the floor painting one of her arms white and the other black, saying: "Do I embrace both cultures? Or do both cultures embrace me?" Outside the theater, the camera captures Rage as he exits down a narrow passage and walks down a small street, which the depth of field makes look even narrower. This may be taken as an iconic representation of his turmoil after this play that performs the questions to which he has not yet found answers. He is perturbed to see staged what he cannot articulate. Pulling back, the camera follows Rage and his two friends, G and T, as they take the overpass. Rage walks ahead of the two others, physically distancing himself from them. Advancing edgily, they get into an animated debate about what it means to be black. His black friend G explains that it "ain't got nothing to do with color." When Rage desperately retorts: "To the white man, a Nigger is a Nigger is a Nigger," G answers: "You keep thinking like that and you're gonna stay a stupid fucking Nigger," stressing the active role that each and every person can play in the construction of their future and their social role. In the obscurity of the night lit by artificial lighting (a symbol of the masks that they wear in the sense that they have not yet found their identities?), the three youths cross the city. They appear to us as a group, thereby highlighting the coexistence of different visions. The visibly angry Rage talks of his pride in being black and the attitude that, in his opinion, a black person should have. At that instant, his friends are ahead of him both in the discussion and physically, as they walk faster than him. But, at the end of the scene, G accuses him of shaving his head for fear that his hair will grow blond. Rage storms off in anger (again to Marcus's), dumping G and T there where they are in the street. This scene again underlines the difference between Marcus, who, with his graying dreadlocks, is at peace with himself, and Rage, who with his shaved head seeks to hide his private fears, not knowing yet who he truly is, and not having accepted his mixed-race identity. Neither black nor white, and not having yet embraced his dual belonging, he is still divided.

That brings us to the third type of duality: that of Rage himself. The dual identity that Jamie/Rage incarnates is already manifest in his two names. His dual being is also represented on the screen in different ways: lit by the two lights, sitting or standing, on the right or left of the screen, both a protector and a disciple. Moreover, Newton Aduaka's camera illustrates his multiple belonging and composite being through the mise-en-scène. Following the edgy Rage's movements, the camera frequently changes perspective. In the sequence discussed here, Rage appears to be mirrored by his shadow, or better still, by his two shadows (both parts of his identity?) that invade the screen. The superposition of Rage's shadow and Marcus's head announces a quasi-filial relationship between them, while also indicating the rapper and the Rastafari's marginality. The two contrasting colors of the dark shadow on the white wall can also be seen to represent the lack of unity that exists in him, the blending that Rage has not yet accomplished. To me, this sequence is also central in the film because it is at this moment that we understand what rap represents to Rage. This can be seen as a mise-en-abyme of what cinema represents to Newton Aduaka: an urgency to speak out.

Rage's epilogue is also a mise-en-abyme, or a *paraphrase* (in Jean-Pierre Esquenazi's sense of the term) of the filmmaker's experience. Like the filmmaker, Rage will produce his rap album himself, independently, but only after having found his own path. Aduaka indeed said, "For me as a director, *Rage* is a very personal story which I more or less lived in the process of making the film."[28] However, rap also represents the voice of those on the margins of society, who, like shadows, are at times invisible, without a voice, not recognizing themselves in dominant media representations.[29] For these youths, hip-hop is a means of expressing their voices and talking about their conditions and neighborhoods (in the film, for example, G, who is not familiar with the working-class neighborhoods, discovers them through Rage's rap, and it is when the latter takes him to his home that G better understands this music). Hip-hop, which inspires the film's aesthetic, rhythm, and montage, is a free art that captures the pulsations of the urban world. Moreover, hip-hop culture often revolves around identity issues and proposes a kind of decolonization of minds, or another gaze that highlights problems and offers alternatives. Born in the African American and immigrant communities of the New York ghettos, this movement has spread all over the world. Young people have appropriated it, with diverse nuances according to their sociocultural contexts.[30] This also explains

Newton Aduaka's choice to select music by independent British rappers—whose songs and words echo the context of the film[31]—enriching a soundtrack in which even Bach's Eighth Symphony finds its place.

To conclude, I chose to analyze this sequence because it perfectly captures the spirit of this feature film, which portrays the seeking of identity in interracial mixing. This extract also helps understand different positionings vis-à-vis cultural hybridity. In this sequence, changes of viewpoint are conveyed in two different ways: either through a change of shot, or a pan, accentuating the fact that the characters are constantly evolving. Even though the plotline is based on the friendship between three youths, two of whom who are not present in this sequence, the extract analyzed offers a good example of the portrayal of plurality. The protagonist's biracialism can be read as a *paraphrase* of the filmmaker's cultural blending and his positioning, which allowed him to look at British society with distance.

CHAPTER 6

Between Fiction and Experience

Juju Factory, by Balufu Bakupa-Kanyinda

This chapter analyzes the composite, syncretic style in which Balufu Bakupa-Kanyinda crafts a storyline set between past and present, fiction and reality, history and forgetting, and in which the dialogues articulate different possible positions. *Juju Factory*[1] is indeed both a mise-en-abyme of the filmmaker's own dilemmas and a portrayal of artistic creation in the diaspora space. This fiction recounts the vicissitudes of Congolese Kongo Congo (Dieudonné Cabongo Bashila), who lives with his wife, Béatrice (Carole Karemera), in the Matonge district of Brussels, about which he is writing a book. Matonge is in the Brussels suburb of Ixelles; due to its large Congolese, and more generally African, immigrant population, it is named after a lively district of Kinshasa in the Democratic Republic of Congo (DRC). Through a mise-en-abyme, city life, certain facets of Kongo Congo and his entourage's daily lives, and historical moments enter the fictional world of the novel and thus that of the film. Kongo Congo is inspired both by "the entrails of his illusions," and by his individual (hi)story, which is also the collective history of his people. His writing is enriched by dreamlike visions and by the ghosts who haunt him, such as, for example, the ghost of Patrice Lumumba, who "roams with no sepulcher."[2] The author writes in the present tense, but unravels the threads of history that connect Belgium and the Congo, much to the displeasure of his publisher (Donatien Katik Bakomba), the eloquently named Belgian of Congolese descent Joseph Désiré.[3] Rooted in the present, driven by commercial interests, the latter dreams of a tourist guide spiced up with exotic details—a kind of invitation to journey in present-day Matonge. Kongo thus must choose between his freedom of expression and the constraints dictated by his publisher. Meanwhile, life goes on around him, with all its complexities and human contradictions, and with the different visions of the many characters, all of whom experience exile in their own way. The publisher does not read the tales that his wife, Bibi (Pascale Kinanga), writes, and she, upset at her husband's indifference, cheats on him with Kongo's brother. Finally, thanks to the efforts of a cultural association, Kongo's book is published, while the publisher loses his job and is left by his wife.

The storyline is structured on different interwoven narrative levels, to which are added archive images and scenes shot in the streets, with passersby, in documentary style.[4] Balufu Bakupa-Kanyinda embraces the freedom to mix forms: black and white sequences are inserted into the color film, reinforcing its heterogeneous style and offering diverse visions of the city. The film's story, Kongo's thoughts, and his novel are like tributaries merging to enrich the narrative flow.

Mise-en-Abyme, Exile, and Artistic Creation

Juju Factory is Balufu Bakupa-Kanyinda's first feature-length fiction film, in which he portrays questions that are very dear to him, such as the opposition between a day-to-day present and a present marked by the past, while also seeking a path to the future. This film opposes a temporality of the pure present, a remorse-free actuality, and a historical temporality that looks at the Congolese people's memory. *Juju Factory* questions the relations between the DRC and Belgium, the role of artists, their link with the diasporic community, and the place of the individual within the collectivity. The notion of "home" and of the elsewhere, the imaginary, the creative act in the exilic universe, and questions of power and artistic creation are all examined here. Born in DRC in 1957, Balufu Bakupa-Kanyinda had an eclectic education, and his cultural and geographic belongings are multiple. The son of Congolese intellectuals, a cinephile, he grew up watching many films, and notably Westerns, in the cinemas of Kinshasa.[5] He began studying medicine, before abandoning this path because he preferred "healing minds rather than bodies."[6] He also preferred storytelling, which, for him, involves generosity and contact with others.[7] After working in film programming at the French Cultural Center in Lubumbashi (DRC), he left his country in 1981 to go to Belgium, which he was forced to leave in 1986 due to his anti-Mobutu militant activities.[8] In Belgium, he studied sociology, philosophy, history of art, and history. He then continued his film studies in France, Britain, and the United States. He has stated, in this respect, that "My mind is pretty free because I am not the product of one [single] school."[9] The actor Dieudonné Cabongo Bashila said of him: "Balufu Bakupa-Kanyinda comes from Congo, but I think I can unmistakably say that he comes a little bit from everywhere."[10] Bakupa-Kanyinda has also said that he lives in "cultural exile."[11] In short, he embodies what Avtar Brah calls multi-locationality,[12] that is, someone who crosses territorial and cultural frontiers; he is a transcontinental and transcultural artist, as is reflected in his composite aesthetics and narrative style.

Balufu Bakupa-Kanyinda is a polyvalent artist. A filmmaker and writer, he has also developed a theoretical, critical reflection, and has occasionally taught cinema, notably at the New York University in Ghana.[13] It is significant that the documentary about him by Burkinabè Issaka Compaoré is subtitled "the poet, the thinker." He has also written plays, which is how he met the actor Dieudonné Cabongo Bashila, with whom he made two major films. All of his works revolve in one way or another around the representation of Africans, history, and exile. It is significant that in 2006, he was also executive producer on the documentary *Who's Afraid of Ngugi?* about Ngugi wa Thiong'o, the Kenyan writer in exile's return home, made by the Malian academic Manthia Diawara. During his studies in Brussels, Balufu Bakupa-Kanyinda studied Congolese history, but, as he asked, "What perspective on the history of the Congo could I be taught in Belgium except that of the former colonial rulers?"[14] He thus started taking increasing interest in the representation of the Other (perceiving himself as "the Other") and in images of black people in contemporary Belgium, which became the subject of his postgraduate research.[15] With *Juju Factory,* he thus reexamines these questions that have inhabited him for a very long time. He does not simply reverse the perspective; through the plurality of his characters and their different truths, he offers a complex viewpoint, seeking to understand the current situation through history and memory.

The complexity of Balufu Bakupa-Kanyinda's gaze also comes from his many travels and encounters. He returned to the African continent for the Ouagadougou Pan-African Film Festival (FESPACO) in 1985, the golden age of Thomas Sankara in Burkina Faso.[16] This Burkinabè experience strongly marked him for various reasons and was at the origin of two films. For the first time, Balufu Bakupa-Kanyinda saw films made by African directors. However, while happy to see them, he perceived them as a prolongation of the colonial gaze, which was all the more shocking for him as he found himself in the country of Thomas Sankara, "the man who appeared to have revitalized the old Pan-African dream."[17] While talking with his colleagues and friends, and in particular with David Achkar and Djibril Diop Mambéty, he decided to make the documentary *Dix mille ans de cinema* (*Ten Thousand Years of Cinema*), a poetic short film built around the reflections of filmmakers, recorded during the 1991 FESPACO.[18] The title was inspired by Djibril Diop Mambéty, who said: "I have an appointment with ten thousand years of cinema."[19] In this film, Mambéty and David Achkar describe cinema as a dream, as an encounter with Others, and as freedom.[20] Thanks to this Burkinabè experience, Balufu Bakupa-Kanyinda also met Captain Thomas Sankara. In 1991, he made a 26-minute documentary about him, *Thomas Sankara*.[21] He got the idea for this film during the 1989 FESPACO when he visited Sankara's grave with John Akomfrah and other filmmakers. The fact that a film containing images of Sankara was removed from the same edition of the FESPACO was also decisive for this project. Balufu Bakupa-Kanyinda's film shows Capitaine Sankara in his anti-imperial struggles, determinedly opposing outside diktats.

The director's voice-over commentary is highly personal. Without falling into myth, he poetically testifies to the hopes that Thomas Sankara inspired in the country. Through this documentary, which joins the long list of works on Thomas Sankara by various auteurs, the filmmaker pays homage to all those who have lost their lives fighting for freedom, and immortalizes the unfinished dreams of an entire population.

Bakupa-Kanyinda is particularly fascinated by political figures. He also made a documentary about the former Gabonese president Omar Bongo, *Bongo Libre*.[22] It is an ambiguous portrait, built around a dialogue between the filmmaker and the Gabonese president, as the powerful images of Libreville in the background contradict the president's words.

Before this, in 1996, Balufu Bakupa-Kanyinda made his first fiction: the magnificent mid-length *Le Damier, Papa National oyé!* (*The Draughtsmen Clash*) about an imaginary dictator.[23] Beyond the metaphor of the game of draughts (checkers), he portrays the relationship between the people and power. Even though the film is not set in a specific country, it is not hard to see where the director—who, it must be recalled, is Congolese—got his inspiration and to take it as an allusion to President Mobutu. Insomniac, the "Founding-President-for-Life" in his leopard-skin hat demands that someone come to play draughts with him. As no one plays well enough, or is brave enough to play against him, he is frustrated and can no longer find a fitting adversary. Everyone lets him win, which is no pleasure. On the night of the film, the dictator thus plays against a man from the streets, a champion in his neighborhood, who accepts the challenge and who symbolically represents the people. In conformity with the rules of the game, the two men sit facing one another, on the same level. The advancement of their respective pieces becomes a dialogue between the dictator and his people. Given that power here is seen as a drug, in order to be able to play on an equal footing with his opponent, "the people" requests to be allowed to smoke some marijuana. The film, which is quite static, is powerfully shot in black and white. It illustrates the improbable meeting of two solitudes: that of power and that of the people. *Le Damier* is about freedom of speech and the freedom to play by the same rules. This same theme of freedom is found in *Juju Factory*, which contains a sound extract of this mid-length film. *Le Damier* also marked the start of Balufu Bakupa-Kanyinda's collaboration with actor Dieudonné Cabongo Bashila (who plays the role of the dictator here) and with the musician So Kalmery, who also created the music of *Juju Factory*.

Bakupa-Kanyinda is not just interested in politics and history; he also made a documentary about the Congolese singer Papa Wemba—*Balangwa Nzembo: L'ivresse de la musique congolaise* (1999)—and another about the Cameroonian football player Roger Milla (*Roger Milla, le lion des lions*, 2006), thereby demonstrating his border-defying Pan-African spirit.[24] His desire to cross borders is also apparent in the different countries that he has shot his films in (notably—in addition to Belgium—in Burkina Faso, Gabon, and Congo), and the fact that he crisscrossed the African continent to make *Afr@digital*.[25] In the latter, as earlier in *Dix mille ans de cinéma* or *Thomas Sankara*, Bakupa-Kanyinda adopted the woven narrative structure of the Congolese *kasalas* (storytellers, who use spiraling narratives and digressions, illustrating their tales with images and allegories), which is also found in *Juju Factory*. In all his films, Bakupa-Kanyinda advances by "within the narrative sphere constantly creating this weave that appears to be a form of de-structuring, but which becomes a form of structuring, because it is intentional."[26] Pointing to the difficulty of finding film funding on the African continent, he identifies digital as a solution that is not only democratizing but also frees expression. He travels the continent exploring existing practices and finds that digital is already widely used. Observing that when it comes to technology, young Africans often suffer from an inferiority complex vis-à-vis Europe or the United States, Balufu Bakupa-Kanyinda invites them to master the technical to express themselves. The filmmaker states:

I have worked in 35 African countries. I know the difficulties with production on this continent. Every day, I am confronted with inferiority complexes. . . . Our role as artists is also to give young people confidence. There is enormous creativity in Africa. Sometimes the most is not made of it because the professional tools are lacking.[27]

Film funding is a thorny issue that Balufu Bakupa-Kanyinda knows only too well—he who in the film milieu is known as "a big mouth" and who has often paid dearly for speaking his mind. For example, *Juju Factory* received only a postproduction grant from the Organisation internationale de la Francophonie (OIF). Olivier Barlet said of the film that it "struggled to find funding."[28] As the director explained:

A film like *Juju Factory* could not be funded by them [the "masters"]. Why? Because a film made by an African in a European setting is not eligible for any European fund. They finance Africans to film depravation back home, stories from their villages, their wells, that's why![29]

Indeed, *Juju Factory* (which had a budget of approximately 500,000 €) was funded by the film crew and actors, who invested their salaries, and the décors were lent by friends (including the police office and uniforms). Only the postproduction was paid for.[30] Unable to block the streets during the shoot, the decision to film people in their neighborhood was also clearly an economic choice. In the film's press kit, Bakupa-Kanyinda explains:

The film was shot on DVcam—above all because it suited the conditions of a small independent production. The film comprised ten people. Olivier Pulinckx, the director of photography, and I were the only two professional technicians. The crew was made up of young people who, for the most part, were discovering their first film.

After *Juju Factory,* Balufu Bakupa-Kanyinda made the short fiction film *Nous aussi avons marché sur la lune* (*We Too Walked on the Moon*) in 2009 as part of the *L'Afrique vue par . . .* project, a collective work comprising ten short films by African filmmakers, funded by the Algerian government for the PANAF Festival in 2009.[31] To commemorate the fortieth anniversary of the Americans' first steps on the moon, Bakupa-Kanyinda invites people not to abandon their dreams. In 1969, *Réveil dans un nid de flammes* (*Awakening in a Nest of Flames*), a collection of poems by the Congolese poet Tshiakatumba Matala Mukadi, was published. In the prolongation of the at the time much-debated Negritude movement, this work was banned in Mobutu's Zaire (present-day DRC). Inspired by poets whom the Congolese youth do not study, *Nous aussi avons marché sur la lune* revolves around texts by Aimé Césaire and Tshiakatumba Mukadi, recited by pupils, led by their teacher. The narrative is poetic and dreamlike. Images of major African figures abound (Patrice Lumumba is ever-present), but we also see the then new American president Barack Obama.[32] This was the first film that Balufu Bakupa-Kanyinda shot in Congo.

This blend of history, politics, memory, and poetry typical of Balufu Bakupa-Kanyinda's creative world is also explored in *Juju Factory*. It is also manifest in the extract that I shall now introduce and analyze.

Sites of Memory, between Past and Present (Extract)

The extract begins 1 h 8' 28" into the film and lasts approximately two and a half minutes. It comprises nineteen shots. It takes place at the Royal Museum of Central Africa and its cemetery in Tervuren and ends in the publisher's office. The characters are Kongo Congo, Béatrice, his wife, and, at the end, the publisher and the manager of the nonprofit association that is publishing the book.

The extract begins in the gardens of the Royal Museum of Central Africa in Tervuren, in the region of Brussels. The pleasant but sad and nostalgic background music (a jazz piece, set to African rhythms and guitar) begins a second earlier, at the end of the preceding scene.

This creates a link between the apparently unrelated scenes, which we shall later discover are part of the same intersecting play of diverse narrative layers. In the previous sequence, Béatrice reads lines from her husband's novel, while Nico, the brother-in-law, and Muadi, his wife, live the same scene, reconciling after having split up. The extract analyzed here continues the same structure, mixing images from the film's plot with the narrative of the novel that Kongo is writing, which constitutes a second diegesis.

We firstly discover the pleasant, well-laid-out grounds typical of Belgian chateaux (a slow pan from left to right), then the Kongo/Béatrice couple walking arm in arm. An imposing cypress offers a foretaste of the cemetery to come.

Next, we follow them inside the museum. Filmed from behind in wide shot, they climb the steps to enter. Even though they are filmed from a slightly low angle, they appear small against the museum's sumptuous classical façade. (Béatrice, at this point, is still unaware of part of the history of the Congolese in Belgium).

A written page is superposed on this image in a crossfade. It is a page of the novel that Kongo is writing. He reads it in voice-over, set to the same background

music: "In the great exhibition hall topped by a high ceiling that gave it the austere allure of a courtroom, next to the old, locked glass door behind which lay a corridor as impassive as . . ." Kongo, here, is the narrator both of his novel and of his real life.

In another crossfade transition, Kongo appears as he writes. His face is visible behind his computer screen. Focusing on his computer, his glasses perched on the end of his nose, he continues reading aloud, this time onscreen: "a prison visiting room, they stopped in front of a Tshokwe."[33]

We are no longer in the grounds of the museum, but in an unidentified place. In this interior shot, Kongo is dressed differently to the rest of the sequence: he is now wearing a checked shirt, not the leather jacket he was wearing before and wears again after. Unlike in the other shots in this extract, in which he is almost always with his wife, here he is alone. Another shot is introduced: Kongo Congo is now writing his novel, or at least a story that appears to be related to the preceding scene. Now, he is simultaneously narrator and the author/creator of his novel. This shot thus introduces discontinuity into the narration.

He is at the same time the writer and the embodiment of the character he is creating, this character himself being inspired by Kongo's life. The to-ing and fro-ing and ambiguities are constant. We do not know whether the narration relates the preceding scene, if it is a fictionalized account of it, or if, on the contrary, the scene is a representation of the novel. The camera approaches slightly, but we rapidly move on to the following shot with a slight fade.

Kongo continues to read out loud the text on his computer: "or a Songye . . . ," as a Songye mask exhibited in the museum appears on the screen.[34]

Then the initial scene resumes. We see the couple visiting the museum as the narration just recounted. We thus witness not only a doubling of the narrative layers, but also a doubling between what we see and hear. In this play of multiplications, we no longer know if Kongo is writing and taking inspiration from his experiences (that we see, and which thus take on the status of flashbacks), or if we are watching the representation of his writing, and thus the fruit of his imagination.

His voice-over continues: "Then he kissed his girlfriend on the lips, for a long time, sliding his hand under her poplin skirt," as the couple reaches and stops in front of the display case of the mask. Kongo puts his arm around Béatrice's shoulders. At this moment, Kongo is both the narrator and the protagonist, but the scene we see departs from the read narration. The character does not kiss his girlfriend, or put his hand up her skirt, as the voice described. The shots of the voice-over narration and the story we see are interwoven, but not identical. We then see the couple looking at the mask. Several images appear in superimposition. Behind the couple, we glimpse other visitors, other statues, and objects exhibited on the wall behind the entrance.

The background African guitar music stops and we hear various sounds, including what sounds like a chiming bell, roaring animals, followed by metallic

industrial sounds. Kongo kneels before the mask (the camera at this point is by its protective glass case; we thus see Kongo through the glass).

As the camera shoots through the glass case, he thus appears blurred; for an instant, his image appears to double in the glass, like in a mirror, as the glass also reflects the arches and other details of the room. He next looks up towards Béatrice, whom we see in low-angle. This shot thus also captures the *high ceiling* described by the narrator Kongo. The camera quickly comes back down and, in a lateral pan, shows other masks.

Unidentified sounds can be heard in the background. The couple continue their visit. Behind them, we glimpse schoolchildren on a guided tour. The camera follows Kongo and his girlfriend's movement and stops with them in front of another wooden mask, this time fixed to a yellowing wall. Silence. Until now, we have not heard them speak. A somber music strikes up. It is a piano piece, which grows louder, then lessens in intensity, like a rhythmic punctuation. It is Western music, different to that of the earlier stringed instrument and its African tones and rhythms. The musical motif underscores and enhances the text. The voice of a disembodied and extra-diegetic narrator takes over and continues Kongo's narration offscreen: "In 1897, in Brussels, during the International Exhibition . . ."

The narrator continues over the low-angle shot of a church spire soaring

skywards: "Three villages were built on the Tervuren ponds to exhibit 267 Congolese. Seven of them, Ekia, Ngemba . . ."

The peaceful, serene image of the little church and its blue stained-glass window contrast with the violence of the historical facts recounted in voice-over, which continues over the same background piano music.

The couple arrive in front of the church. An insert shot shows gravestones on

the ground as the narrator's voice continues: "Mpemba, Zwao, Sambo Kitukwa, and Mibange died here. They are buried in this spot."

A high-angle panning shot shows the seven tombs, stopping on the last one, that of Mibange. The pan pivots slightly until we can read "Mibange soldat Congo Belgique 1897" (Mibange, soldier from the Belgian Congo, 1897).

In a medium close-up shot, Béatrice, not taking her eyes off the tomb, asks Kongo next to her to explain.

The first dialogue between the two characters thus begins: "Someone must have told them it was a short-cut to heaven," Kongo answers impassively, also looking down. After raising and lowering their eyes again, without actually looking at one another, Kongo continues: "They brought them here to . . . exhibit them." The brief pause in his words stresses the gravity of what he is about to say. Their eyes meet briefly and Béatrice sighs: "You're right, Matonge indeed started here." Here, a second temporality experienced by the protagonists predominates: that which definitively connects them to the colonial past. Then, in silence and in medium close-up, the couple, seen from behind, look at a plaque on the wall written in Dutch, in memory of these seven Congolese.[35] A close-up of the plaque. The voice-over of the extra-diegetic narrator comments:

> In Brussels in 1897, several Congolese exhibited in a human zoo to demonstrate the benefits of colonization were felled by the Belgian sun. The plaque on the church

wall claims that they died in a heat wave. A murderous summer. The true success for the penetrative force to civilize the virgin forest.[36]

Meanwhile, the shot changes and we now see an old, yellowing black-and-white photo, typical of colonial photography. It is a photo of a Congolese village: young black women dressed in the white missionary dresses of the colonial era are in front of a thatched bamboo hut.

Alongside, people are looking at the hut, maybe visitors at the Universal Exhibition.[37] A pan zooms out to reveal the photo in its entirety. The piano stops.

After a black frame, we are in the publisher's office. A young white woman, one of the people in charge of the association due to publish the book (Stéphane Bissot),[38] is sitting opposite him, looking annoyed as Joseph Désiré says in voice-over: "We have a problem. Our writer needs to get back to the subject, i.e., Matonge Village." In the absence of any other background sound, we hear only their voices.

The following shot shows Désiré at his desk in a shirt and tie, speaking on the phone to the director of the association.

Interweaving Styles and Forms

The extract chosen presents a series of stylistic and narrative elements that are representative of the polymorphous and composite structure of the film, notably its different intersecting narrative layers and temporalities, and the historic and documentary elements woven into the fiction. While its discourse is at times excessively explicit and the mise-en-scene uneven, the filmmaker's multiple cultural belongings and his preoccupation with identity-based issues are found in the film. This extract comes shortly before the epilogue. The conflict between writer and publisher, which constitutes the plotline of the film, is about to be clarified. It is a major turning point, which shows the writer's deep-lying motivations, such as, for example, the importance he accords to the past and history. His narrative choices move further and further away from the exotic tourist pleasures dreamed of by the publisher, who, thirsty for profit, lives in the present, with no interest in the past. Two different conceptions of time are at play, then, which I shall analyze. The film portrays a temporal hybridity that combines with the characters' dual belongings. Nonetheless, to better understand the antagonism between Kongo and his publisher, who respectively appear at the beginning and end of the extract, the articulation of the film must be considered. They respectively embody the opposition between the idea of the present with roots in the past, and that of a present cut off from history.

The beginning of *Juju Factory* establishes certain elements that help understand the constant alternation of different styles and narrative layers. The film's dreamlike, allegorical opening depicting the protagonist's dream is followed by a series of shots that announce the spirit of the film. Quasi-documentary color images show several emblematic sites in Brussels: the planetarium; plaques showing street and district names, but also memorials; and notably the statue representing a black man's head, or the slave memorial representing a black man holding his children in his arms, his feet chained, which the camera lingers briefly on in fixed close-up. These shots are intercut with those of Kongo at his computer, writing his novel, *Matonge Village,* and with scenes of a black-and-white report on the neighborhood's inhabitants. As Olivier Barlet notes: "The film boldly makes forays into documentary reporting to capture echoes of the inhabitants' relationship to their neighborhood."[39] This clearly reveals the film's complex aesthetics, which mix different diegetic layers, styles, and languages. The at-times poetic fictional narratives of the book and novel are woven into images of the real, filmed in a rawer manner, at close hand. Throughout the story, three constantly woven narrative threads are thus distinguished, portraying:

- daily life: that of the neighborhood, relayed through documentary or report-like images; the main characters sometimes feature in these, and sometimes do not;
- the story of Kongo, his novel, and the dilemma of forgetting the past as the publisher wishes, and the presence of colonial history that the author seeks;
- colonial history, which appears in the form of different archeological, or even filmic, documents.

These three layers overlap both in the film's narration and in the second diegesis, the novel that Kongo is writing, as already seen in the extract. Moreover, this narration is based on an analogical play in which the two diegetic layers (the film plot and the story of Kongo's novel) constantly interweave.

From the outset, approximately three minutes into the film, we are given the key to the narrative when a woman from the neighborhood (in the black-and-white report-style scene) explains: "Matonge is tucked between the EEC and the galleries, the luxury district." The entire film plays on the in-betweenness in which Matonge is caught. This neighborhood where most of Brussels's African population lives is torn between those who conceive of today's life as a present to be lived, and those who seek the roots of their migration in the past and in the terrible history linking Congo and Belgium.

This duality becomes manifest in a scene shortly afterwards. During a dinner, Kongo, Béatrice, Nico, and Muadi are in the midst of a deep discussion. While all Congolese, they share their different visions of the neighborhood, exile, belonging, individual and collective responsibility, and history. Most of the characters are African; here there is no Manichean division between blacks and whites. The filmmaker therefore does not adopt the style of the Westerns that he used to watch in his youth and which he deplores: "Western have good guys and bad guys, and not much in between."[40]

This scene is filmed in close-up and in a series of shot/reverse shots that accentuate these oppositions, but also in medium shots, which convey the idea of overall complexity. For Kongo and Béatrice, the present stems from the past and tends towards the future, whereas for Muadi, only the present counts. She does not question the past, nor the reasons for her presence in Belgium. The publisher adopts the same position. The opposition between these two temporalities is thus at the root of the conflict between Kongo (who looks to history to understand the roots of the present—and who finds them in the Tervuren cemetery) and the publisher (who thinks only of the present moment and refuses all historical traces in Kongo's novel, claiming that they are irrelevant). This opposition is portrayed in the extract chosen. The spaces of the Kongo/Béatrice couple and that of publisher Joseph Désiré contrast to the point of being separated by a black frame. The museum, the cemetery, the plaque on the wall, and the colonial photograph are historical markers that Kongo seeks out of an obligation to remembrance and, at the same time, in a quest for his complex identity. Contrastingly, Joseph Désiré's office (which ends the extract), closed within its four walls, represents the present. He demands that Kongo "stick to the subject"—that is, the description of present-day Matonge, with no reference to the past. *Juju Factory* not only questions the relations between power and art, but also poses in a parallel manner the question of the role of the artist in society. The film shows the latter's precariousness: the bailiff who persecutes Kongo for his debts quizzes him: "Mr. Congo, why do you refuse to apply for welfare? . . . If you can't pay, stick your pride in the trash and go and knock on the welfare office door. And why don't you look for a proper job too?"

Driven by the quest for profit, the publisher thus enjoins Kongo to forget about history and to portray Matonge as a nice, exotic neighborhood, free of the wounds of the past, and to write a "neutral" story, without positioning himself. Through the conflict between the publisher and writer, whose motto is "it's better to sleep with an empty stomach than full of shame," the filmmaker also questions the construction of imaginations in exile and the freedom of artistic expression.

This same duality is found in the titles that each proposes for the book: for the publisher, *Matonge Village*, which evokes the quotidian character of the present, free of the weight of the past; for the writer, *Juju Factory*, rooted in history. The novel is finally published with the same title as the film, *Juju Factory*, highlighting the extent to which the two diegeses are intertwined. Far from a Hollywoodian happy ending, the book's publication can be seen as a paraphrase for the fact that the film *Juju Factory* indeed exists, even though the filmmaker did not concede to the possible constraints imposed by the funding bodies. Like the book in the fiction, the film in real life was also made with the backing of the nonprofit association Artspheres.

Moreover, this (bilingual) title reflects the filmmaker's multiple belongings and composite identity, as he mixes a word rooted in certain African cultures—*juju*, which Balufu Bakupa-Kanyinda describes as a protective amulet that gives the wearer the "faith" that they are out of harm from evil[41]—and the English word "factory," which brings to mind Andy Warhol's Factory, whereas the film is in French and shot in Belgium. "Factory" also seems to suggest that one must construct one's own *juju*, or the self-confidence needed to have the strength to say what one wants to and not what others hope to hear. Self-confidence is particularly important for Africans in exile (like Kongo Congo), who may suffer from a colonization complex or from being an immigrant. For Kongo, for example, *juju* becomes vital to assert himself as others (the publisher, society, and so forth) ask him to forget a painful part of his story, of their story, of history.

Both *Juju Factory*—the book and the film—adopt a similar structure in which the imaginary and production realities are interwoven. The novel's story echoes that of the film, in which, moreover, the main character is placed in the same situation as Balufu Bakupa-Kanyinda. The latter, who hails from Kasaï, states: "Once again, we have the woven, disjointed structure of the *kasala*: Kongo Congo's life, the life around him, his history, and his imagination form the waters of the same river, which gives rise to his book *Juju Factory*."[42] The filmmaker explains that the force of *kasala* oral narrative resides in the emotion that the narrator conjures through images.[43] The two fictions (the book and the film) are thus imbued with their authors' experiences. The book is an illustration of Kongo's life; he, in turn, illustrates the experience of the filmmaker. Balufu Bakupa-Kanyinda explains: "In the writer's perception, there lies an ensemble of perspectives constructed by a multitude of experiences and encounters with people in life. Kongo's writing indeed conveys "his" perception of the society he frequents, based on his own environment."[44] We clearly understand that Kongo's environment is the same as that of his author, Bakupa-Kanyinda. "[Kongo's] life resembles that of most of my writer, poet, playwright, and actor friends," the filmmaker confirms.[45] Thus, in the same way that elements of the filmmaker's life enter the film, elements of the characters' daily lives enter Kongo's novel. For example, we find the episode in which a student cousin living in university halls in the suburbs comes to Brussels to buy 450-euro shoes, then has no money left to get home. Here, we can read another critique of the attitude of certain Congolese people in Europe. The Congolese are famous for their elegance, Congolese dandies being known as *Sapeurs,* a term derived from the acronym *SAPE,* or the Société des ambianceurs et des personnes élégantes (Society of Ambiance-Makers and Elegant People). Kongo Congo mocks the contradictions of the young people who, once they've reached Europe, believe they are in the Land of Cockaigne and do not know how to prioritize their spending. Elsewhere, the film's scenes illustrate the narrative of the novel.

In the extract chosen, the two diegetic layers blend and merge, in keeping with the narrative devices of the *kasala* employed throughout the film, and interweaving both the roles of the characters and fiction and reality. The ambiguity is taken to the point that we do not know if the scene in the museum is a "real" scene that inspired the novel, or whether it is a representation of it. We cannot distinguish whether what Kongo writes/recounts materializes, or whether he takes inspiration from what happens to write (for example, the Songye mask, but also his novel's protagonists, who find themselves "in the great exhibition hall, topped by a high ceiling"). Noteworthy, too, is the multiplicity of narrators and the plurality of roles that Kongo Congo, who doubles into two people, takes on as he occupies different positions, going from writer/creator of a fictional world, to narrator, to the protagonist of his novel's plot. Sometimes he is both physically present onscreen and, through his voice-over, the narrator. The protagonist's duality is already present in his name, "Kongo Congo," which evokes the two Belgian names for this African country in French and in Flemish.[46] But "Kongo" is also a relatively common name in DRC, after the ancient kingdom of Kongo. He becomes the archetype and collective subconscious of a people, beyond his own destiny and his historical, social, and individual circumstances. The names "Kongo" and "Béatrice" can also be taken as a reference to traditional (Kongo) and Christian Africa (Béatrice).

The shots of Kongo writing constitute an interruption in the narrative and create spatio-temporal discontinuity—spatial because he is situated in a different place to the rest of the sequence set in the Tervuren museum and cemetery. Here, he wears a checked sports shirt and is thus dressed differently from the rest of the sequence too, in which he wears a leather jacket. The shot is thus temporally fragmented because Kongo at the same time writes and narrates the story (of which he is at times the protagonist). In this image, we see him at his computer, indoors. It is the only shot in the sequence where he is wearing glasses, as if they played the function of changing his point of view, role, and diegetic level.

Here Kongo is no longer coupled with Béatrice; he is alone, is the narrator, and moves the narrative forward. The writer's relationship to this work constitutes one of the driving narrative threads of the film. Shortly before, a page of Kongo's novel appears full-screen: a fixed image that repeats many times like a leitmotif in the film (at times we see the text directly on his computer screen). This shot introduces another layer of narrative complexity and stylistic hybridity for the written words, and the fixed images participate in a moving narrative. This is notably the case at the end of the extract when the camera sets in motion the fixed photograph of the colonial exhibition, which is slowly revealed by a pan and a zoom out.

At the start of the film, newspaper pages are also visible. The dreamlike beginning, which represents Kongo's dream, shows articles from Belgian papers about the Matonge district, often stigmatized by the media as being violent. The papers are in French and Flemish, for once united in their (negative) vision of this African enclave in Brussels. The newspaper pages are intercut by shots of the city. It is in this sequence that Mobutu's leopard-skin hat makes its first, fleeting appearance and the black-and-white photo of Lumumba appears for a second, set to the sound of gunshot, evoking his assassination. It is also in this dream that the only images of Africa appear in the entire film. The introduction of newspaper articles about Matonge is similar to the procedure used by John Akomfrah in his "cult" documentary *Handsworth Songs* (1987), which recounts the race riots in Birmingham in 1985 from a different point of view to the official version broadcast by the media. It is a way of bringing two opposing visions of a same reality into dialogue, and, at the same time, offering an alternative to dominant representations. This is also found in the fiction short *Lebess* (Hedy Krissane, 2003), in which the expectations of a Tunisian immigrant in Italy explode in the shock of the reality of social tensions also fueled by the media.

The Iranian scholar Hamid Naficy identifies the use of inscriptions and written texts in films as characteristic of diasporic cinema.[47] In his work on the recurrent aesthetics of exile and diaspora film, Naficy also refers to the presence of means of communication—often a link with the country of origin—and of transportation, by which the protagonists travel during their exile. Regarding the telephone, a prime means of long-distance communication, *Juju Factory* contains an emblematic scene. Kongo is lying peacefully on his sofa when the phone rings. It is someone from DRC asking him for money. Here, the phone not only is representative of the ties with the geographically distant family characteristic of the exilic condition, but also highlights the dependency of those still at home who believe that everything is easy in Europe and money readily available.

In the extract studied here, not only does the written word appear; we also often witness a doubling of images and words (via the voice-over). Throughout the film, passages of Kongo's novel are read by different voices: Kongo's, the narrator's, Béatrice's, the publisher's, or that of the woman in charge of the association responsible for publishing the book. At times, several voices are superimposed. The doubling of these expressive forms and the use of diverse film languages indeed characterize this feature film.

Most logically, the film plays on the interaction between the characters' stories—those of the film and the novel, which at times coincide—and history. The figures of Patrice Lumumba and Mobutu not only inhabit the narrative, but haunt Kongo. The filmmaker explains: "From the perspective of *Juju Factory,* the Congolese population's Belgian exile is a burning question that still haunts the dark side of Belgian politics that had Lumumba assassinated and created Mobutu."[48] Patrice Lumumba, an emblem of the revolutionary Africa that fought for liberation and was always assassinated, features several times and in different forms. Lumumba is a reference. As will be seen later, he is also cited in *L'Afrance,* and in other films, such as *Kinshasa Palace* (Zeka Laplaine, 2006). Here, Lumumba appears in Kongo's dream at the start of the film, his photo hangs in Kongo and Béatrice's apartment, and street youth rap about him. Here, too, the characters go from the "reality" of the first diegesis to the novel, and vice versa. As he walks down the street, Kongo thus bumps into the rapper, whom he was just creating in the fictional universe of his novel. Lumumba's face appears several times superimposed over shots of Brussels or of the church. When his image materializes inside the church, it is accompanied by the sound of gunshot, recalling his murder. Here, the montage points to the Catholic Church's responsibility in the assassination of Lumumba. He is also evoked again via the archive recording of the speech he gave in Kinshasa on 30 June 1960, the day of Congo's Independence. He thus also represents other assassinated African political leaders or emblematic figures (such as Thomas Sankara, Amilcar Cabral, Mehdi Ben Barka), and activists, journalists, or students (such as Norbert Zongo, Boukari Dabo, Guillaume Sessouma, and Ken Saro-Wiwa). In *Juju Factory,* we also see an excerpt of the documentary *Assassination Colonial Style: The Execution of Patrice Lumumba,* by Thomas Giefer (2008).[49] This confers another layer of complexity on *Juju Factory*'s narrative structure, adding a variety of film languages and styles. The figure of Mobutu also features several times in different forms.

If we adopt Kongo's point of view as he seeks his history and past, we better understand the signification that the visit to the museum takes on at the beginning of the extract analyzed here. From the very first shots, the tone is set. We immediately notice a contrast: the beautiful, pleasant gardens, the melodious birdsong, the pleasant music, but also the presence of cypresses, the tree typical of cemeteries and a symbol of mourning in many countries.

Kongo and Béatrice seem small next to this tree, a presage of death, as they do before the museum's façade. They appear to be crushed by the monumentality of the patrimonial museum that embodies memory. This building that Léopold II had constructed for the Universal Exhibition in 1897 later became the Royal Museum for Central Africa. It is an incarnation of Western memory—one that does not acknowledge the cruelty of Belgian colonization.[50] Seeking their history, Kongo and Béatrice will be confronted with it. They visit the museum and the graves of their compatriots, victims of colonialism. Precisely because the museum only contains masks considered art objects, they must go elsewhere, beyond the museum, to find their memory in the form of the Congolese graves. Béatrice traverses the present and history with Kongo. One may wonder whether the name Béatrice is an allusion to Dante's *Divine Comedy,* the couple's path bringing to mind a crossing of the hell of Matonge's history.

The visit to the museum's exhibition rooms finely highlights the gap between what, for the Belgians, is art and what has a ritual function for the Congolese. The two characters appear to be in a somber mood (perhaps due to this contrast). The piano music that sets the visit to European rhythms accentuates this divide. The visit to the tombs then takes on a dramatic tone. It is indeed a historic tragedy, to which they feel heir, and it is a way of integrating the real into the fictional universe. Just before, over a shot of a mask, the narration of the seven Congolese's deaths during the 1897 Universal Exhibition begins. This narration is accompanied by the same music, which contrasts with the background melody at the start of the sequence when Béatrice—and the spectator—does not yet know where Kongo is taking her. Later, the extra-diegetic narrator will again recall the murderous nature of colonization—murderous both literally and metaphorically, as Jean-Marie Teno also states, calling colonization a cultural genocide.[51]

The death of the seven Congolese is also recounted in another fiction, *Pièces d'identités (I.D.,* 1998), by the Belgium-based Congolese filmmaker Mweze Ngangura.

Dedicated to the African diaspora, *Pièces d'identités* also references other historic facts. The film also includes archive images (of Lumumba and of Independence Day, for example) and the statue of Léopold II in Brussels, a veritable archetype of colonial violence (the same statue seen in *Juju Factory*). Mani Kongo, an old Congolese king, comes to Belgium to find his daughter, there where his symbols and traditional knowledge do not hold the same significance. It is interesting to note, for that matter, that after a string of diverse and multiple adventures, the film's protagonists are reunited at a party in the Matonge district. The title is eloquent too. Not only does *Pièces d'identités*—literally "identity papers"—contain the word "identity," the title plays on an array of possible interpretations: identity papers, in the sense of the documents one needs to exist legally; a *pièce* ("play") in the sense of a show, a theatrical representation in which everyone plays their role; but also and above all in the sense of reconstructing and identity-in-pieces. This comedy poses the questions of cultural identities and colonial history. The situations reflect the identity-based questionings of the Congolese (and Africans in general) living in Belgium, and those of the former Belgian colonizers back from Congo and seeking who they are. The latter are inhabited by the memory of a mythical, imaginary Africa, and miss their past lifestyles and local domestic workers who were at their service. They are lost, both here and there.

The way in which events marking a people's collective history impose themselves in fiction can be observed here. It is not surprising that in *Juju Factory,* the narration concerning the Congolese who died after having been exhibited before Belgians in search of exoticism begins with a shot of a mask, which embodies two attitudes before the present and history. Removed from their history in the Belgian museum and considered art objects, these masks represent specific symbols to the Songye or Tshokwe peoples and are destined to fulfill important social and ritual functions.[52] Masks are indeed present throughout the film: at Kongo and Béatrice's, at Niko and Muadi's, but also on the wall of the bar where the protagonists often meet. Moreover, they repeat like inserts, for example when the "teller of fantastical stories" pretends to read his history in a notepad whose pages are completely blank. This subtle irony on the part of the filmmaker reinforces the fact that most African cultures are essentially orally transmitted, which caused Westerners to think that Africa was not civilized, for it possessed no written traces of its civilization.[53]

What emerges here is a historical continuity: today the masks are on show, exhibited as the Congolese were and effectively dehumanized as exotic objects. The role of the mask in *La Noire de . . . (Black Girl,* Sembène Ousmane, 1966) also comes to mind. The mask hanging in Diouana's boss's house in Antibes is nothing more than an exotic art object, to be shown off to friends on return from the colonies. In the film, we see this mask pass from hand to hand, crossing time and space, according to which its function changes.

The presence of other visitors in the main exhibition hall recalls the fact that the museum—which for Kongo is a place of history—only has artistic interest for the other visitors, who associate the exhibits with a certain exoticism.[54] Contrastingly, Kongo and Béatrice are alone before the Congolese tombs. They discover this forgotten chapter of Belgian and/or Congolese history. Before the dead, Béatrice concedes: "You're right; Matonge well and truly started here." She thus finds a historical response to what Matonge represents today and highlights the weight of the history that links Congo and Belgium. The camera lingers on the names of the two countries, written side by side on Mibange's grave. By showing emblems of memory, or historical proof, such as the statues, the commemorative plaque on the church wall, and the graves, Balufu Bakupa-Kanyinda roots his fictional universe in a specific context, creating connections and positioning himself.

Moreover, through the publisher character—who, let us not forget, is called Joseph Désiré, like Mobutu (echoing the names of Kabila, father and son, too)—the director makes a critical nod to the European financial institutions and to the Congolese and African political class. The filmmaker's position at the interstices of cultures and societies gives him the right distance to pose a critical gaze on both Africa and Europe. Through the figure of the publisher, he criticizes the European funders who at times demand exoticism from African films. The character Joseph Désiré is a slave to the system. He has been formatted by Belgian society to steer artistic creation and censors. On the wall of his office, we can see a poster of the comic book *Tintin in Congo,* an emblem of the Belgians' distorted representation of the Congolese. At the same time, his despotic manner recalls certain indoctrinated African leaders, who are blind, deaf, cynical (Joseph Désiré does not read the tales that his wife writes), and uninterested in the cultural development of their countries. Like state presidents, his portrait hangs in both his home and office. Towards the end of the film, Kongo ironically advises him to "try something else and become a Congolese politician." We then see him walking alone in a dark street in the Brussels night, dreaming of beer, music, "fountains" of whisky, sighing, "and if I catch that Kongo, I'll send him straight to prison and make his wife Béatrice my trophy," echoing the attitude of most Congolese leaders. Joseph Désiré thus goes to question "[His] Lord," Léopold II. Before the imposing statue of the king on horseback (up on a pedestal)—mocked and animalized here by neighing sounds—Joseph Désiré is shot from high-angle, as if from the king's point of view, rendering him tiny and even more ridiculous. After this, Joseph Désiré enters a Catholic church and begins to recite "Our Father." The filmmaker thus makes another parallel between Belgian colonization and Catholic evangelization, which—particularly in Congo—were intimately tied.

It can be concluded that Balufu Bakupa-Kanyinda's cultural hybridity, which is turned towards the future, yet at the same time connected with his roots and the history of his people, is clearly reflected in *Juju Factory*. He has indeed stated, "Like Kongo Congo, I am but a link in a chain. I belong to both my people's and my individual history. The experience in question here is that of exile. The history of that exile is political."[55] The film's plot and multifaceted style illustrate the filmmaker's struggle to exist and to make his films, but also his multiple cultural belongings.

Juju Factory is the epitome of aesthetic syncretism, then. Black-and-white inserts, report-like sequences, still images, archive recordings and images, and an excerpt of a documentary are all integrated into the color fiction. A variety of narrators alternate; real and fictional are interwoven. Different styles and languages occupy two diegetic layers, in which different temporalities and conceptions of times cohabit.

CHAPTER 7

In-Between Places

Notre étrangère, by Sarah Bouyain

his chapter explores the search for identity in an in-betweenness (between two countries, two languages, two cultures, two mothers, but also between fantasized memories and present reality). It analyzes the montage and film style used to portray this quest in *Notre étrangère* (*The Place in Between*),[1] whose very title reveals the complexity of belongings that this fiction portrays. Amy (Dorylia Calmel)[2] is a biracial young woman who lives in France with her stepmother and half-brother. After her French father's death, she returns to Bobo-Dioulasso in Burkina Faso looking for her mother, whom she has not seen since she was eight years old. Looking for her roots and herself, Amy thus returns to her birth country, which she feels she belongs to, but where she is treated like a foreigner—where she is both "notre" (our) and "étrangère" (foreigner). Unknown to her daughter, her mother, Mariam (Assita Ouédraogo),[3] has meanwhile left Bobo-Dioulasso for Paris, where she works as a cleaner and lives in an immigrant workers' hostel.

The two women's journeys in opposite directions is told in a parallel montage between Bobo-Dioulasso and Paris. Amy is a foreigner in Burkina Faso, her birth country, and Mariam is a foreigner in France, where she lives as if holding on tight to her melancholy. Her solitude opens the narrative.[4] Her gaze lost during the whole film, the mother appears to be a passive spectator of her own life, apart from when she teaches Jula to Esther (Nathalie Richard), a manager in the company where she cleans. Then Mariam feels she has a value; she can make a contribution and share the knowledge that she was unable to hand down to her daughter. Esther is the only person with whom Mariam has a friendship, until she discovers that Esther is studying Jula to adopt a Burkinabè child. This, she is unable to bear, because the pain of having had to let her own very young daughter, Amy, go is still too acute. In Bobo-Dioulasso, in the family home, Amy only finds her mother's sister, Aunt Acita (Blandine Yaméogo),[5] who raised her and considers her a daughter, but who does not immediately recognize her. Acita drowns her worries and pain in alcohol. She lives with Kadiatou (Nadine Kambou Yéri), the young maid who helps in exchange for board and lodging. These two lone women have found one another and have an almost familial relationship. Kadiatou is a key character: she will interpret for Amy, who no longer speaks Jula and can thus no longer communicate directly with her aunt.

Portraying Cultural Hybridity

Sarah Bouyain's artistic path is a fairly unique one. Born in France, biracial, she spent a lot of time at the cinema as a student.[6] Having always been interested in stories and drawing, interested in painting too, she decided to train as a camerawoman as her parents "panicked" at the thought of the visual arts.[7] After a first degree in mathematics, she won a place at the Louis Lumière National Film School in Paris. She then worked as camera assistant in advertising and on various documentary and fiction films, including Idrissa Ouedraogo's *Le Cri du cœur* (*The Heart's Cry*) and *Afrique Mon Afrique;* Henri Duparc's *Une Couleur café* (*Coffee Colored*); *Nikki de Saint Phalle,* a documentary by Peter Schamoni; then was an intern camera operator on Luc Besson's *Léon.* After working with these major filmmakers, Sarah Bouyain felt the need to devote herself to her own projects in order to tell her own stories.[8] *Notre étrangère,* her first fiction feature, was indeed born out of personal necessity. While the screenplay was written in collaboration with Gaëlle Macé, the fiction is infused with elements of the filmmaker's own experiences. The screenplay evolved into various versions over years of writing, and again during the shoot.[9] Nonetheless, the director stated: "In the end, my film, more than the screenplay itself, is faithful to what was deep inside me."[10]

    Notre étrangère was initially born from the idea of film about acquiring the

Jula language.[11] For the filmmaker, who is inhabited by two cultures—French, via her mother, and Jula, via her father—making a fiction about learning this language meant putting her own experience and family story on the line. For Sarah Bouyain, who makes a cinema of images rather than dialogues, basing her film on a language may have seemed odd. Yet, as "a language also contains a vision of the world," learning it also constitutes a way of entering a culture.[12] This language henceforth becomes emblematic of connections and cultural belongings, or of the difficulty of defining them. Indeed, the narrative is also centered on hybridity (both biological and cultural), a question that has always inhabited her. Bouyain had already addressed dual heritage in her collection of short stories *Métisse Façon* (*Mixed Style*).[13] These are again tales that move to-and-fro between Paris and Bobo-Dioulasso in Burkina, where Rachel travels to look for her father. The questions of maternity/ paternity, family relations, and identity quests were already present.

Bouyain's documentary *Les enfants du Blanc* (*The White Man's Children*) also focused on this subject.[14] In it, she tells the story of her grandmother (the daughter of a French army officer and the woman he abducted) and the violent history of colonial interracial relationships. Beyond the historical account, the discovery of her grandmother's biracialism creates a strong bond between them: "It was quite personal because, in a way, I was confronting my grandmother's biracialism with my own."[15] As Olivier Barlet describes, "in all of her literary and cinematographic works, Sarah Bouyain takes *her* biracialism as the subject."[16] The fictional realm of *Notre étrangère* is an example of this. This Franco-Burkinabè coproduction embraces two languages, two cultures, two countries—to which mother and daughter only in part belong—and different attitudes and ways of positioning oneself. This duality is clearly expressed through the alternating montage, often with no transition, from the vicissitudes of Mariam in France to those of Amy in Burkina Faso, as if they had switched places; each is there where the other is supposed to be. The silences at times impose themselves between the two languages, like an abyss that, in the beginning, might seem insurmountable, leaving no place for a true cultural hybridity, but that remains an ambiguous and interstitial position. The English title, *The Place in Between,* illustrates this well. Indeed, already its title *Notre étrangère* expresses an intrinsic duality that is reflected in the narrative structure.

Notre étrangère offers a female viewpoint of typically feminine concerns, such as the question of maternity. But, through Amy's individual story, Sarah Bouyain questions the cultural identities of a community: that of multiracial people. The quest theme remains primordial in it. Similar quests can, for that matter, be found in films by other multiracial directors, notably Congolese Zeka Laplaine, whose father is Portuguese (*Le Jardin de papa/The Garden,* 2004, and *Kinshasa Palace,* 2006), the Franco-Guinean Gahité Fofana (*Immatriculation temporaire,* 2001), the Senegalese-born Franco-Vietnamese-Guinean Mama Keita (*L'Absence/The Absence,* 2009, and *Le Fleuve/The River,* 2003), the Mauritanian-Malian Abderrahmane Sissako (*La Vie sur terre/Life on Earth,* and *Heremakono/Waiting for Happiness*), but also in *L'Afrance,* as shall be seen later. Although set in different fictional universes, their characters journey from one country to another in quest of themselves, crossing identity boundaries and seeking their complex selves.[17]

In *Notre étrangère,* the narrative setup is established from the start, when mother and daughter are still in Paris, in order to signify the distance of their lives: Mariam with her solitude, her barren room, and the Jula classes she gives Esther; Amy still in Paris with her white family (her stepmother and half-brother), in her colorful room full of objects and bursting with life. However, and even if in the background, the map of Africa on her wall becomes the focal point of the frame and this young woman's life. This map gives us a sense of a missing piece in the puzzle of her life—a void that she must fill. During the first ten minutes of the film, we discover her present life and the mystery surrounding her past, including the life of her real mother. The alternating montage accompanies their vicissitudes during the whole film, even when Amy goes to Burkina, imposing a huge vastness between them. Yet distance sometimes helps one to see things differently and to find oneself. It is in Burkina Faso that Amy eventually discovers her mother's address in France, as she does a part of her past that she was unaware of and needed to know to advance. The film thus places Amy's departure point in Paris, where she now lives. We see her getting ready to leave, and in the extract chosen here, Amy has just arrived in Burkina. We are thus witness to her marvel at (re)discovering her birth country and part of her family.

The Native Land: The Shock of Rediscovery (Extract)

The extract analyzed comprises four scenes, made up of a total of fourteen shots. It lasts 4' 15" and takes place thirteen minutes into the film. The main character is Amy and the action takes place entirely in Burkina Faso, but it is as if this scene were framed by two scenes of Mariam in France. In the preceding scene in Paris,

Mariam, standing still on a station platform, passively watches the train she has not taken pass.[18]

In the scene following the extract, Mariam is in the barren room of the hostel in Paris.[19]

Scene One: Bobo-Dioulasso, the Home Compound Yard

Shot 1: 13' 45"

A shot of a shut gate. Silence. The top of a man's head appears above the gate; his hand opens one of the two doors from the outside. Amy appears on the screen, framed by the open gate and the wall, in an African wax cloth dress, looking lost.

This shot follows a long scene in which a tailor accompanies a smiling Amy on his moped. The tailor is Amy's only contact in Bobo-Dioulasso, the only person whose address she has. In the previous scene, she arrives from France, and we see her, in European dress, in a tailor's shop where she must deliver a packet. From the very first image in Burkina, Amy appears to feel her foreignness and decides to have a dress made out of local cloth. It is the tailor who then gives her a ride to her family's home. As they ride along, the city is seen through Amy's eyes: in subjective shots, Amy rediscovers her birth country, which she no longer recognizes. As Barlet writes: "Here, [the filmmaker] thus situates herself through Amy's point of view."[20] Even

when it technically is not a true subjective shot, the camera illustrates Amy's point of view. At times, we also see her in the shot, but we always get the impression that we are looking through her eyes. It is also through this type of mise-en-scène that dual belonging and a dual gaze play out. It is as if Amy herself sees herself looking.

In the shot before the extract, the moped stops and the man nods in the direction of the offscreen gate. We expect, then, to see the gate from the outside, in a point-of-view shot. This being so, the framing gives the impression of a shut gate seen from the street outside, whereas just after, we discover that the camera's focus point is inside the yard. To give more force to this moment without dialogue, the European music that accompanied the ride through the city stops and a heavy silence descends, accentuating Amy's uncertainty. The music was in a minor key, repetitive, alternating highs and lows as if in an unending spiral—a sad music. This Western melody (composed by French musician Sylvain Chauveau) that accompanies Amy's errantry, as if it were resonating from inside her, accentuates her foreignness and the allogenous universe she bears inside her. Here, Amy's set expression contrasts with her radiant face in the previous scenes.

The tailor, who was in the background and half-hidden by the gate, leaves without a word, and without her turning to say goodbye. He can do no more for her; now Amy must continue her heuristic path alone. Still lost, not moving, she takes the time to look around the yard from right to left. Then she advances slowly, uncertain.

Shot 2: 14' 04"

A subjective panning shot of the yard, from left to right. The hand-held camera wobbles, as unstable and shaky as Amy. The yard appears big and empty. No one is there, just pots and pans on the fire, and laundry tubs, and sheets hung to dry in the sun.

On the right, finally, the house, the door open, a print curtain billowing in the wind. No one currently seems to be there in this solitary setting.

Shot 3: 14' 22"

The camera is now focused back on Amy, who, still at the entrance, almost frozen, alone, timidly comes into the yard, in silence, with no background music. A distance is thus established between the setting and the character. A medium long shot shows Amy in her entirety. The framing makes her appear isolated. Disoriented,

she nervously holds onto her bag while continuing to look around. Amy appears to be a stranger to this place that, as we later learn, is the house she grew up in. A young female voice suddenly greeting her from offscreen makes her jump. A slow tracking shot to the left leaves Amy isolated to the right of the frame and reveals the young Kadiatou, who—stopping hanging up the washing for a moment—asks her in French: "Can I help you?" The fact that the teen addresses her in this language accentuates her foreignness. French is the language of colonization, of the

authorities, of school, and the one people use to communicate with foreigners. The two young women remain at a certain distance—the camera too. They are filmed from a 45° angle.

An empty space stretches between them. Amy, in sneakers, to the right of the frame, apart, ill-at-ease, as if she did not dare enter this space, whereas Kadiatou, barefoot, is at ease in her daily world.

Another voice is heard offscreen: that of an older woman this time, calling "Kadiatou." Another slight tracking shot, but the woman is not shown. Kadiatou addresses her like a mother: "Mummy!" Amy is often isolated by the camera, kept at a distance by the mise-en-scène; she is not part of the life in this yard.

The tracking shot continues. Amy suddenly advances rapidly, impatient to discover who is there, quickly exiting the frame. Looking concerned, Kadiatou follows an instant in the direction of the house. A panning shot accompanies her, now filming Kadiatou in medium shot in the center of the frame until she approaches the door of the house. She exits the frame; the camera lingers on the open door, its curtains half open. Then, the curtain opens and Acita appears, framed by the door. The fixed camera films her frontally. The slightly low angle gives her an imposing air. She advances unsteadily towards the camera with the befuddled look of someone who has been drinking. We see her through the leaves of a tree, whereas Kadiatou, appearing tiny in the bottom left-hand of the frame, goes up the steps to help her, but Acita brushes her away.

For a moment, Acita just stands there, perplexed (one imagines she can see Amy, without really seeing her), then, without a word, turns and goes, pushing Kadiatou (still at her side) away again.

We guess the intimacy and affection between them. The two women are framed together, physically close to one another, whereas Amy is often alone on the screen, isolated by the camera.

The camera starts tracking again. For a short instant, we see just the branches of a tree and then Amy, alone, in profile and medium close-up, rooted to the spot.

Surrounded by leaves and trees, disoriented, she remains paralyzed for a few seconds. Accompanying music strikes up with a crescendo; Amy turns and flees.

Shot 4: 15′ 44″

Acita goes back in the house, followed by Kadiatou, the two filmed from behind, still together. Remaining fixed for four long seconds, the camera continues to focus on the door, with its shut curtains. The door marks a threshold that Amy does not yet dare cross. The music grows louder.

Scene Two: Exterior, Bobo-Dioulasso

Shot 5: 15′ 51″

The music continues in transition; no dialogue. The camera is now inside a moving car, showing the city through the windscreen.

The car's turning a corner produces a tracking effect; this is still Amy's point of view. The slightly dirty window blurs our vision. In the background women's voices talk indistinguishably in Jula.

Shot 6: 16' 00"

The music continues in transition; in a reverse point-of-view shot, the camera, now outside and in medium close-up, shows Amy looking lost and taciturn, sitting among three Burkinabè women who are chatting merrily in Jula, indifferent to her presence. The two women in the back on either side of her lean forwards, thereby excluding her from the conversation and relegating her to the background. The other women gently accompany the swaying of the vehicle as it drives on an unsurfaced road. We can tell that this is a collective taxi.[21]

Third Scene: Bobo-Dioulasso. A Hotel. Exterior/Interior

Shot 7: 16' 23"

The music is still playing in transition; Amy crosses the grounds of a hotel, stressed and nervous, her face worried. The sad, repetitive music appears to accelerate with her growing uncertainty. We see her walking fast from different angles, first in profile, then in frontal shot. Her frenetic movement contrasts with the calm surroundings.

Shot 8: 16' 30"

Framed from behind, in a hurry, Amy takes the key from the concierge. Still with no dialogue, the same accompanying music underscores her sense of foreignness. She goes around a column, an obstacle that she is unable to confront and thus circumvents. Previously fixed, the camera now follows her and accompanies her movement, tracking almost imperceptibly.

Shot 9: 16' 35"

Amy goes up the empty, cold white stairs without bumping into anyone. We see her appear through the glass balustrade; the camera waits until she reaches her floor, then follows her briefly as she heads down the corridor, only briefly showing her body, cutting her head from the frame.

Shot 10: 16' 37"

Shot in low angle through the corridor windows, we see Amy pass then disappear from sight. For a short instant, we glimpse the empty landing of the hotel, with its interior windows. Silence.

Scene Four: Bobo-Dioulasso, Interior, a Hotel Room

Shot 11: 16' 40"

Silence, no music. Amy closes the door to her bare, white hotel room and goes to sit in silence on the edge of the bed.

The fixed camera was awaiting her in the room. The frame adjusts slightly. The shot remains almost fixed for eighteen long seconds of heavy silence. The only movement and sound come from Amy's breathing.

Shot 12: 17' 01"

The point of view changes. A long (eight second) close-up of Amy seen from the opposite side.

Not only has the direction of the camera changed, but the young woman has changed out of her African dress and back into her European clothes.

The camera descends to show Amy's hands as she sketches the family home in a pad resting on her crossed legs. The house she silently draws is empty. There is no music, only the sound of the pencil on paper. The pencil remains on the shutters of the doors to the house. An eraser is placed next to the pad, on her legs, suggesting that at any moment, Amy may need to correct her memories.

Shot 13: 17' 09"

A bare white wall and an interior door, slightly ajar. The phone rings. Wrapped in just an orange towel, Amy exits the bathroom and rushes to answer.

The camera follows her. It is as if she no longer knows which clothes to wear; she is "uncovered," alone in her solitude and her questionings.

A medium long shot: Amy stands behind the bed. Her stepmother's voice

calling from Paris asks how she is. Through this call from afar, from someone to whom she is nonetheless very close—closer than her own mother—her everyday life comes flooding back in.

Shot 14: 17' 24"

A close-up of her foot and on the nervous, anxious wiggling of her big toe. Silence. Her stepmother breaks her silence: "Amy?"

The camera tracks up to Amy's bent head, her face in profile. She explains on the phone: "I found the house, but my mother wasn't there."

A weak light shines from a lamp on the bedside table, too far away to light Amy's face. The room key by the lamp reminds us that the young woman is not at home; she is in a neutral place—a hotel room.

"I don't get it. Didn't she know you were coming?," asks her stepmother.

"No," Amy replies, her face in close-up against the white backdrop of her hotel room wall.

Her stepmother brings her back down to earth. "What did you imagine, just showing up like that?"

The camera comes to a halt on her face in close-up.

– "Listen, I had no number or address, who do you think I could've asked?

– I thought your father . . .
– You know he never spoke about her!"

She sits. The camera again tracks up her body, stopping in close-up on her bent head. On the other end of the phone, her stepmother continues:

– Sorry. You said you found the house?
– And my aunt.
– Didn't she tell you where your mother was?
– She didn't recognize me.

Amy looks up, her mind made up: "I'll go back again tomorrow."

The next day, Amy returns to the family home. On this second visit, we see her meet her aunt properly. It is she who introduces herself: "Aunty, Aunty. It's me, Amy." This time, her aunt runs to embrace her, in tears, crying out her name: "Aminata!" The young woman whom everyone in France calls Amy becomes Aminata again in Burkina. This time, the two women are framed together, their faces close. They lace hands, without talking. Amy's expression is again uncertain and troubled. After a long silence, her aunt leads her to sit in the shade of a big tree (as a "European," she cannot withstand the Burkinabè sun) and their in-part impossible conversation begins. The aunt speaks in Jula, a language that Amy no longer understands. When Kadiatou comes back with drinks, she, like a mediator, translates.

In-Betweenness and Self-Reconstruction

I chose to analyze this extract because it portrays the rediscovery of the homeland, or the moment at which the émigré's memories and fantasies come into collision with "reality." It illustrates well the questions of dual belonging and of reconstructing one's identity. In this passage—as in the entire film—the point of view chosen is Amy's. Her life is for the moment suspended; not yet able to define herself, she is double. She feels foreign in Burkina. In this work, various elements indicate that Amy is perceived—and perceives herself—as different. She does not feel as if she completely belongs to this society, whose language she no longer speaks—a first marker of integration. In shots, she is often near a door, on a threshold, sitting on the edge of a bed. She also appears on the edge of the frame, on the margins, and is several times alone on the screen or separate from the other characters. This contrasts with the shots of Amy in Paris, in which she is always smiling and framed in proximity with her stepmother or her half-brother, notably the shot in which Amy removes something from her stepmother's eye, or the shot where she is sitting with her brother on the bed in the intimate space that is her bedroom, which she lets him have. This intimacy with her Paris family accentuates the distance she initially feels from her family in Bobo-Dioulasso.

In Burkina Faso, Amy is not at home. Before moving into her aunt's, she stays first at the hotel, in a bare room, a "no-man's land" that recalls the hostel where Mariam lives in Paris. This hotel room can indeed be seen as a kind of interstitial place, a place of transition, an antechamber that accompanies her quest. Other elements throughout the film also highlight her foreign condition: people call her "white," she falls sick as soon as she arrives, and she does not know how to tie her wrapper like the other women do. The taxi driver charges her a higher fare, like a tourist; her aunt and Kadiatou invite her to sit in the shade as the sun is too strong for her. And, of course, Amy does not speak the local language. During the whole film, the words her aunt addresses her with in Jula are not subtitled; spectators not speaking this language are thus placed in Amy's position and espouse her point of view. At times, their dialogues remain moments of impossible communication; at others, Kadiatou translates. This social and linguistic alienation is a feeling that Sarah Bouyain knows well. She explains: "Through Amy's journey, I wanted to show what I feel each time I go to Burkina, where I'm considered white, foreign, even though I consider it to be my country." Bouyain continues: "For me, it was important to situate my gaze as European right from the start of the film. Even though I am biracial, my gaze in this film is more European than African."[22]

The repeated nostalgic European music is voluntarily at odds with the context. The melody that accompanies Amy's voyage and her rediscovery of this city reflects her state of mind and recalls that her perspective is one of an outsider. Amy's interior space is even more at odds with the context and the other characters. The music, which is also often present in the scenes with no dialogue, brings us closer to Amy's thoughts. We see through her eyes and feel her emotions. These dialogue-free scenes structure the film. This recalls Luc Dardenne's reflections when he said, referring to Wittgenstein, "Don't make characters say what they cannot. They cannot step out of their situation to say it in words."[23] Feeling an outsider echoes the mother's situation in Paris, even though their social conditions are different. Mariam is truly a foreigner, whereas Amy was born in Burkina and has come back in search of her history. Moreover, the to-ing and fro-ing of the subjective camera (Branigan's *point of view*) and Amy's onscreen presence evoke the duality of her gaze; she sees herself not only as an outsider looking in, but also as being part of the country (and being part of the picture).

Amy is both from and excluded by Burkinabè society. This ambivalence is also highlighted by the ambiguity of the human presence in the empty courtyard, or by presence/absence of the offscreen voices. During her first visit, Amy sees no one in the yard, but the hanging washing and the pots on the fire indicate that the house is inhabited. The yard is also an interstitial place, an "in between" the outside (the street) and inside (the house). Amy remains in this space, neither in nor out, which clearly illustrates her dual condition as a foreigner (outside) and a local (inside). Being from a country, a culture, is not something abstract; Amy must reconstruct her history and her being, rediscover her markers and (re)define her place in Burkina and in the world.

The extract chosen begins with a shut gate, a barrier. Later, we notice the constant presence of doors (shut, open, ajar), which appear to be thresholds, barriers, or frontiers separating spaces that Amy must cross.

During the narrative, mother and daughter appear to blend into a single character, whose duality is manifest. Both women are looking for a missing piece in order to be able to reconstruct their identities in their entirety. Their identities can only be complete through a unity, a coming together of two parts, two cultures, two countries, and two languages.

In the film, Amy must thus overcome obstacles (the column, the stairs, the silences . . .) before uniting the two entities, before finally reaching selfhood. Initially, she is in a state of separation, of confusion (a body with no head, the lamp not illuminating her face, the scratched and dirty taxi window). She is divided, has two names (Amy in France; Aminata in Burkina), is often framed from different points of view in the same scene; she constitutes a dual character with her mother and switches between European and Burkinabè clothes. Her way of dressing is significant throughout the film, reflecting her two unresolved belongings in a constant toing-and-froing between the two. Her external appearance reflects her inner incertitude. This remains so until the final scene of the film, when she finds her mother's address in Paris and when she finally appears to have found her equilibrium and own synthesis as she wears an African top with European trousers. Furthermore, she is in Africa, but the European music that inhabits her is omnipresent. She is physically there, but excluded from conversations. In this respect, the film's initial idea, based on language as a form of belonging, is still present. Bouyain indeed explains:

> To me, the main subject was language as an affective object. When you can speak a language, it brings you closer to its speakers, both intellectually and physically, in the sense that you articulate hitherto unfamiliar sonorities, which become yours.[24]

She continues: "When I lost my father in 2000, I had the impression that the only way to prove that I was Burkinabè—beyond my identity papers—was to speak this language."[25]

The filmmaker draws on her own experience. During her long childhood vacations spent in Bobo-Dioulasso, at her grandmother's, she lived similar situations to those with which Amy is confronted. Biracial, light-skinned, Sarah Bouyain was repeatedly labeled foreign, even in her father's home village. As she did not speak Jula, she often felt excluded from conversations, especially in the family courtyard, the ultimate site of meeting and sharing. "Stuck in the family courtyard in Bobo-Dioulasso," she would have liked to have made friends and spoken with people, but she "couldn't bear the '*toubabou!*' that kids called to her as soon as [she] took a step outside."[26] This same compound yard in Bobo-Dioulasso was to become a key setting for her films. It is indeed this empty yard that we see through Amy's eyes at the beginning of this extract. The following scene also evokes this emptiness, the absences, the dichotomy between memories, the imagined return, and reality. Amy joins Kadiatou in the yard and questions her. The two young women sit side by side on a little low bench. Amy chops onions while Kadiatou plucks and guts the chicken (which the "foreigner" is probably not used to preparing). The fixed camera frames them in a frontal medium long shot, the camera positioned indoors, looking out through the door. They are thus doubly framed. Certain questions remain unanswered; Kadiatou tells Amy nothing about her love life, for example. When Amy asks: "Before, there were loads of people in this yard. Where have they all gone?," the camera is now to the side, filming them in profile, and closer up to better capture Amy's confusion, at times masked by Kadiatou's head. The days when she lived there and knew everything are over; now it is Kadiatou who is at home in this house and knows all its secrets. We learn that after the death of Acita's husband, people withdrew as the money ran out. Kadiatou left her village after her mother's death. After going around all the families in Bobo-Dioulasso, she found refuge at Acita's. "That way, we keep each other company," the young woman explains, having since become a kind of adoptive daughter to Acita.

Here, Amy is confronted with reality. This is how individual paths reconfigure in fictional worlds, which may represent collective experiences.

The extract chosen is also significant because it represents the long-dreamed-of, long-imagined reunion. Amy will not find her mother in her childhood home, however, only her aunt, who appears unsteady on her feet, an instability that mirrors her marginalized social position as a woman on her own with no children. Through the questions that her stepmother asks her on the phone at the end of the extract, we discover that Amy has come looking for her mother without finding out where she is, as if it were obvious that she would find her exactly where they last saw one another, fifteen years before, as if time had stopped. That explains Amy's malaise and disquiet, which we perceive from the very first pan in the sequence. The migrant condition indeed often makes people define their identity through an idealized and fixed memory of a home that no longer corresponds to reality. Amy's memories belong to an imagined Africa, to static places and situations, reconstructed in her head. As the filmmaker explains: "I also wanted to stop speaking about *Africa*—that is, of a quasi-imaginary place—in order to talk about today's Burkina."[27] Sarah Bouyain explains that this imaginary Africa relates to her father's stories and memories:

> I get the impression that what I've tried to explore in my work is the distance that exists between the real Burkina, past and present, and the Burkina that was passed on to me through what my father and my grandmother told me. (So, it's not surprising that most of my stories are set in Bobo-Dioulasso, a nostalgic town if there ever was.)[28]

Recalling her trips to Burkina, she states: "My memory of these vacations is profound boredom and great solitude, completely unlike the thrilling stories that my father used to tell me about his childhood."[29] It was these feelings of boredom and monotony that made Sarah Bouyain take the time to observe everything that went on around her: "I remember sitting there, with nothing going on, with nothing moving, even if I did also talk a lot with my grandmother. The sensation I have of it is very static."[30] In her mise-en-scène, this translates into an often-static camera, a slow rhythm, and the fact that very little takes place in this courtyard. The lengthy—and at times very lengthy—shots give the characters time to exist.

The shots here are units unto themselves. They portray a succession of present moments that, very slowly, compose a narration. The force of the montage resides above all in the alternation between the scenes in France and in Burkina Faso. Here, the static camera and slowness of the shots allow us to observe the details and, at the same time, to perceive Amy's nervous movements, which are at odds with this space, but which inject her fast, constantly on-the-go "Parisian" attitude into it. It is as if she were "deterritorialized." Finally, the narrative is constructed from a kind of toing-and-froing between fiction and life. As the filmmaker remarks: "I didn't consciously realize it was a film that drew on so many elements of my and my family's lives."[31] To avoid identification between her and her character, however, the director originally imagined Amy as black, but, in the course of writing and rewriting the screenplay, she became biracial. Bouyain recounts:

> As for Dorylia Calmel [Amy], I met her at the time when the character I had written was black, not biracial. One day the producer pointed out to me that she looked biracial and asked me whether that might be confusing. In the end, three or four months before the shoot, I decided that the character would be biracial because it seemed more appropriate. The reason for my initial reticence was that I didn't want it to be too close to my own life.[32]

The screenplay underwent another, almost unconscious change when it also became a film that revolves around a woman and her maternal relationships. As the director described:

> There was a turning point when I wrote the film. At first, I was convinced this was a film about identity and language. One day, my producer called me and said: "Listen, Sarah, you're absolutely going to have to rewrite your director's statement because your film is first and foremost about motherhood." It took me a day or two to get over the shock and to face the obvious. So yes, my film also talks about motherhood.[33]

Notre étrangère indeed questions uprooting and (experienced or unfulfilled) motherhood. Acita has no children and her niece was sent far away from her. Mariam was not able to keep her daughter with her. Esther, a single woman, dreams of adopting a child (whom she looks to Africa to find). The film thus also raises the question of transnational and transcultural motherhood. Amy has a Burkinabè biological mother, an aunt who raised her as if she were her own, and a kindly

French stepmother. The filmmaker's female sensibility inhabits this fiction, in which men are essentially absent and, for the most part, do not have glorious roles. Among them, the taxi driver, for example, treats Amy as a foreigner and rips her off; the two men she meets in a bar and who she thinks are friends of her parents try cheaply to seduce her. The only positive male figure is the tailor.

The intersection of cultures and gender, and her own personal and artistic path have shaped the person and the filmmaker Sarah Bouyain has become today. She is biracial, and thus straddles two cultures, but is also a woman: "I position myself on the border of two continents. . . . As a result, I have a specific gaze that belongs neither to one nor the other. It is obvious that, as a woman, I can only but write with my feminine sensibility."[34] In *Notre étrangère,* we may also interpret the question of motherhood as an allegory of belonging to a country. In Amy's case, she has several maternal figures of reference. She belongs to two societies and has two cultures. Her heuristic path thus consists of finding herself as a woman, of finding her unity in the different facets of her being. Speaking about her character in conversation with Catherine Ruelle, Sarah Bouyain explained:

> When she is in France, her spirit is preoccupied with Africa, and when she is in Africa, she realizes to what extent she is French. There's a constant toing-and-froing going on in her head, and in the heads of a lot of people who live like that, in a condition of dual belonging.[35]

Similar issues are indeed found in Franco-Congolese filmmaker Claude Haffner's documentary *Noire ici, Blanche là-bas* (*Footprints of My Other*), 2012. This evocative title perfectly captures the ambivalence of viewpoints and perceptions.[36] Franco-Ivoirian Isabelle Boni-Claverie's short films also address this question of identity, notably *Pour la nuit* (*For the Night,* 2004), a fiction that portrays the quest of a young mixed-race woman in Marseille.[37] In her latest documentary, *Trop Noire pour être Française? / Too Black to Be French?* (2015), she reverses the viewpoint and poses contemporary France a social question through the prism of her personal family history.

In the oxymoron of its title, *Notre étrangère* bears this ambivalence of belonging to a society while at the same time being excluded from it. This duality is reflected in the mise-en-scène, which broaches questions that are very present in the director's own life. "My Foreigner" was what her grandmother used to call her, uncertain of how to treat her, or what to give her to eat,[38] advising her to stay sitting so as not to get tired, and not to remain too long in the sun.[39] Bouyain continues, explaining how in Burkina Faso, the title "foreigner" is honorary, but how painful it felt to her. The film is not a sociological essay, however, but a fiction that tells the story of a young woman trying to reconcile herself with herself. It is Amy's (European) point of view that we adopt, but it is an intimate gaze, far from folklore. Sarah Bouyain indeed also fought to impose her choice of film poster,

> to not have a poster with an eternally red background. The distributor wanted to adapt the image of the film and label it "African cinema," claiming that if the film didn't fit into a slot, it wouldn't attract viewers, which is paradoxical, given that African cinema is not exactly popular![40]

Notre étrangère portrays a quest for identity rather than a geographic rooting. For Amy, the trip to Burkina Faso and the search for her mother symbolize the quest for a part of herself—her African part, which she felt disconnected from, but which she always bore in her heart. It is interesting to remark how far Amy travels to find her mother, who, like her, lives in Paris. However, the journey that she undertakes is an interior one too. She will only be able to find her integrity and her equilibrium via a displacement and a decentering that opens other points of view to her, other ways of seeing, until she is able to rediscover (or reconcile herself with) a part of her being. It is precisely the physical displacement that engenders the perceptual decentering that allows her to gain distance, and thus to see differently. Just as mother and daughter are connected by their quest, Mariam's perspective also changes. The epilogue in France follows a scene that takes place in the family courtyard in Burkina, in which Amy's brother in France phones to give her her mother's address. The following shot takes us directly to Paris and the narrative ends in a cyclical structure: Mariam is at work, as at the start of the film. She looks at herself in the same mirror, but as if she were seeing herself differently, as if something in her life has changed, and a smile reappears on her face. From this open ending, we can imagine that as Amy finds her mother, she allegorically finds a part of herself and will be able to reassemble and reconstruct her being in both France and Burkina.

The character Amy, who is both "ours" and "foreign," and her identity quest translate the world of the film director. We find this multifocal vision in all of the characters—all women in different situations—who belong to different cultures and generations, and who each face their daily lives in their own ways. Acita and

Kadiatou, both of whom are Burkinabè and live in Burkina, face life differently. Acita, who is older, only speaks Jula and seems trapped in her suffering. She embodies the sorrow of a marginalized, childless woman. Kadiatou, who is younger and bilingual, becomes a bridge between the cultures and generations. And while her private life is shrouded in mystery, she faces life with a smile. Mariam, the emigrant who bears an unresolved weight inside her, is unable to reconstruct herself elsewhere, unlike the woman she shares a room with in Paris, who is an immigrant too. While also bilingual, Mariam does not seek to connect with others; she remains unconnected, whereas Amy is determined to unite both her belongings.

It may thus be concluded that *Notre étrangère* is a portrayal of the director's own experiences, her world, her preoccupations, and her own identity quest. It is clear in her interviews that this question of dual belonging has always inhabited Sarah Bouyain. Being biracial, she is of dual heritage—that of the colonized and the colonizer. As she puts it: "Belonging to two cultures . . . navigating between two families separated by so much distance, whether geographic or cultural, separated too by the legacy of colonization, at times you feel obliged to choose between your two countries. Must you choose between your two parents?"[41] Bouyain decides not to choose, and dedicated her film "To my family, here and there." Or as she states: "All my life, I'll never stop navigating and oscillating in between. I will always be an outsider in both countries. But ultimately, it's not a problem for me. A dual culture is also a richness, in the discomfort it gives rise to."[42]

CHAPTER 8

Interior/Exterior Worlds

L'Afrance, by Alain Gomis

This chapter questions the ruptures and transformations that take place in people's lives in the diaspora space. It studies the strategies by which, as they become aware that their identity is being reshaped, individuals manage to imagine different futures to those that seemed set out for them, as the protagonist of *L'Afrance* illustrates well.[1] Senegalese El Hadj (Djolof Mbengue) is a history student in Paris. His present is steeped in his personal past and in history. He lives in foreign-student halls of residence, a world rich in diverse human trajectories, in a Paris far from the tourist spots. He has been in France for six years, but believes it his duty to return to Senegal, where he plans to participate in his country's development. As time goes by, his life becomes more complicated, and his perception of himself and his destiny is painfully called into question. After failing to renew his visa on time, he is arrested and spends several days in detention. He then finds himself working as a laborer, even though he does not belong to the working class, as his companions point out to him. He tries to find his path in the shady milieu of selling false papers, but does not fit in there either and his efforts fail. El Hadj, who bears a Muslim name, thus lives in an imaginary space, in "Afrance"—neither France nor Africa, but both at the same time—or in a "non-France" (an a-France, or France with an alpha privative).

He is inspired by the Independence leaders (notably the Sékou Touré of the early years—about whom he is writing a dissertation—and Patrice Lumumba), or by writers such as Cheikh Hamidou Kane. However, contrary to the protagonist of *L'Aventure ambiguë* (*Ambiguous Adventure*), he renounces both suicide and return.[2] Feeling alienated from the outside world, he often takes refuge in the shower, which becomes the prime (non)place where he lets his rage rip. Under the water of the shower, the memory of his past in Senegal and the idea he has of himself haunt him. He is consumed by a feeling of guilt. Over time, he becomes aware that he is now also an outsider in his home country, an observation that is all the more painful. He abandons his fiancée back in Senegal and starts a relationship with a French woman, Miriam (Delphine Zingg). The narrative, which opens in Paris with the voice of his father (Thierno Ndiaye Doss) heard in a recorded letter, concludes with El Hadj's return to Dakar, where he informs his father of his decision to remain in France and to teach there. His father then recounts his own migration when he was young and his own father sent him from the family village to Dakar, the capital. For the father, this exile was undertaken unconsciously, not by choice.

Myths of Return

Alain Gomis was born in Paris to immigrant parents, his mother coming originally from another region of France and his father from Senegal. These two types of migration, which marked his Paris childhood and existence, are reformulated in the film through the characters of El Hadj and his father. Passionate about cinema, Gomis has long watched all sorts of films, from the works of Djibril Diop Mambéty to Jean Vigo, science fiction, Italian comedies, Japanese films, and Swedish films.[3] He studied art history, then did a master's in film studies. Partaking in video workshops, he filmed reports in Paris about young people of immigrant descent, a theme that is particularly dear to his heart. Right from the outset, his cinema has questioned identities and belongings, whether in short or feature films shot in France or in Senegal.

Tourbillons (*Whirlwinds*, 1999), his first fiction short (12½ minutes), contains the seeds of all the themes of *L'Afrance*. It is the story of Ousmane, a Senegalese student in Paris, torn between his life in France and the return home. Like *L'Afrance*, *Tourbillons* was already inspired by *L'Aventure ambiguë*. This short film, which unfolds in a hip-hop universe, portrays the "whirlwinds," or contradictions and complexities of this Senegalese student's life in his final moments in France, before he crosses the line of "no return." Ousmane "can sense that he is living the final moments in which he is still able to make the decision to return to Senegal. But is it already too late?," the film synopsis states.[4] The *tourbillons,* or whirlwinds, of the title perfectly capture the jerky, rich aesthetic of this short film. It can indeed be seen as the starting point of *L'Afrance,* in which El Hadj surpasses this threshold and can no longer turn back. The loop is looped in Gomis's feature film *Tey* (*Today,* 2012), in which Satché returns to die in Senegal after living abroad for years.

The question of return is also found in other diaspora filmmakers' films, as shall be seen later with *Teza.* But it was already present in Ababacar Samb Makharam's short film *Et la neige n'était plus* (*There Was No Longer Snow*), which illustrates the psychological shock suffered by a Senegalese student on return from France, whose interior monologues express his distress at no longer knowing where his place is—or in *Concerto pour un exil,* by Désiré Écaré (*Concerto for an Exile,* 1968), which recounts the path of a disillusioned student who returns to Ivory Coast after his studies in France, or again *Le Retour d'un aventurier* (*The Adventurer's Return*). More recently, the question of return was found at the center of films such as *L'Absence* (*The Absence,* Mama Keita, 2009), *Testament* (John Akomfrah, 1988), and *Le Jardin de papa* (*The Garden,* Zeka Laplaine, 2004).

L'Afrance was shot shortly after *Tourbillons* and translates a need to further the exploration of exile and identity that so deeply concerns the director. This feature film is also a universal story of human destiny. Featuring a spatial duality that mirrors the narrative, *L'Afrance* is the first film that Alain Gomis shot partly in Senegal. Even though most of the story takes place in Paris, Dakar is present in the protagonist's memories from time to time, woven into the narrative, and in the final scene. The narrative is not linear; it progresses through flashbacks that disrupt the present-tense narration.

The principal source of funding for this film, shot mainly in Paris, was the CNC *avance sur recettes,* or Advance on Earnings Fund (Centre national cinémato-graphique). For his first feature film, the young filmmaker thus enjoyed favorable conditions compared to most of his colleagues, who had to learn early to juggle with shoestring budgets. Gomis recounts that after spending two years rewriting his film, he no longer knew where he was going, yet was at the same time aware he needed to shoot it: "At one point, I nearly didn't make it, but it worked out in the end. Anyway, they'd have had to have killed me to stop this film being made."[5] These difficulties quickly rid him of his naiveté and forced him to understand certain funding methods. He continues:

> I came to understand the television system, which doesn't fund films like this due to the subject (not commercial enough), or the cast (too Black). African films flop, they kept telling me; which is true, but I don't think that is due to being Black or White. The problem is when you don't conform to a commercial, standardized, and reassuring form of narrative.[6]

Alain Gomis's work is auteur cinema. He was accordingly selected at the Venice Film Festival in 2007 for *Andalucia,* and at the Berlin Film Festival in 2012 for *Tey.* His fourth feature film, *Félicité,* won the Silver Bear Award in Berlin in 2017 and the Golden Stallion Award at the FESPACO the same year.

To make *L'Afrance,* he assembled an artistic and technical crew that has continued to work together since. He notably began his collaboration with the film's protagonist, Senegalese actor Djolof Mbengue,[7] who has since played in other films of Gomis and also cowrote *Tey.* Gomis also worked with the French actor (and later director) of Algerian descent Samir Guesmi, who played the main role in *Andalucia.*[8] Among his regular actors is also Delphine Zingg (Miriam in *L'Afrance*). Finally, ever since his first short film, and in most of his works since, the soundtracks are composed by his brother, Patrice Gomis, a tandem that recalls Djibril Diop Mambéty and Wasis Diop.

L'Afrance was commercially released in France on 30 January 2002 and distributed by Cine Classic. It was selected in official competition at the Sundance Festival in 2002, and won several awards in major international film festivals, notably the First Film Silver Leopard (Locarno 2001), the Audience Award at the Milan African Film Festival (2002), the Golden Bayard (Namur 2002), and the Best First Film Award at the FESPACO (2003). Gomis went from feature to short film, next making *Petite Lumière* (*A Little Light,* 2003, 13 minutes), which he shot entirely in Senegal this time. A girl named Fatima keeps opening and closing a refrigerator door, intrigued about whether the light remains on when it is shut. She goes out into the street and wonders if people are still there when she shuts her eyes, if the world truly exists or whether it is the fruit of her imagination. An allegory about knowledge and the diverse perceptions one may have of the world, this play on light and obscurity evokes cinema itself, and recalls Senegalese filmmaker Djibril Diop Mambéty. To explain cinema, Mambéty described his poetic universe as follows:

Making films isn't hard. When you shut your eyes, you see darkness; but if you shut them even harder, you begin to see little stars. Some of them are people, others animals, horses, birds. Now, if you tell them how to move, where to go, when to stop, when to fall, you have a screenplay. Once you're done, you can open your eyes: the film is made.[9]

With this poetic short film, Alain Gomis again confirmed his composite culture. He took "another convincing and magnificent step into his style of the in-between," wrote Olivier Barlet.[10] His following short film, *Ahmed,* made in 2006, is the adaptation of a screenplay by the high-school student Michaël Morena.[11] James Campbell played the leading role.

Gomis's second feature film, *Andalucia* (2008), again addresses the themes of migration, marginality, and the quest for identity. Yacine lives in a trailer on the edges of society in a world inhabited by marginal figures. Ridden with doubts and existential anguish, fleeing his past and his origins, he loses himself until he runs into his childhood friend Djibril, who forces him to confront himself and to redefine his place. In the trailer of this film, set to diverse rhythms, the protagonist, Yacine (Samir Guesmi), is described as "from here, . . . from elsewhere." The director's statement tells us that "Yacine is born in France. Yacine is born a foreigner."[12] As Axel Zeppenfeld describes in *Les Cahiers du Cinéma, Andalucia,* which enters Yacine's dreamlike, lyrical world, can be described as "accompanying its hero's rapture."[13] I personally prefer, however, the term protagonist to hero as Yacine is completely human. His heroic self is perhaps precisely not being a hero, but rather accepting himself as a mere human searching for himself. The film's title represents an interior "non-place," the protagonist's initiatory dream—he who, in the Paris suburbs, fantasizes about his journey to this region of Spain, Andalusia, the epitome of cultural blending, a mix between the Arab and Western worlds, where the end of the film is set. As in *L'Afrance,* the narration is not linear. Following the moments lived in the immediate present, the small pleasures of the protagonist and the characters who gravitate around him, the narrative is fragmented and poetically disarticulated.

Like *L'Afrance* and *Petite Lumière, Andalucia* was produced by Mille et Une Productions. The following year, in 2009, Alain Gomis, Newton Aduaka, Valérie Osouf, and Delphine Zingg founded Granit Films, which aims to develop "themes relating to identity questions in the broadest sense."[14] His first production with Granit Films, *Tey* (*Today,* 2012), was a positive experience.[15] Shot entirely in Senegal, *Tey,* like Gomis's previous works, "questions identity and narrative deconstruction,"[16] and plays on the aesthetic, on sensations, and on the atmosphere more than on the story itself. The narrative plunges us into Satché's last day, knowing that he will die that night. Played by the famous American musician and slam poet Saul Williams,[17] the Senegalese protagonist returns home to die after having lived part of his life in the United States. In the course of the day, which is an interior voyage, he traverses both Dakar's neighborhoods and various periods of his life. It is a film that addresses human intimacy. It poses fundamental questions, such as the meaning of life and self-reconciliation. Satché returns home to die and at the same time returns to the sources of his being. In *L'Afrance*, the question of return is portrayed as a dilemma; in *Tey*, it becomes a final, inevitable destination.

Tey is interesting in Alain Gomis's path on several counts. It is first of all the film that brought him to the attention of a wider audience. In France, all Gomis's previous feature films were released in cinemas, but it was the latter that met with public acclaim, even if some critics and spectators found it too elitist and intellectual. It is no coincidence that the DVD of *L'Afrance* came out in June 2012—that is, ten years after the film—after *Tey* had been selected in several festivals.[18] It may be noted that Alain Gomis lived for a year with his family in Dakar to shoot *Tey*. This was in 2012, at the time of the presidential elections and the peaceful demonstrations that took place in the streets of Dakar. Gomis thus became a reporter and filmed real events in the streets. Some of his images of the Dakar street demonstrations were later included in the fiction of *Tey*. This process is particularly interesting given that the film is above all dreamlike and timeless. Thus, as in *Teza, Juju Factory, Testament,* or *Kinshasa Palace,* elements of the real or archive images are interjected into the fiction in a stylistic mix that reflects the filmmaker's composite culture. This formal mixing was already present in *L'Afrance*, in which historical elements merge with the fiction via El Hadj's master's thesis on Sékou Touré and the snippets of speeches by Patrice Lumumba, the political leader of Congolese Independence (then the Belgian Congo).[19] In *L'Afrance*, fiction and historical reality intertwine.

As its title—a contraction of "Africa" and "France"—illustrates well, the film represents both territories and neither of them. It is also the "non-France" of the alpha privative, the France that El Hadj cannot really enter, which is not totally accessible to foreigners. "Afrance" is situated in the divide that exists between the mental and real territories. "L'Afrance is this world in which you live on just one foot, in transit, constantly planning the Return."[20] For those who inhabit the diaspora space and who navigate multiple groups, the notions of home, belonging, and identity are constantly questioned and never fixed. It is precisely this dreamlike confusion between Paris and Dakar—a fusion of two cities that merge together in an internal whirl beyond time and space—that this film begins, and whose opening sequence shall be analyzed below.

Beyond Space-Time (Extract)

The extract chosen is the film's opening, which lasts about five minutes. It consists of a sequence comprising a long audio letter recorded on a tape cassette that the protagonist's father sends him, and which is heard over a succession of real images, or images imagined by the protagonist. The continuity of the audio letter serves to link the discontinuous images. The latter are at times from the present, at times from different periods in the past—the recent past and the distant past, in both France and Senegal—bringing together several generations and two languages. This extract is comprised of twenty-three shots of varying durations: from 1' 13" (for the first shot) to 2 or 3 seconds. The first shot is situated in an indefinite place; the other shots alternate between Paris and Dakar. Those set in Senegal refer in general to the past. Either they illustrate the letter that El Hadj's father has recorded for him, or they belong to his childhood or his recent and distant memories. This extract introduces many key elements that feature throughout the film.

Shot 1: 00' 15" (Unspecified setting, greenish backdrop)

Straight after the beginning of the credits, which are set to a black backdrop with no music, the face of a thirty-something black man (who, we will soon discover, is El Hadj, the protagonist) occupies the left three-quarters of the frame. His head is slightly bowed, his eyes shut. A fraction of his face is cut by the frame.

In the background, a blur of noises: a continuous, distant whistling sound haunts El Hadj for a few seconds; the sound of waves; the cries of a gull; the singing of crickets; croaking frogs; market hustle and bustle; the sound of rainfall; and distant, indistinguishable voices.

El Hadj lifts his head and looks up. The actor's name (Djolof Mbengue) appears at the bottom right of the screen. Completely still, his eyes alone swivel while the names of the other actors scroll by. At times, he ever so slightly moves his head, his gaze constantly lost in the distance. He is fleetingly lit by a ray of light, and a smile

Djolof Mbengue

plays on his lips. He resumes his serious expression while continuing to move his eyes. He leans into the center of the frame before rapidly resuming his position to the left. A flash of light falls on his face at the same moment that a high-pitched sound is heard over the murmur of distant voices. The honking of a horn makes him turn his head, without us knowing if the sound is real or in his imagination. He blinks rapidly, his head tilted skywards. The camera gently accompanies these movements before becoming static again, filming his distress. His eyelids blink, his face still as drops of water begin to run down his face; at this point, the director's name appears. Drops continue falling on his face. He does not move for an instant, his eyes shut, a smile playing on his lips. For the entire duration of this lengthy shot (1' 13"), we see just the protagonist's face.

Shot 2: 01' 28" (Senegal, as we discover later)

The bow of a pirogue cuts through the waves, appearing to follow the sun's reflection on the water, vertically dividing the image into two symmetrical parts. Tracing a straight line, like a directional arrow, the bow points to the path home. In the distance, on the horizon, land (Dakar?). The camera is on the advancing pirogue; the title *L'Afrance* appears on the screen.

A ship horn signals that the boat is going to land; it is *returning* to the port in the distance. The siren is replaced by a man's voice-over, in Wolof (which confirms that

*El Hadj,
j'espère que cette cassette*

this shot is located in Senegal): "El Hadj, I hope that this cassette finds you in good health..." We thus learn the protagonist's name. The pirogue continues to advance.

Shot 3: 01' 41" (Paris, as we later learn)

El Hadj is sitting on his single bed in his room, to the left of the screen. He puts the tape in his cassette player. He is dressed in white, his yellowish shirt open, and is wearing a little leather pouch around his neck. We see him in profile, the framing giving the impression of a *huis-clos,* a place of confinement, with no possible way out. The cassette player is by the window, facing the spectator. Books lie open on the desk, to the right of the shot. It is a student's lodgings, tiny and bare, with institutional furniture, but clean and tidy. The wall is decorated simply with photos of key African Independence leaders, such as the black-and-white photo of Patrice Lumumba.[21] A shut window, masked by a net curtain, gives a glimmer of yellowish light that shines in from outside. The camera slowly approaches El Hadj, who remains framed in medium shot.

He sits comfortably on his bed, leaning back against the wall behind him. The camera follows him and, slowly homing in on him, now shows his face, which appears next to the portraits stuck to the wall behind him.

Comfortable, barefoot, he looks at home, but the pouch around his neck suggests that he is voyaging, in transit, and must protect his most precious possessions.

He takes a pillow and tucks it behind his head to listen to his father's words, recorded in Wolof (right after, we get the confirmation that it is his father's voice): "El Hadj, I hope you are fine, that your studies are going well, and that you are in good health. I received your letter, and I'm delighted that you have nearly achieved your objectives . . ." The camera comes to a halt.

Shot 4: 02' 05" (Senegal, an unspecified town)

The decor changes; we are now in an apartment in Senegal, the camera remaining static for the entire shot. We see over the shoulder of a man to the left of the frame. In front of him, to the right of the frame, a middle-aged woman, her head covered with a white cloth, is sitting on a sofa with lace headrests. On a table, in the middle of the shot, a cassette player is center frame, a microphone on the table next to it. It is this means of oral communication that carries the voice of the older generation back home across the ocean. This type of player allows people to collectively record and listen. Behind the smiling woman—who listens attentively in silence—we can see the bottom of an open window.

It is a typical Dakar-style window, protected on the outside by bars. Contrary to El Hadj's confined room, here there is an opening to the exterior. Despite the bars, this image of an open window gives the impression of an opening onto the world. It is as if we can feel the air circulating.

et que tu fasses grandir
notre nom.

The house looks comfortable, giving an indication of the family's social status, which is later confirmed by the man's declaration that the shop is doing well. The father speaks, facing his wife—that is, also facing the outside. The same voice that accompanied the previous shots is now embodied, onscreen: "And that you are honoring our name." The father asks El Hadj to send news more often, so that his mother does not worry.

Shot 5: 02' 16" (Paris)

El Hadj is in his room in Paris: a close-up of his pouch, from which he takes an old, slightly yellowed black-and-white photo of his mother when she was young, as the stereo continues to play his father's voice recorded on the cassette.

In front of the camera, El Hadj's close-up hands hold the photo, which to begin with is visible to the spectator. Then the protagonist looks at it; it thus ends up upside down on the screen.

He passes his hand over his mother's photo, as if caressing her; then the camera follows his hand as it rises to caress his own face, as if to reinforce the connection between him and his mother—as if to receive her maternal protection and blessing. We see El Hadj's face in close-up, hidden behind his hand; finally, his almost expressionless face appears before our eyes. He listens to his father's words, his

ta mère s'inquiète

eyes shut. He opens his eyes a second, then shuts them again, as if to plunge back into his intimate world, into the realm of his thoughts and dreams.

Shot 6: 02' 32" (Dakar)

A close-up low-angle shot of a woman holding a little plastic bag filled with red fruit juice (maybe bissap) that is frequently sold in the streets in Senegal. In this sensual image, drops of water glisten on her smiling face, set against the blue sky. She lifts her head to drink. The sea is heard in the background, set to the father's voice-over, which continues: "Awa also asks for your news every day."

Shot 7: 02' 36" (Dakar)

El Hadj with his fiancée Awa (whom the father has just mentioned) on a beach, near to the shore. The sea is to the left of the shot. The line between the land and sea divides the image diagonally. They are still on the edge of the Senegalese land.

El Hadj has not yet taken the step that will lead him definitively to the other side of the ocean. He is lying near the rocks and looking at his fiancée, who, her back to us, is drinking. Lost in the environment, their bodies stand out thanks to their blue swimsuits. The voice-over continues over the sound of the waves crashing on the shore.

Shot 8: 02' 43" (Dakar)

Three men surround a bed where someone lies dying. The window is open; outside it is dark. The recorded voice speaks: "We celebrated the anniversary of your grandfather's passing." The father's voice-over mentions the imam's call to prayers. The man nearest the window—the protagonist's father—is counting his prayer beads. The hand of the man on the right of the bed lies on the dying man's brow, whom we better discover as the camera tracks slowly forwards. They pray. The voice-over strikes up again. Here, spatiotemporal discontinuity is conveyed in the mention of the anniversary of the death and the death itself.

Shot 9: 02' 59"

El Hadj is naked, sitting in the right-hand corner of his shower, his head lifted as he leans back against the wall under the running water. His eyes shut, his black body contrasts with the white of the shower basin and the tiled walls that shut him in on three sides, as if he were alone with himself, as if there was nothing else in the world apart from him.[22]

The father's voice-over continues, asking him to think of his sister too, "who hopes to follow the same path as you." The camera is static. El Hadj too is immobile; only the slight movement of his stomach as he breathes indicates that he is alive.

à ta sœur,

Shot 10: 03' 06" (Dakar)

El Hadj remembers back in time. A child, he is in school in Senegal. The teacher calls "El Hadj," confirming that this is indeed the protagonist as a child.

He is reading a text in front of the class. In front of the blackboard, he takes the place of the schoolteacher who, brandishing his menacing-looking ruler, is

to the left of the frame. They are filmed at a 30° angle. On the wall between the teacher and pupil hangs a map of Senegal. To the right of the young El Hadj, the blackboard is visible. The child is thus in the middle, between the map of Senegal and the blackboard on which the date (which is not entirely visible) and the title of the book he is reading (Cheikh Hamidou Kane's *Ambiguous Adventure*) are written in French. The camera is in the back of the classroom, filming the other pupils from behind. The young El Hadj's voice is superimposed on that of El Hadj's in the present, the two voices reading aloud a passage of the novel: "They would learn all the ways of joining wood to wood, the art of convincing without being in the right, but would what they would learn be worth as much as what they would forget?"[23]

Shot 11: 03' 26" (Dakar)

El Hadj as a child, filmed from behind, prays on a rooftop terrace, in the shade of a hanging sheet, with his father and another man. The present-day recorded voice of his father resumes in voice-over, reminding him to continue to say his prayers.

Shot 12: 03' 28" (Dakar)

The same terrace seen from the opposite direction. Father and child are frontally framed in medium shot, their hands over their faces, the washing hanging in the background. They then uncover their faces, and the father's voice-over continues (referring to the prayers): "that we hand down from father to son." The child lowers his hands and raises his head; his father puts his hand on his shoulder. They look at one another, smiling, as the voice-over continues: "I put my trust in you."

Shot 13: 03' 40" (Unspecified place)

An slightly low-angle extreme close-up shot of present-day El Hadj fills the screen. The father's voice ends in voice-over: "I am certain that you will do what is best." Drops of water run down his face, which he turns slightly, closing his eyes, as if to return to his memories, or his inner world.

*je suis sûr
que tu feras pour le mieux.*

Shot 14: 03' 48" (Dakar)

A slightly high-angle shot down at a street in Dakar, full of cars and people dressed in colorful prints. A slightly high-angle pan accompanied by somewhat strident, slow flute music reveals the rest of the street. Everything is in movement: the cars, the people, the camera.

Shot 15: 03' 57" (Dakar. Continuous sound)

The same street filmed from the opposite direction. People are moving; the place is bustling with life. A high-angle shot shows the passersby before the camera descends towards the ground.

Shot 16: 04' 04" (Paris. Continuous sound)

A similar high-angle shot now looks down on Paris, at big paving slabs in a pedestrian zone. A red, white, and blue plastic bird (the colors of the French flag) swoops, drawing our attention to a white man performing on a pedestal in front of a handful of spectators, who are white for the most part too, gathered around him to watch, while the plastic bird flies away and out of the shot.

Shot 17: 04' 09" (Dakar. Continuous sound)

The same street, again in a slightly high-angle shot. Dakar's characteristic blue and yellow communal buses and yellow and black cabs circulate. The neighborhood is animated; we can see "real" daily life. The camera accompanies the advance of a communal cab.

Shot 18: 04' 14"

Still in Dakar, a man dressed in a boubou walks down the street, the camera following him in high-angle. At first, he is half hidden by the branches of a tree, before emerging to become entirely visible. On the sidewalk, he crosses paths with other men sitting on chairs in front of their shops, also dressed in boubous.

Shot 19: 04' 20" (Paris. Continuous sound)

The same setting as shot 16. The same plastic bird cuts swiftly across the sky and frame. A young man on rollerblades, dressed in shorts and a vest T-shirt, jumps a strap strung between two barriers before a group of immobile onlookers. Another young man follows him and does the same jump. The camera initially follows them, then comes to a halt.

Shot 20: 04' 26" (Dakar. Continuous sound)

The same Dakar street is now filmed from the other direction. A high-angle shot down as a street hawker pushes his yellow soft-drinks cart, his head hidden beneath a parasol. The camera follows him.

Shot 21: 04' 32" (Paris)

A high-angle shot down at the same Paris setting: a tourist spot where street hawkers display their wares. The red, white, and blue plastic bird continues flying. A rapid pan shows the (white) tourists and (black) hawkers, the former who are mainly strolling, the latter still. A red, white, and blue parasol protects a hawker who is standing there.

Shot 22: 04' 36" (Dakar)

The same Dakar street, teeming with people and traffic. A slow upwards tilt shot reveals the buildings.

We spot a mosque: the Mosque of the Divinity in Ouakam, with its minarets. Further in the distance, the sea and a sliver of sky. A bird is spotted flying.

Shot 23: 00:04' 46" (Paris)

The plastic bird comes crashing to the ground, filmed in high angle. A hand picks it up—El Hadj's—and shows it to a friend. The two men are filmed in low angle: El Hadj, his back to the camera; his friend, who is black too, faces the camera. The crowds around appear to disappear, and we see only the two friends, who hand each other the plastic bird. "Chérif, for sure!" says the friend, recognizing one of their friend's trinkets. The second character exits the frame, revealing the Eiffel Tower behind him, lit up in the twilight. El Hadj remains alone on the right side of the image, which is cut in two by the Eiffel Tower (imposing, but in the background), the lights on it reading "Year 2000." Seen from behind, El Hadj crosses the frame and in turn exits, revealing the tourists behind him kneeling to look at the souvenir trinkets laid out on the ground.

The extract chosen ends here. The film continues with a wedding party scene. The camera is in the room, the door opens, and the couple—a white woman and a black man—appears before their friends gathered for the celebration. In this scene, numerous inserts from the recent past reveal the protagonist and his friends. It is the first time that we see El Hadj in a convivial setting, and it is here too during this celebration of this interracial marriage that discussions about returning home are first heard. El Hadj says to the groom's mother: "I'm finishing my master's, then I'm going home." Between the expatriate Senegalese, the debate is heated. There are those who wish to build their lives in France, and those who see it as a temporary passage. El Hadj argues: "If no one goes home, things won't just never get better, it'll be the end!" It is also at the party that he meets the French woman, Miriam, who later becomes his girlfriend. But I wish to return to the first scene here.

Personal Rebirth

I have chosen to analyze the opening because it already contains many of the elements that characterize the film. The extract is indeed very rich in references that help us understand the film in its entirety, as many of the factors that later turn out to be central to the narrative are established. For example, it introduces one of Alain Gomis's preoccupations that is of particular interest here: the quest for, and redefinition of, the self at a junction between cultures. Already, the first lengthy close-up of El Hadj (1' 13") invites the spectator to enter the character's psychology and his interior world; we can sense his torment and the weight of his condition. Indeed, the use of close-ups and extreme close-ups is a characteristic of Gomis's cinema. Here, El Hadj is not to the center of the image; we thus perceive an imbalance in the shot, which reflects his instability. Right from the start of the narrative, Alain Gomis thus underscores the heart of the film: "a human caught in the whirlwinds of his contradictions."[24] During the entire extract, El Hadj is silent, but we sense his internal existential turmoil.

The extract starts simply, before becoming more complex. Space, time, reality, and imagination alternate throughout the entire sequence. At first, the alternation is geographic, then becomes temporal. The two countries—France and Senegal, as they are later identified—are interwoven. Moreover, the narrative follows diverse temporalities: the present in Paris mixes with the recent past, when the father recorded the cassette in Senegal; El Hadj's distant past in Dakar with his fiancée before his departure six years earlier; and finally, the even more distant past when El Hadj was a child. The narrative becomes more complex and the images increasingly intertwine. The rhythm accelerates and slows. In memory, space and time are not limited; we can grasp the simultaneity of events and the ubiquity of places. Here, the montage is predominant, not the individual shots, whose meaning comes, rather, from the successive ensemble. The director indeed describes what he was trying to capture:

a mental universe, a mix of memories and hopes, fragments of Africa reconstituted in France. It is this all and this nothing that El Hadj, the main character, experiences at the start of the film, where time and space do not exist, where everything is possible, where everything is dreamed, where the native land lives in one's memory and projects, killing the real present and dilating borders.[25]

It is clear, then, that the director deliberately blurs the diverse temporalities, giving the film its depth, and inscribing in it the language of hybridity.

The image of the past clearly situates who this man undergoing a full-blown identity crisis in France is, and why the memory of his home country prevents him from fully living the present elsewhere. We know from his father's voice that "the shop is doing well, very well, thanks be to God." He has not migrated for economic reasons then—as the image of his parents' comfortable home shows too—but rather due to ideological and cultural aspirations: El Hadj has chosen to study history and return to Senegal to contribute to his country's development. We later discover that his master's thesis is on Independence and Sékou Touré, a "hero" he wants to measure up to (or at least the early Sékou Touré, who refused a "domesticated" Independence, who said "no" in the 1958 referendum,[26] and who "held his head high"—as El Hadj explains to Miriam—and not the despot he became later). Through this prism, history enters the fiction.

El Hadj had a peaceful social existence in Senegal: a family, a sister, a fiancée. Like Samba Diallo in *Ambiguous Adventure,* he was educated into the values of the Quran (as his name also indicates),[27] and also attended "the new school." This is clear in the shots of his childhood. We therefore understand everything that he would feel he were betraying if he decided to remain in France. In the shots filmed in Paris, he is almost always alone, whereas in Senegal, other characters accompany him, which reinforces the impression that he belongs to a community.

The first image of what we later learn is Senegal—the bow of a pirogue that advances in the water—evokes the impression of travel, of a faraway place on the other side of the ocean. The pirogue is also emblematic of fishing, a highly developed activity in Senegal, and thus a local rooting. Yet at the same time, the vessel heading back to the port already evokes the idea of return, which haunts the protagonist. The straight line of the sun's reflection on the water evokes the duty to return that inhabits El Hadj, as if his destiny were all planned, with no alternative. In this respect, this inevitably recalls an image in *Testament* (John Akomfrah, 1988), in which Abena—a Ghanaian journalist who lives in London and who returns to Ghana twenty years after the coup d'état that overthrew Nkrumah—is sitting in the bow of a boat sailing on the river. The camera's focus point is also on the boat. Her interior monologue rests on an overlay of past and present, a first-person voice and another in the third person. In *Testament,* we can sense the feeling of guilt of she who abandoned her country and the struggle of her compatriots.

It is precisely this idea of a duty to return that torments El Hadj and stops him from really constructing himself in France.

Later, this concept is illustrated by the symbolism of the pink flamingo. A down-and-out in the street says to El Hadj: "We are flamingos; one foot in the water, the other in the air, our wings folded." That is all the clearer as, in an earlier scene, an African friend in the university residence said to him: "For me, home is where my two feet touch the ground." El Hadj is here, but dreams of "there." He is in Paris to fulfill his duty to study, but his soul is in Dakar, where, deep down, he is afraid to return for fear of also feeling an outsider in Senegal, which would be worse still. As the shot in the shower suggests, at this point, he is still a prisoner of the rigid idea he has of himself; he is mentally trapped. He does not let life transform him and is not yet ready to accept the changes taking place within him. *L'Afrance* indeed poses the question of what it means to be foreign—and what one is foreign to. The filmmaker explains:

> The sense of being a foreigner in one's own country was very close to me in more ways than one. It is this sense, this pain that animates El Hadj: what he's scared of is becoming an outsider back in Senegal. I'm an outsider in France, and in Senegal; that's my biracial condition. It's both a quality and a shortcoming.[28]

Although born in France, Alain Gomis—like Sarah Bouyain—grew up immersed in the paternal myth of return. As Gomis describes:

> I grew up hearing my father planning our *imminent* return. I saw cousins come to study in France *for five years.* And, even though I was born here, to a French mother, I know how hard I find it to say: *This* is my home. El Hadj, the lead character in the film, embodies our concerns: those of my father, who no longer says he'll go home one day, but who wonders where he'll be buried. And mine, having to confront a time-space without fleeing, relying on an elsewhere. And no doubt, all of our concerns.[29]

The filmmaker thus draws on his experience, reorganizing it into a fictional universe. But he draws on other films too: for example, *Mémoires d'immigrés* (*Immigrant Memories,* 1997), by Yamina Benguigui (also the daughter of immigrants). This is a three-part documentary that recounts the existence of Maghrebi men, women, and children in France. "I remember a woman in the film saying that they never repaired anything in her family, for example when a faucet broke . . . because they knew that they were going home," says Gomis.[30]

The extract chosen clearly illustrates the state of limbo in which El Hadj lives, in the expectation of returning home. In shot 3, for example, he is in his room in Paris, but Senegal and Africa are present, not only in the materialization of his memories, but also through the photographs on his wall and the photo of his mother in his pouch. The upside-down image of his mother evokes the reversal of mother-son roles. Senegal is also present through the words in Wolof that his father recorded. The film begins in Wolof, then, but the main language spoken in the film is French. The choice of an audio letter corresponds perfectly with Senegal's predominantly oral tradition. The radio-cassette player—an instrument of communication par excellence, especially when one is far away—is an essential presence, which operates as a sort of continuity between shots 3 and 4, respectively situated in Paris and Dakar. Thousands of miles apart, and in different time-spaces, the radio-cassette player remains at the center of both shots.[31]

The two domestic spaces are thus connected. That of the student room in Paris appears confined. El Hadj is alone, shut in this room, the window closed; he does not communicate with the exterior (at least, not for the moment)—whereas the parental home in Senegal gives the impression of an open, airy space. El Hadj lives as if suspended in an in-between, neither in Senegal, nor in France, but in this "Afrance" that he has constructed in his own mind. For example, when he shuts his eyes in the shower, which is the symbolic space of his universe (shot 9), he is no longer listening to his father's words, but enters his own world and memory. He becomes a child again, returning to his childhood values. Indeed, the following shot (in the school) acts like a warning: not to flee like Samba Diallo, not to forget what he has learned.

From the moment we see this shot in the shower, we understand that this intimate territory represents a specific place, a space in which El Hadj talks to himself. In the show, he learns to free himself of the armor he has built around himself. It is the space of his interior truth; he is naked (like everyone at birth, or rebirth); he can no longer lie to himself. On several occasions, the shower scenes are filmed in close-up. This way of filming very close gives the impression that the camera wishes not just to enter the character's world or body, but also his deepest intimacy: his soul. "If I could have placed the camera inside his body, I would have. I really wanted to get inside. I wanted us to be him, for us to enter his body and spirit. Certain reactions are also conveyed via the skin," Gomis states.[32] The shower thus appears several times: El Hadj takes refuge there, inhabited by his memories, his sense of duty, his feelings of guilt and failure. Twenty-four minutes into the film, it is in the shower that he evokes the complexity of the colonial subject, incapable of defining him/herself other than in relation to France. Then shots of Dakar are seen while he continues to ruminate. His hits his head against the wall, beneath the running water; a close-up of his hand, then of his leg, reveal his trembling body. He takes his head in his hands, declaring desperately over the images of Dakar:

> Chérif, listen to what Sékou Touré said: the colonized African's consciousness evolved under the alienating and assimilating influence of French culture. Until now, we have asserted our desire for liberation at the same time as we have our inability to define ourselves outside the French context. That is one of the traits of the colonial subject, who acts like a slave, always hesitant when it comes to asserting himself independently of the master.

After 49½ minutes, we find him in the shower again, crouching—almost in a fetal position—his hands clasping his knees, his eyes staring, filmed at a 30° angle. In an interior dialogue with Awa, he explains to her why instead of bringing her to France, it is he who will come home to join her (he still has not yet abandoned his idea of returning). Without moving from his corner, he proclaims: "In any case, I wasn't going to remain a foreigner all my life!" In another later sequence, still in the shower, filmed in profile, his head resting against the tiles, he seems indifferent to the water running down his almost entirely visible body. He violently smashes his fist against the wall, letting his rage and disappointment rip. There is a brief sequence in *Teza* too in which Anberber, haunted by the nightmare of his recurring memories, takes refuge in the shower also. He is filmed almost from behind, his raised arm against the wall, in a position that El Hadj is seen in too.

In *L'Afrance*, these scenes are incredibly powerful. Gomis said of them:

> The shower is the territory where he collects his emotions and tries to convince himself. He even tells himself as he pummels the wall: "I *have to* go home, because

there are all those people who say you have to go on . . ." There's this intimate space but there's also the outside world, so at some point you have to get out of the shower. . . . That's it, this film is the story of someone who has to get out of the shower![33]

It might be said that the shower represents Afrance, this in-betweenness that one has to step out of to become oneself; that is, the sum of both worlds.

Paris and Dakar alternate in the protagonist's head, in the shower, and in the reality of the narrative. The continuity of the sound over shots 14 to 23 establishes a link between the two distant countries that are visually separate in the images. During this rapid succession of parallel shots at the start of the film, we see touristy Paris, unlike in the rest of the film, which is set in the students' residence, the detention center, a long way from the picture-postcard Paris. Afrance (a-France) is also one that we rarely see represented. "That of foreigners," as Alain Gomis insists, "that which exists in detention centers like those in Paris beneath the feet of the thousands of tourists who visit the Latin Quarter every day."[34] He continues: "It was important to me that the fiction focused on places and populations who are so rarely represented in the country I was born in. My deep desire was to make a film about humans."[35] Indeed, it is interesting to remark that the protagonist of this fiction does not represent a symbol, but simply a person-in-the-making, who must accept, accommodate, and even surpass his incapacities and multiple determinisms. The foreign students' residence or the detention center indeed represent hybrid spaces; they are not France or Africa (like the hostel where Mariam lives in *Notre étrangère*). They might be seen as confined spaces, but in the student residence, for example, the students are free. This is another France, with which the filmmaker is also familiar. Referring to the detention center, Gomis confided:

A relative of mine had a problem with his papers. I went to see him at the detention center. It was a hell of an experience. I have French nationality; he doesn't. Suddenly, although like me he'd never committed a crime, he was in prison. It's a question of exclusion. I'm biracial and you constantly ask yourself who you resemble, what you belong to."[36]

The captivity images in the film are indeed very powerful.

In the extract chosen, the vision of Paris is pretty idealized: a plastic bird embodies the colors of France; a mime artist performs for tourists; two youths on rollerblades execute the same jump for the onlookers; trinkets are sold as souvenirs to tourists, who, at this moment, are far from their "real" daily lives. The irony remains that these trinkets are illegally hawked by African immigrants. The fact that the wind-up bird flies like a maniac, out of control, can be seen as a warning to El Hadj about his possible destiny if he loses himself in the French capital where the Eiffel Tower shines. Like jewels, these beads of light offer a fantasy dream of Paris that will turn out to be very different in reality. These shots show us touristy Paris, the Paris of appearances, of artifice, and not the Paris where people live. It is no accident that the only shots of classic, touristy Paris—that of the city center and its monuments—are found in this extract of *L'Afrance* and in the scene in which El Hadj is taken into custody, through the barred window of a police van. Even though his profile is present in the frame, we see the capital as if through his eyes, through the window of the vehicle that serves to separate him from the City of Light, which will never be completely accessible to him unless he finds the means to truly belong. We see everyday Dakar, on the other hand, with its quotidian activities and ordinary life. The shots of Paris are, furthermore, marked by an impression of immobility: the mime artist on a pedestal, rooted in the ground; the spectators who stop to watch him; the hawkers, almost all of whom are standing still; and the tourists who stop to look at their wares. After accompanying a movement (for example, the flight of the plastic bird, or the youths jumping), the camera also stops still. Dakar, in contrast, is shown in perpetual movement, which the camera follows (the bus, the pedestrian, the drinks seller pushing his cart), or simply the pans, tilts, and tracking shots. The series of shots in Senegal indeed ends with an upwards tilt (shot 23) that slowly shows the sea and sky, as if the camera were looking up to explore what lies on the other side of the ocean, or as if to point to the distant horizon. Here, the minaret of the Mosque of the Divinity in Ouakam, the immediate suburb of Dakar, imposes its verticality. A real bird swoops, free in the sky. The sky and sea also evoke the hope of freedom. The following shot shows the red, white, and blue plastic bird crashing to the ground in Paris. The minaret is replaced by the verticality of the Eiffel Tower: the secular, tourist symbols of Paris, on the one hand, and the religious symbols of Dakar on the other. The narrative then continues with El Hadj's adventures in the French capital.

These initial images of the two imbricated cities illustrate the hybridity or the duality that inhabits El Hadj. He lives between the two, and for the time being, these two parts remain separate. He is haunted by the idea of return and cannot manage to envisage himself any differently. His thoughts are still set, like him stuck in his shower. As if in a metaphoric prison, he is unable to fully live there where he is, at

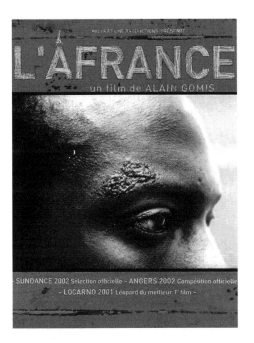

present, yet at the same time he is unable to leave too. Is he washing himself of the sin of having left his country? This image and El Hadj's position bring to mind the scene in which the father of the protagonist (played by an actor) in *Allah Tantou* (David Achkar, 1990) is in the same position inside his prison cell. The confined universe of the shower may evoke the interior prison, the barriers that El Hadj himself erects. At the same time, it evokes existential, primordial human solitude. Torn between two contradictory impulses—accentuated by the alternation of time and space—he is stuck and cannot advance. It is as if he were immobilized in this position. His dual being is at play, as is made clear throughout the film: two countries, two languages, two women, two El Hadjes (the child and the adult, whose voices are fleetingly superimposed), two Frances (that of tourists, and of immigrants, who do not have the same access), two Senegals (the real and imagined countries). Moreover, it is not by chance that the film begins in Paris—even if this is not specified at the start, which universalizes his existential angst—where El Hadj lives as if he were just passing through, listening to his father's recorded voice. Nor is it by chance that it ends with El Hadj in Dakar, informing his father of his choice to remain in France to teach.

In the epilogue, then, he accomplishes a synthesis of the personality that he was painfully seeking throughout the film. It is interesting to note how the stigmas of suffering are literally embodied in El Hadj.

Not only do we feel his malaise through his body in the shower—a body that, at other times, we see sweat and so on—but the poster of the film has already borne the signs via his scarred eyebrow.

El Hadj is confronted with a dilemma, with the feeling of betraying himself, between the "memory of the man he was, the image of the man he hoped to be, and the acceptance of the man he can feel he is becoming."[37] He is also confronted with the image that others have of him. As the filmmaker explains: "I didn't want to make a film about a Black guy in a white country, but precisely about someone who is capable of saying: 'I'm sick of being the Black dude, I am Senegalese,'"[38] someone who can thus affirm what he is, fearlessly, freed of his own self-image. During his first meeting with Miriam in her studio, he indeed says to her: "Fifty years ago, people used to say: 'Negros are savages, all they can do is play drums'; today they say: 'Blacks are amazing, they've got rhythm in their blood.' I'm sick of being the Black dude, I am Senegalese." This echoes what is also said in *Bamboozled* (Spike Lee, 2000).

The choice of accepting his life in France indeed comes after all the trauma and interior struggles he endures to finally be able to abandon not only his dream of return, but also the "heroic" image he had of himself, to finally become, and accept, who he is. Later, we see El Hadj, rock bottom, in front of the Pompidou Center, shout at a friend who has come looking for him: "I fuck the El Hadj that you knew!" This scene is emblematic of a rebirth, of accepting a new identity. He can now accept what he has become. But this transformation is painful; a part of him must die to be born again, as a caterpillar must die to become a butterfly. The fact that this scene takes place in front of the Pompidou Center, a typically Parisian space, is significant given that the film is mainly shot in the foreign students' residence, in places off the beaten track, far from the tourist centers. Accordingly, Gomis cites James Baldwin (exiled in France): "Yet, it is only when a man is able without bitterness or self-pity, to surrender a dream he has long cherished or a privilege he has long possessed that he is set free—he has set himself free—for higher dreams, for greater privileges."[39]

In conclusion, *L'Afrance* translates the director's dual culture, both in its form and content. Its style encompasses both cultures, through a narrative situated predominantly in France, but inhabited by Senegal and Africa, and in which different languages cohabit. In this sense, it can be said that it is a *paraphrase* of part of the filmmaker's universe, in both content and form.[40]

This fiction remarkably illustrates the reconstruction of identity and the interior transformation of a character caught between a "here" and "there," which can just as equally be inverted. It encompasses different countries and languages, with a nonlinear narrative style in which fiction and real, actual and virtual, present and past, dreams and reality constantly intertwine.

CHAPTER 9

Worlds in Construction and the Intellectual's Return

Teza, by Haile Gerima

T he following pages explore the painful path to reconstructing identity after the turmoil of history and migration, and the return to the homeland—a return that is not a backward step, but a new beginning, which requires overcoming disillusionment, rethinking former ideals, and imagining a new world. *Teza*[1] indeed recounts the path of Anberber (Aaron Arefe), an idealist intellectual who does his studies in Germany, and who returns home to his village in Ethiopia.

Although equipped with all his "modern" knowledge, Anberber is incapable of meeting the needs of his people. Tormented and undergoing a full-blown existential crisis, he takes refuge in his childhood memories, which are nonetheless soon broken by nightmares that make his life a misery. In the 1970s, he left to study biology in Germany, with the dream of "curing all diseases" and of contributing to the spiritual and political renaissance and cultural development of his country. Anberber (whose name means "courage" in Amharic) and his friend Tesfaye ("hope") become involved in political activism against the Negus Haile Selassie regime. In Germany, Tesfaye (Abeye Tedla) has a child with a German woman, Gaby (Veronika Avraham), which sends Anberber's girlfriend, Cassandra (Araba Evelyn Johnston-Arthur), into a rage. Not listened to, as her emblematic name suggests, she predicts the destiny of the child, who will later be abandoned by his father.[2] Indeed, following his revolutionary, political passion, Tesfaye returns to Ethiopia, leaving his wife and child in Europe. As Cassandra predicts, the child will be victim to racism, as she was herself as the biracial child of a Cameroonian man deported from Germany when her mother was pregnant with her.[3] Unable to stand the racism that she felt was directed at her daughter, her mother committed suicide. Driven by this same racism, a group of German extremists throw Anberber out of a window when he is in East Germany after the fall of the Berlin Wall. He loses a leg in the fall. At the beginning of the 1980s, after the 1974 overthrow of Haile Selassie, Tesfaye then Anberber return to Addis Ababa to participate in the future of the country. They try to put their knowledge at the service of the communist revolution in full swing at the time in Ethiopia, but only experience frustration and repression. They find a torn country under the regime of General Mengistu and the Derg junta. After Tesfaye's violent death, which happens just as he is about to return to East Germany, Anberber replaces him in this mission and will again be confronted with his past and his disillusionment. Anberber only definitively returns to his village in the 1990s. That is the moment when the film begins. After having reconstructed his past, he will get together with Azanu, a marginal figure taken in by his mother, and begin his life in the village again.

Haile Gerima, Cinema, and Memory

Haile Gerima describes himself as "a Third World independent filmmaker."[4] His father, an Orthodox priest, teacher, historian, author, and theater director, played an important role in the resistance struggle against the Italian invasion. Gerima was born in 1946 in Gondar, in the northeast of Ethiopia, on the banks of Lake Tana, where *Teza* is set. The young Haile acted in his father's plays, which initiated him into traditional Ethiopian theater. This experience influenced his way of telling stories. Yet the narrative and aesthetic structures of his films also come from his maternal line. His mother and grandmother were traditional storytellers, and he spent his childhood before the arrival of electricity listening to these stories that they used to tell around the fire at night.[5] In addition to this immersion in traditional storytelling, the young Gerima worked at the ticket office of a cinema, where he was able to watch many films. He thus grew up with American movies (Westerns, Tarzan, and so forth), which perturbed his childhood.[6]

Haile Gerima left for the United States at the age of twenty-one, after having studied theater in Addis Ababa and meeting Peace Corps volunteers, one of whom was a teacher who, "impressed by his talent,"[7] helped him obtain a scholarship for the Goodman School of Drama in Chicago. He thus hoped to continue his career as a theater actor in the United States. However, still young and not at all prepared for this intercontinental journey, he found himself thrust into a completely alien culture, still in the throes of racial segregation. It was 1967: Haile Gerima advocated for civil rights and became involved in the Black Power movement and the Black Panther Party. He did not directly take part in the struggle, however, preferring to use his camera as a weapon. On arrival in the United States, the young Ethiopian felt lost in a white America until, to his great surprise, he found his place in the black community, which embraced him as one of their own. Thanks to African Americans, Gerima was able to rehabilitate his past and culture, and to "legitimate aesthetic criteria [his father and people] had transmitted" to him.[8] As he confided to Frank Ukadike: "African Americans embraced me and, in fact, made me self-confident and realize that not only white people can claim the right to make movies."[9] Gerima says he belongs to both Ethiopia and Black America.[10] This definitely forged his political and black consciousness. He nonetheless holds dearly to his roots and defines himself as African, not African American: "I could never be an African American because the cultural shaping of my childhood took place in Ethiopia."[11]

Gerima was shocked and disappointed to discover a theater world that asked him to drop his accent and to conform to a society that was completely alien to him. He was above all stupefied to learn the place to which black people were relegated on the stage. "All the Romeos and Juliets are white people," as he put it.[12] Not managing to find roles to play in Chicago, he decided to try Los Angeles, where he entered UCLA theater school. Yet after meeting the African American filmmaker Larry Clark, he "by chance" found himself in a film class. At UCLA, where Angela Davis, the Black Panther icon, taught, he discovered the writings of Malcolm X, Frantz Fanon, W. E. B. Du Bois, Amilcar Cabral, and Che Guevara, but also the emerging cinema of the South. He very soon became part of an international, intercultural group of filmmakers—the Los Angeles School of Black Filmmakers—who were fighting against Hollywood's cultural hegemony. Along with other filmmakers, including Charles Burnett, Larry Clark, Julie Dash, Billy Woodberry, and Ben Caldwell, he organized screenings of films from all horizons: Cuba, Brazil, Argentina, Senegal, Italy, and France.[13] With these young filmmakers from diverse countries, he questioned the possible plurality of film language: "You say: What's cinema? What's cinema? There is a cinema like what we see in Hollywood and there is another. . . . We said, 'we need to create a new cinema!'"[14]

In *Les Cahiers du cinéma,* Yann Lardeau analyzes Haile Gerima's work—and in particular his early films—as a cultural exchange between different societies:

> While certain American filmmakers were seeking to reconnect with the past, to seek the roots of a continent, a land, a culture from which they had been stolen and which, for them, represented a founding myth, Haile Gerima looked at the empire through the eyes of an African. That is why, even though people tend to place him at the head of the Roots Movement, he appears, on the contrary, to be guided by the opposite movement, bearing the cultural struggle of the Third World, like the two sides of a single cultural territory. African culture is present in America; there is a Black continent that continues to exist in America, just as there is an Anglo-Saxon Europe that continues there too. There was a colonialism inside America, just as the Third World was subjugated to the social values and economic force of Western imperialism. . . . Film integrated into African American culture cannot stop at just changing the content. . . . The film language itself, the montage, the relationship to the sound and image had to be rethought and remodeled in contact with African American culture."[15]

At the same time, Gerima embraced the cause of the pioneers of African cinema (such as Mauritania's Med Hondo, or Senegal's Sembène Ousmane), who, for their part, looked to historical and colonial memory and fought for cultural liberation after Independence. For Gerima, bringing other (hi)stories to the screen and telling them in his own way was a social and political commitment.

He rapidly launched into experimental cinema with *Hour Glass* (1971), a 13-minute short film, shot in Super 8. Director Larry Clark was the cameraman. This film, which is more allegorical than realist, represents through an audacious montage the rising consciousness and self-(re)discovery of a young black man having grown up in the United States in a family of white culture. He first seeks to integrate, playing in a basketball team, but truly finds his identity thanks to the writings of Frantz Fanon and the figures of Martin Luther King Jr., Malcolm X, and Angela Davis. This first, youthful work already contained many of the seeds of Gerima's cinema. Passing behind the camera gave him control over what he was doing; it was at this moment that he laid the foundations of his path as an independent filmmaker, which would be a "struggle inherent to a cultural liberation movement," as Yann Lardeau describes.[16] Next, during his studies, he made *Child of Resistance* (1972), a mid-length experimental surrealist work in black and white, inspired by the incarceration of Angela Davis. In it, Gerima expressed all his anger as a young African having recently arrived in the United States. Through the portrait of a woman (whose look and hairstyle recall those of the Black Panther activist), he explores the discrimination, social injustices, and their psychological effects on black people in the United States in the 1970s. Mixing abstraction and a nonlinear realist narration, his style bears the influences of Italian neorealism and Buñuelian social consciousness. According to Françoise Pfaff, it is "one of the most stylistically daring films of Black African cinema."[17] With the exception of certain works by John Akomfrah, these words from 1988 remain true today. The leading role of *Child of Resistance* is played by the African American actress Barbara O. Jones, who would also later play the protagonist of *Bush Mama* (named Barbara-O in the credits). Made as his master's thesis, *Bush Mama* (1976) was Gerima's first feature film, for which he had an exceptional camera and lighting man, the director Charles Burnett. In the film, Dorothy, a black woman from the Watts ghetto in California, raises her daughter while her African American husband is in prison, despite being innocent. After a certain number of violent confrontations with the system, she finds herself "pushed . . . over the line from which there can be no retreat," in the words of George Jackson.[18] The film is another surrealist fiction, but this time rooted in reality. The film is not a call to violence; it recounts black people's coming to consciousness and resistance in a hostile society. Haile Gerima gives black people a different representation to the passive role assigned to them in the Hollywood imagination, still present in more recent films, such as *Cry Freedom* (Richard Attenborough, 1987), or *Mississippi Burning* (Alan Parker, 1988), in which black people are either spectators, or victims waiting to be liberated. As Greg Thomas writes, Gerima's early works (and particularly the *Hour Glass—Child of Resistance—Bush Mama* "trilogy") are strongly influenced by black militant figures, such as Angela Davis and George Jackson (via his prison letters, published under the title *Soledad Brother* in 1970).[19] It is interesting to note that this "trilogy" was released on DVD after the success of *Teza*.[20]

Although Ethiopian, Gerima thus became "a leading figure in Black American cinema."[21] His first films were shot in the United States, in English. At the time, Gerima believed that they had to be in English, until the day that he saw *Mandabi* (*The Money Order,* Sembène Ousmane, 1968), shot in Wolof. For him, this was a sort of "individual, personal revolution."[22] The same night, he started to write

Harvest: 3000 Years in Amharic (*Mirt Sost Shi Ami*).[23] This fourth film was the first that Gerima shot in Ethiopia. Charles Burnett sees the genesis of *Teza* in *Harvest: 3000 Years*.[24] The film is the saga of a peasant family exploited by the feudal regime in power at the time. Restored by Martin Scorsese's World Cinema Foundation, it was presented at the Cannes Film Festival in 2006 in the Cannes Classics section. This two-and-a-half-hour black-and-white film was shot in 1974 during the summer vacation just after the overthrow of Haile Selassie. According to the director, it was the only possible moment to make it: before, the film would have been blocked or censored by Selassie's bureaucrats, and later, it would have been by the military junta. Indeed, the *New York Times* reported that this film caused Gerima problems with the Derg, the communist military junta that succeeded Haile Selassie.[25] Gerima considers this film to be "a miracle," which was only able to see the light of day thanks to its collaborator's passion, as he had no other resources than the motivation of the crew. Referring to his films' funding, Gerima claims: "Money would not have made my films better."[26]

In 1976, he began teaching the aesthetics of Third World cinema at Howard University in Washington, DC. With the black community and Howard students, he shot *Wilmington 10–USA 10,000* in 16 mm. This two-hour black-and-white and color documentary, which was released in 1979, narrates the story of ten civil rights activists (nine black men and a white woman) who were imprisoned in Wilmington (North Carolina) because they dared to speak out against racial injustices and denounced police violence.[27] As the subtitle suggests, beyond these ten people, this was the struggle of a multitude of black people across the United States.

The preoccupations of black people throughout the world and his own cultural alienation are at the heart of Gerima's oeuvre. In 1981, he made *Ashes and Embers*.[28] This feature film recounts the difficult return and psychological alienation of an African American Vietnam War veteran, Nay Charles.

Gerima returned to documentary in 1985 with *After Winter: Sterling Brown*, funded (with a tiny budget) by Howard University and devoted to the African American poet and critic Sterling Brown.

Gerima's following work, *Sankofa* (1993), deeply touched the African American community and brought the filmmaker to a wider international audience.[29] Shot in Ghana, this fiction begins in the Cape Coast slave castle.[30] Made with a million-dollar budget, the film made three million dollars, which allowed Gerima to open the Sankofa Cultural Center and bookstore, a venue well-known to Washington's black community. *Sankofa* tells the story of slavery and the African diaspora. The title highlights the importance of memory and the past: in Akan, *sankofa* is a bird that looks backwards to advance. Mona, a black American model who has forgotten her roots, is visited by the spirits of slaves. She goes back in time and becomes Shola, a slave on a North American plantation, who fights for her freedom. It is important to note that the film is entirely shot from the slaves' point of view, with a nonlinear narrative form that uses flashbacks and flash-forwards, weaving together different characters' points of view. A journey in search of roots is also at the heart of *Through the Door of No Return* (Shirikiana Aina, 1997). Shirikiana Aina, Gerima's wife, is an African American filmmaker, born in the United States where she lives and shares her husband's combat. She is also the cofounder of the Sankofa Cultural Center in Washington and the coproducer of the film *Sankofa*. In *Through the Door of No Return,* the filmmaker follows her father's traces, an African American who died in Ghana on a business trip. She goes to the place that saw the departure of millions of slaves, who were never to return. The reverse path is found in *Little Senegal* (Rachid Bouchareb, 2001), in which Alioune, a guide at the Gorée Island House of Slaves (Senegal), crosses a point of no return when he goes to the United States to find his family's descendants.

The theme of slavery is also found in *Le Passage du milieu* (*The Middle Passage,* 1999), by Martinican Guy Deslauriers, who, through the narrative voice of a slave, retraces the crossing of a slave ship from Senegal to the United States. As Savrina Chinien writes, this ship is a "metonymy for the centuries of horror, . . . a way of re-reading the history told via the patrimony of colonial stereotypes."[31] It is clear how much these positions differ from that of Steven Spielberg in *Amistad* (1997), in which the slaves are relegated to a passive position of waiting. In this film, the slave revolt is a pretext that opens the narrative but lasts only ten or so minutes in a two-and-a-half-hour film. The rest of the film is told from the point of view of the white abolitionist characters, who are given all the responsibility and glory of the slaves' emancipation. While there are a few shots portraying the black protagonist according to the Hollywood codes of an enhanced individual hero, the rest of the black characters are often filmed in groups, in long shots, not enabling spectators to grasp their identities. Their heads hung, they rarely speak. At times, they are just heard whispering without us being able to actually make out what they are saying. "The black characters thus only speak through a simultaneous translation provided thanks to the generosity of the white man. At the end of the film, in a tearjerker of a scene, the black character says, 'thank you' [in English] and the white character manages to pronounce an African expression," Olivier Barlet states.[32] Unfortunately, this representation did not change in *Lincoln* (Steven Spielberg, 2012), in which the struggles to emancipate slaves appear to be entirely the doing of the American president. *Twelve Years a Slave* (Steve McQueen, 2013), on the other hand, offers a different point of view. (The film marked McQueen's consecration as the first black director to win an Oscar for Best Foreign Film).

Haile Gerima's cinema portrays black people's active resistance, which is so often silenced elsewhere. This is true not only in *Sankofa, Bush Mama,* and *Child of Resistance,* but in all his films. This is above all a resistance to cultural imperialism. For Gerima, only resistance can heal cultural and psychological alienation,[33] and this resistance also lies in the form and aesthetics of his works:

> Like my father, my grandmother, my mother, I heard stories with a different temperament. It's not only the story, but also how you tell the story. So, the storyteller also has to assert his or her temperament, otherwise you will be uniformized into a fascist structure, a fascist narrative structure that dictates one way of telling a story.[34]

Gerima then made *Adwa, an African Victory* (1999), which narrates the Ethiopians' victory against the Italians at Adwa in 1896. Before that, he made the documentary *Imperfect Journey* (1994), which was a BBC commission, traveling Ethiopia from Gondar to Addis Ababa in the company of the writer and journalist Ryszard Kapuściński.

Each film constitutes an evolution in Haile Gerima's career. It can be said that his is a human and artistic journey in which all his films are linked by the common thread of history, memory, and the condition of African Americans or of Africans, and the reconstruction of their identities. Whether it is black people fighting for their existence and claiming their African American identity or their African roots, or a black American returning from Vietnam, or the Ethiopian people under the yoke of feudal power, all of his films pose the question of identity. This question reached its apogee in *Teza.*

Gerima began writing *Teza* in 1993 when he finally obtained some funding. This was possible thanks to *Sankofa*'s participation in many major festivals, and thanks above all to the fact that it was selected in competition for the Golden Bear in Berlin.[35] Nonetheless, it took him fourteen years to gather the film's budget. The eight-week shoot took place in Ethiopia in 2004, but it took another two years to get the rest of the money to shoot in Germany (six days) in 2006. *Teza* won various awards in major international festivals.[36] At the Venice Festival, Wim Wenders said to Gerima: "I hope the whole world will go to see your film."[37] *Teza* was indeed a success in cinemas in many countries.[38] However, it is not really awards that interest Gerima, but rather the possibility of funding his next film. For him, the urgency of storytelling is such that it is not unusual once he has received an award to see him disappear into his hotel room to work on a new screenplay. In *Teza,* as in most of his films, Gerima worked with nonprofessional actors (the exception being Barbara O. Jones).[39]

At the time of this book's writing, Gerima was working to complete the project *Adwa Part II: The Children of Adwa,* which he has been working on for about twenty years. This is a memory-based reconstruction of the Italians' return to Ethiopia in 1935, when they killed Ethiopian resistance fighters en masse, using poison gas that was forbidden by the 1922 Geneva Convention (in *Teza,* Anberber's father was also killed by the Italians).

Fragmented Selves (Extract)

The extract chosen begins twenty-five minutes into the film, lasts approximately 3 minutes and 5 seconds, and is comprised of fifty-six shots of varying lengths. (The first lasts 1 minute 20 seconds, the others a few seconds). Although the film is set in Ethiopia and Germany, and while several languages are spoken in it, the extract chosen takes place entirely in Ethiopia, in Anberber's home village, which explains that all the dialogues are in Amharic.[40] It nonetheless contains many elements that help grasp the spirit of the film.

Shot 1: 25' 22"

Filmed in profile, Anberber is sitting at the top of a hill, slightly bent over, his chin resting on his walking stick. He occupies the left side of the frame. He is wearing an overcoat and a kind of military cap. The rising sun, still low on the horizon in a sand-colored sky, gives off a gentle light, which highlights Anberber's silhouette only, without really showing the features of his face.

We first hear just the natural sounds: the tweeting of birds, the rustle of the bushes. A few seconds later, a melancholic jazz music strikes up. Anberber remains still (15 seconds)—this could almost be a still photo, if the shrubs were not blowing

in the wind—then lifts his head to look at the sky and the horizon. His face can be made out more clearly. The camera stays on him. His interior monologue in Amharic strikes up: "I am so numbed. Everything's gone topsy-turvy. I have no memory of my past."

Shot 2: 25' 45"

Anberber gets up from the base of the monument he was sitting on (which bears the engraved inscription "Colonna Storace 12 April") and starts to walk with the help of his stick.

 The interior voice continues: "How am I to fulfill the expectations of my family? Where can I go? Where can I escape to?" He now appears small, on his feet in the center of the frame. The arid landscape and its sparse vegetation are revealed as the shot grows lighter.

Shot 3: 25' 49"

Part of his still dark, undefined silhouette, in profile and slightly low angle against the beige shades of the sky, cuts across the image vertically. Limping, he advances with his stick, the tapping sound of which accompanies each step.

The camera follows his movement. He is now seen from behind, almost completely camouflaged by the landscape, masked by the branches of the shrubs.

His image slowly fades away, giving way to the dawn landscape. In the background, the hills rise behind the branches of the shrubs. The music stops, giving way to the birdsong and sound of the wind.

Shot 4: 26' 1"

An interior. On a bed, a child is lying on his side, wrapped in a checked blue cover that only shows his face. The bed is covered with a cowhide, the color of which blends in with the wall.

We know, from the previous scene, that this is Anberber as a child. After a few seconds, stringed Ethiopian music strikes up, different to that at the start of the

extract. The child raises his head, propping himself up on his elbow as if to listen to Anberber the adult, who asks: "Did you ever imagine a world other than this village? Please tell me."

The camera runs along the child's body in a left-to-right pan and continues until it stops on Anberber, in profile, looking at the child. We now see that the child is dressed in traditional Ethiopian clothes, in a long beige cotton shirt, the sleeve of which is torn at the wrist.

We now see his opposite profile against a black background, his beard graying, his expression tortured. He continues: "Was the world you traversed as you foresaw it?" Anberber is dressed Western style, in a casual gray shirt and beige jacket.

Shot 5: 26' 19"

A close-up of Anberber's mother as she eats and observes him attentively, her expression anxious. Like Anberber's in the previous shot, her face stands out against the black background, separating her from the décor.

The perspectives complement one another. The imagination brings reality to life.

Shot 6: 26' 20"

The two characters, Anberber child and adult, are together on the screen. The youth lying on the bed and the man sitting facing him look at one another. Placed behind the adult, the camera adopts his point of view and appears to observe the youth with him.

Shots 7–8: 26' 22"

Shot/reverse shot of Anberber adult and child, while the man pursues his questioning: "Do you have any memories of your journey? Did you have any foreknowledge of it?" In close-up, the silent child looks attentively into the camera.

Shot 9: 26' 28"

In profile on the right of the frame, Anberber continues his imaginary dialogue with the child. His mother, at first standing at the edge of the frame, passes behind him. Her hair is plaited in cornrows and she wears a long, off-white colored traditional dress with Ethiopian motifs on the front and an Orthodox cross around her neck. She looks at Anberber, then in the same direction as him, towards the child. Then, with great concern, she looks at Anberber, then turns away again. The camera follows her, framing her now standing, her head lowered. She looks in the same direction as Anberber, who is now offscreen. Anberber continues: "As you traveled, did it all turn into a hazy dream?"

A subjective pan to the left from the mother's point of view shows the bed where the child was lying, now empty.

This is her point of view, she who does not see the same thing as Anberber.

She sits on the bed, thus taking the child's place, while leaving half of the dark

frame empty. The Ethiopian music gradually fades, and soon only the voices are audible.

She leans forward a little, appearing to seek an answer in vain. She is seeking to be reassured: "Who are you talking to?"

Shots 10–13: 26' 45"

Shots/reverse shots of Anberber and his mother. She questions him insistently: "Are you alright?," while Anberber, in profile, perplexed, remains immobile in the same position.

Shot 15: 26' 51"

Anberber from behind, partially visible to the right of the frame, looks at the *injera*[41] cooking on the crackling fire.

Shot 16: 26' 56"

A long shot. Anberber is sitting on a bench in front of his house, leaning back against the wall, his hand resting on his again visible walking stick.

He is alone, small, dressed in more or less the same beige colors as the houses (round, with twig and adobe walls and thatched roofs) and the nature around him—that of an arid, rural landscape. His open overcoat reveals his white shirt. The only other living beings are the chickens pecking in front of him. The sounds of chickens and goats punctuate village life. Offscreen, people in his mother's house are talking about him and his malaise.

Shot 17: 27' 00"

"Some evil has possessed him. Maybe he got bewitched when he was abroad," a man says in voice-over, while onscreen we can see Anberber's distress, isolated by the camera in a medium close-up shot. Once again, he stares into the void, looking crushed.

Shots 18–22: 27' 01"

Inside, Anberber's mother, brother, and uncle, sitting together around the fire on which a soup cooks in a clay pot, discuss whether he might be cured by holy water.

His uncle stokes the flames, fanning them with his feathered stick. A series of close-ups of the people in the room. His brother says that they cannot leave

Anberber to suffer in this way. His mother explains that "Those who've been abroad don't know about holy water."

Shot 23: 29' 15"

A long shot of a lake. Anberber is paddled along in a canoe by a middle-aged man. A group of men are sitting on the rocky shore.

Shots 24 and 25: 27' 18"

They land and greet the men, who are wearing traditional clothes: long tunics and blankets. Seen from behind, Anberber follows the priest, who carries an Orthodox pastoral baton up a forest path.

Shot 26: 27' 26"

A long shot. They reach and enter a stone hut with a thatched roof. A tracking shot reveals a man sitting on the ground at the entrance to another hut and the camera stops on him.

Shot 27: 27' 33"

A group of traditionally dressed pupils recite prayers, while in voice-over Anberber says: "My whole memory is blocked. I don't think holy water will work."

Shot 28: 27' 37"

Anberber and the priest are face to face on either side of the fire. The protagonist is seen head-on, dressed in Western clothes (a dark casual shirt and beige jacket), and the priest from behind, wearing a traditional tunic and a turban. This contrast in clothing style reflects how much their attitudes differ at this point. Anberber is filmed sitting lower than the priest. The camera is placed next to the priest, as if to accompany the latter's perplexed gaze as he tries to pierce Anberber's internal world.

Shots 29–37: 27' 39"

A series of shots/reverse shots of Anberber and the priest against a dark background, cut off from their surroundings. In the middle of these shots is one framing the two characters together. The priest advises trying holy water, at least to reassure his mother. He invites Anberber to believe in it, arguing that "even your modern medicine only works if you believe in it." This series of shots ends with an image of

the two men and a pan to the right, revealing the pupils sitting on the huge roots of a tree, singing the same prayers.

Shot 38: 28' 04"

A long panning shot of the sepia landscape in the mist and the silhouette of the village huts. We hear the crowing of a cockerel and rather sinister birdsong.

The camera pauses a few seconds, then rapidly zooms out and in again, which allows us to briefly glimpse the lake in the distance. This camera movement is accompanied by the desperate cry of a man. The image wobbles and the camera zooms out again.

Shot 39: 28' 24"

Tadfe (Anberber's mother), who is milking a cow, drops the container she was holding.

Shot 40: 28' 25"

Tadfe and a young woman, Azanu, run. In profile against the landscape that constitutes their natural milieu, their faces are almost superimposed. The mother bends and the camera homes in on Azanu an instant.

Shots 41–52: 20' 29"

A series of brief, fragmented shots follows: the mother running, seen from different angles, at times in entirety, at times parts of her body (her legs, head, back); people on a hillock looking on; a close-up shot of an old woman sitting at the entrance to a house; a dog; the mother again, from behind, rushing to Anberber's house.

Intercutting these shots, two very brief images of a wounded man on a hospital bed, wrapped in bandages, with only his eyes and mouth showing. We guess it is Anberber. Bloodstains are visible on his raised arm, which appears to be attached to a drip.

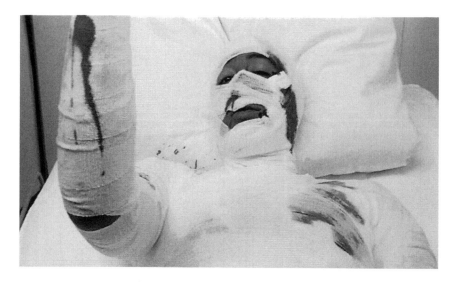

Shot 53: 28' 38"

On his bed in the middle of a nightmare, Anberber twists and turns and shouts out in torment. His mother comes running and tries to calm him. He struggles anxiously.

Finally, Anberber grabs onto her, pulls himself up, and they cling to one another. Dressed in white and lit by the daylight that filters in through a little window, his mother becomes the focal point of the image.

Shot 54: 28' 49"

While his mother, still unaware of what happened to Anberber in Germany, questions him in voice-over, we see Azanu in profile outside, looking worriedly into the house.

Shot 55: 28' 52"

Mother and son clutch each other tightly, their faces hidden as they hug. The mother looks downwards and says, desperately: "So you've come back to me disfigured?"

Shot 56: 28' 54"

A point-of-view shot of the prosthesis that his mother caresses incredulously, crying, "Did they mangle you up, my son? Is this your leg?"

In the following shot, she hugs Anberber again, crying as she desperately exclaims: "Did they send you back to me all cut up, my son?"

An Aesthetics of Reassembly

Right from the first shot of the extract, Anberber is alone, on the edges, looking down at the village, which he is thus able to observe from a distance (with the eye of those who have left and returned). He is dressed in Western clothes, unlike the other villagers. The nostalgic jazz in the background accentuates Anberber's intimate universe, currently remote from the rest of the community. We can make out his silhouette alone because he is still in fragments, lost. His interior voice, which declares that he has forgotten his past, not only explains his distress, but gives us an important entry point to the narrative. This extract also generates the rest of the film, comprising a nonlinear structure of bits of broken dreams and a range of memories that gradually come back to Anberber in pieces. This spiraling structure indeed recalls Gilles Deleuze's analysis of time and "image time."[42]

We immediately notice that Anberber is leaning on his walking stick, which is almost always present on the screen, either entirely or in part, like a reminder of his tormented path and his both physical and psychological mutilation. We later discover that he lost a leg in Germany following a violent racist attack in which he was thrown out of a window simply for being black.[43] And when he starts walking with his stick, he limps, highlighting his difficulty and the fact that his path and his step are still uncertain. Like his step, his memory limps. It is precisely this difficulty that Anberber has in remembering his past that drives the film, in which his memory returns in "recollection-images."[44] The silhouette, then the fade that makes the character disappear (shot 3) convey his ghostlike, evanescent aspect, the loss of his substance and memory. This is also highlighted by the fact that the jazz music disappears at the same moment as his silhouette. Following Deleuze, it can be said that the linking of these images is significant, as "When we cannot remember, sensory-motor extension remains suspended and the actual image, the present optical perception . . . enters into relation with genuinely virtual elements."[45] Different examples of "genuinely virtual elements" can be found in *Teza*, in the recollection-images, dreams, nightmares, and hallucinations. As Deleuze writes, the correlate of the optical-sound image is given to us by "the disturbances of memory and the failures of recognition."[46] We are confronted here with the time-image rather than the movement-image. On several occasions, Anberber searches his memory and questions his past: "Where did I go? What happened to me there? Where did I lose my leg?" These questions are similar to those that Deleuze cites when he discusses the flashback in Fitzgerald and Mankiewicz ("What happened? How have we arrived at this point?").[47] It is a story "that can be told only in the past.[48] The narrative necessity for adopting flashbacks and images of different natures that form in the protagonist's imagination and on the screen becomes manifest henceforth. *Teza* is characterized by its Mankiewiczian nonlinear development of the characters, a procedure that "instead of dispersing the enigma, [refers] it back to other still deeper ones."[49] In this respect, "Time's forks thus provide flashback with a necessity, and recollection-images with an authenticity."[50]

Teza is indeed structured like a puzzle around the protagonist's identity quest, which the spectator pieces together at the same time as the character. The idea of an enigma that must be solved, of recomposing a fragmented identity out of snippets of different phases of the past, is present from the opening images. During the credits, these comprise a ritual song of Ethiopia's Gypsies, who are Orthodox Christians and who travel the country encouraging people to detach themselves from their material belongings. This music, which accompanies shots of traditional paintings, is itself an essential part of Ethiopian memory. This is already manifest in the image of Anberber, wounded, while his interior voice enjoins him: "No! I am not dying! Not before I see my poor mother!" Olivier Barlet, for whom the opening sequence of *Teza* is simply stunning, describes it accordingly:

> A puzzle rhythmed with chants, a storm, fire, traditional illuminations, veils, memories of childhood, of the accident, the ensemble woven together by a fluid camera and powerful music. The whole film is already present, but we do not know so yet: cultural rooting, childhood, memory, trauma and exorcism.[51]

Then, at dawn, the child Anberber walks through the dewy grass, as Anberber adult's interior voice evokes "My childhood—so vivid!," thereby offering a key to the interpretation of the images of his memory. Next, Anberber child invites Anberber adult to follow him back in time. The latter announces: "I see youngsters from my village playing Enkokilish." His memory comes to life on the screen: around a fire, the youths play this traditional game that consists of solving riddles then assembling the answers, which resonates with the narrative form of the film. The first words of the film, spoken by an unidentified voice-over, ask: "Where is the wise man to untangle the riddle?" For Anberber, the key to the enigma will reside in the reconstruction of his memory. The final riddle introduces the title, *Teza* ("morning dew" in Amharic), which then appears on the screen. "I saw it when I left. When I returned, it was gone," challenges one lad. The title indeed evokes passing childhood, just like the dew that appears in the morning, gradually disappears in the day, and is no longer there by night. Yet dew re-forms each day, which recalls that the cycle of life continues with each generation.

After this complex opening, which introduces *Teza*'s "puzzle and enigma" structure, the narrative begins in Anberber's native village in the 1990s, which will prove to be the main narrative thread. He has returned after a long absence, having lost a leg and the memory of what happened to him in previous years. Gradually, images of different moments of the past come back to him, as if in concentric circles. That is what is referred to as the "spiral" structure, in which the central point, the most "contracted" circle, is the present containing all the pasts. Following Deleuze, it can be said that the past manifests itself "as the coexistence of circles which are more or less dilated or contracted, each one of which contains everything at the same time and the present of which is the extreme limit (the smallest circuit that contains all the past)."[52] Drawing on Deleuze, who himself refers to Bergson, it can be said that *Teza* portrays a "non-chronological time" in which the actual present contains all the "sheets of past."[53] Every time, Anberber, who struggles to recompose the shreds of his evanescent memories, has to go looking for his recollections in a different moment of the past. His experiences (his childhood in the village, his studies in Germany, and the political struggles of the 1970s, then those in the 1980s back in the Ethiopian capital, and again back in Germany) thus take shape and structure the narrative of his life up until the present. Each time, he must thus "jump into a chosen region [of the past], even if [he has] to return to the present in order to make another jump."[54] In the sequence before the extract chosen, for example, Anberber adult, like a spectator observing the scene, watches himself as a child playing with his friends in Lake Tana, which delimited his childhood world.

During the first half hour, the narrative is set in the protagonist's home village, during the film's present moment (the 1990s). Anberber is confused and lost. No longer recognizing himself in the changed village life, he attempts to take refuge in his childhood memories, which appear in brief inserts. Anberber the child thus becomes a character unto himself, even if he is only seen by the spectator and by Anberber the adult, who at times appears almost afraid of this vision. At times, in both the extract chosen and elsewhere, the adult character observes the child (shot/reverse shot); at times he observes him while being present in the same frame (shot 6). In these shots, present and past coexist, confusing the actual and the virtual.

"In Bergsonian terms, the real object is reflected in a mirror-image as in the virtual object which, from its side and simultaneously, envelops or reflects the real: there is 'coalescence' between the two. There is a formation of an image with two sides, actual and virtual," writes Deleuze.[55] Often, these "two-sided" shots, these direct images of time, are not announced by fades, or by any filmic element that might allow the spectator to grasp the semi-virtual (or actual and virtual at the same time) nature of these images. It is the young actor who renders the character of the child recognizable, for example, in the scene on Mussolini Mountain in which Anberber is sitting with the children—among whom is himself as a child—as they play at being the first to spot the rising sun.

Elsewhere, this takes place as in the extract chosen, Anberber addressing the child, who nonetheless remains voiceless and does not really enter into dialogue with him. In the eyes of the other characters (his mother, for example), the child disappears. In the sequence chosen, this "coalescence" of the real and the virtual is taken to the point where Anberber adult asks questions of the child that refer to later moments of his life, to which the child cannot of course respond: "Do you have any memories of your journey? Did you have any foreknowledge of it? As you traveled, did it all turn into a hazy dream?" (shots 4–9). These are questions that he poses to his current self but addresses to the child. We are confronted here with what Deleuze calls a "crystal image," which refers "on the one hand, to a small internal circuit between a present and its own past, between an actual image and its virtual image; on the other hand, they refer to deeper and deeper circuits which are themselves virtual, which each time mobilize the whole of the past."[56] One may note, here, the irreducibility of the crystal-image, which "consists in the indivisible unity of an actual image and 'its' virtual image."[57] The memories of other characters in the film are actualized (those of Azanu, for example, when she tells Anberber the reasons for her social marginalization). But the character and her image-recollection are not simultaneously present on the screen. During her husband's second wedding ceremony, out of her mind with jealousy, Azanu kills her child whom she was carrying on her back by throwing him on the floor in a moment of uncontrollable rage. Since this tragedy, she is rejected by her community and husband, who still pursues her, wanting to kill her. Taken in by Anberber's mother, she pieces herself back together thanks to the latter's kindness, just like the marginalized Kadiatou in *Notre étrangère* who finds comfort after having been taken in by Amy's aunt. In a scene in which she is with Anberber beneath a tree, the right side of which has died but whose left side is alive, Azanu begins her narration thus, while the camera, in low angle, runs along the branches of the tree: "Gaché Anberber, see this tree? It's the story of my life. On one side, it hangs onto life; on the other side it has collapsed and is decaying."

Coming back to the extract: the only character to participate in the crystal-images is Anberber. We understand at this point that Anberber's present is infused with his past. This co-presence of the present and his past recalls the film *Roma* (Fellini, 1972), which is also constructed out of the scattered memories of different moments of Fellini's life. An hour and a half into the film, when the countess remembers her meeting with the pope, her present-day image coexists on the screen with images of her past. In this scene, the countess enters into a real dialogue with her recollection-image. She becomes identical to the other virtual characters; they can no longer be distinguished. Anberber, on the other hand, seems to remain on another level, an observer of the scene in which he participates. In shots 7 and 8, he probably expects no answers from the child; he contents himself with asking the questions. In *Roma,* the sequence abruptly ends, without returning to the film's present, and another scene unrelated to the previous one begins in Trastevere. In *Teza,* however, the recollection-image of the child disappears and the scene continues with other characters (shot 9). In this scene, the Ethiopian stringed music—which differs from the jazz at the beginning of the extract, when present-day Anberber is alone on the mountain—is associated with Anberber's childhood and disappears at the same time as the image of the child.

In the first part of *Teza,* images from the more recent past (Anberber wounded on a hospital bed) appear very briefly at times. In the extract chosen, the montage cuts jarringly from other images of daily village life in the film's present tense to these shots (48 and 51), with no stylistic differentiation. This montage does not yet allow the spectator to understand the story. Mixed with the present-day images, the virtual image of the wounded Anberber are part of his nightmare, and we then see him struggling and shouting in his bed. The shot is announced by a desperate cry and a tracking shot of the blurred landscape (like the protagonist's memories, which are still impaired and blurred), then a violent, rapid zoom out/ zoom in, followed by another zoom out. As if disturbed by the uncontrollable events, the camera wobbles, thereby illustrating Anberber's psychological state as he struggles in his bed. As Deleuze states, here the camera "is no longer content sometimes to follow the characters' movement, sometimes itself to undertake movements of which they are merely the object, but in every case it subordinates description of a space to the functions of thought."[58] At times we hear Anberber's inner thoughts, as is the case at the beginning of the extract when he is sitting on Mussolini Mountain (shot 1). This mountain gets its name from the fact that in 1936, the Italians of the Storace Column raised their flag in conquest, or to signal their invasion, depending on the point of view. For Gerima, this mountain situated in his home region is crucial:

> The shooting locations are extremely important to me, because every time I climb this mount, for example, I think of my own personal evolution. I'm in one reality

and I'm suddenly transported into another. So I think: "How can I put that in *Teza?*
How does Anberber's world change in him? How can I turn abruption into a form?"[59]

This mountain—"my childhood playground," Anberber calls it—has a particular signification: not only because it is the main site where the protagonist goes
in search of his memories, but because it also evokes the collective memory of the
people. Thanks to Anberber's interior voice, we know that the monument where
he sits on Mussolini Mountain is the last to the memory of the victims of Italian
colonization still standing. Historical memory is also present through the reminders
of Italian colonization and the archive images—the overthrow of Haile Selassie,
the fall of the Berlin Wall—that the protagonists watch on television. At the start
of the film, the returning Anberber is celebrated as the son of a "hero" who "died
only after chopping off countless Italian heads," one of those who was gassed and
killed during the battle of Tekezé River. Anberber is left fatherless by the Italian
war. For him, these historic events belong both to his personal memory and to
collective memory.

Anberber also seeks his past in the beauty of the landscape that he contem-
plates from the top of Mussolini Mountain. But these contemplative shots are often
rapidly interrupted, as if to signify that he is not allowed to escape and to abandon
himself dreamily to his childhood memories; the past must serve to reconstruct his
present. These landscape images, like those revealing the ordinariness of daily life
as they appear like inserts in the narration, represent "only pure optical and sound
situations," which Deleuze calls *opsignes* et *sonsignes*.[60] Here, it is no longer time
that is subordinated to movement; by a reversal, the movement is subordinated
to time. In the extract studied here, these images show Anberber's states of mind.
We understand that Anberber is frustrated by his inability to face the current
situation. His frustration is clearly expressed in the scene in which Anberber is
framed next to his suitcase full of books (including Karl Marx's *Capital* and other
economic theory books) that do not help him understand contemporary Ethiopia
at all. His brother exacerbates his frustration: "After all those years abroad, what
do you have to offer your poor mother? We can't make stew out of books, can we?"
Towards the end of the film, Anberber has another nightmare, shown in images,
that illustrates his powerlessness before contemporary reality. In it, he is almost
buried under wheat pouring out of the holes in the sides of a granary. He struggles
in vain to block the holes with pages of his books. The priest explains the meaning
of this dream to him:

I think the grain in your recurring dream stands for our people . . . and the granary stands for our country. The holes in the different parts of the granary represent our country's chronic problems. Your attempt to block a hole and stop the leak, and your rushing to stop even more holes and leaks, all this represents your frustration with the existing situation. . . . The book you tear up and use to plug all those holes is a symbol of the knowledge you absorbed. As it appears to me, the nightmare that haunts you day and night shows you've found your education useless for confronting the realities you're faced with.

Indeed, he is confronted with himself and with a violent reality he did not expect. The Derg military junta has crushed the hopes that Anberber and his friends placed in Marxism and the anti-imperial struggle. The socialist revolution—a model imported from abroad—in which they dogmatically believed has failed. In a previous scene, Anberber witnesses soldiers capturing children to enroll them in their war. When he sees a child get killed before his eyes, he sighs: "It was my childhood they killed today." This terrible scene on the hill is masterfully filmed through alternate shots of the pursued child (dressed in green) and Anberber as a child (dressed in beige), who replaces the former in Anberber's eyes as he powerlessly watches the scene.

Anberber discovers a country at war. *Teza* indeed does not spare on certain scenes of violence, filmed in quite a raw, but nonetheless spectacular manner (the abduction of the youth; the child killed by the soldiers; the bloody murder of Abdul, a comrade in the struggle and friend of Anberber; the lifeless, bloody body of a man killed by the revolutionaries; the violent murder of Tesfaye; Anberber's defenestration). Throughout the film, we also perceive another form of violence— one that is less visible, more subtle, and psychological. This violence is social: a constant and silent violence derived from the powerlessness felt before the needs of the people. Several times in the film, Anberber is confronted with demands he cannot satisfy. The villagers come to ask him to heal their children, for example. In the extract chosen, as he sits on Mussolini Mountain (shot 1), he asks himself: "How am I to fulfill the expectations of my family?" In this metonymy, the family represents the entire village. This resembles the filmmaker's own experience; these are situations that face an "exiled Ethiopian returning home."[61] Incapable of being useful to his people, he is cut off from them and alienated. He cannot take action, but only perceive this action. Anberber is indeed no longer part of daily village life; he observes it as an outside spectator, distant from the others. He embodies what

Deleuze said about Italian neorealism: "the character has become a kind of viewer," who "records rather than reacts."[62] Contrary to his experience of political struggle in Germany (the 1970s and late 1980s) and in Addis Ababa (1980), where, with his friends and comrades, he was active, in movement, here Anberber is remote from the others, immobile and isolated by the camera too. He is alone on Mussolini Mountain, alone with his thoughts, framed alone when he is with the priest—from whom he is separate because they no longer share the same beliefs—while the pupils recite together the prayers that he appears to have forgotten. In this scene, the shot/reverse shot against the dark background that isolates the two characters accentuates the separation that exists between them at this moment. Anberber is placed lower than the priest, who holds the traditional wisdom that Anberber has forgotten (shot 28). It is the priest who takes him in the canoe, because he is not in control of his life at this point; he is not in charge. Anberber sits alone, outside, while his family members are united inside the house. The image of Anberber sitting alone in his corner is a recurrent image. At times, he holds his radio against his ear, as if to highlight the link with a reality exterior to the village.

In shot 17, in which he seems to be slumped against the wall, his eyes empty, it appears that his quest for his past has reached an impasse. He can no longer go back and no longer knows how to advance. Shortly after the extract, however, he finally agrees to partake in the holy-water exorcism ritual and part of his memory comes back to him. It is his voice-over that announces this, and the narrative shifts to Cologne in the 1970s. During the first hour of the film, brief sequences of his past in Germany (generally of a duration of about two-and-a-half minutes, at times a few seconds) intersperse the present-day narration. Sixty-eight minutes into the film, the construction is reversed, and the narrative thread becomes that of the 1980s—firstly in Addis Ababa and then in Germany, where Anberber returns before definitely coming back to the village. In this part, the memories of Germany in the 1970s are present through flashbacks.

In this part, the present-day village images become brief inserts, as if to recall that we are witnessing the actualization of the protagonist's memories. The virtual appears to become actual, and vice versa. As Deleuze describes: "Distinct, but indiscernible, such are the actual and the virtual which are in continual exchange."[63]

The narrative is always driven from Anberber's point of view. His is nonetheless complemented by that of his mother, the two characters now forming just a single complex one. It is via her point-of-view shot (shot 56) that the spectator discovers the prosthesis that incarnates Anberber's disintegration, he who has come back mutilated and "all cut up," as she puts it. He is thus fragmented; he must reconstitute his being, shattered by his different life experiences. He is often filmed fragmentedly too, as if in bits and pieces: behind branches, behind a fence, a door, a window, behind the skeins of wool that his mother spins, or the washing hanging in the sun. This fragmentation is also mirrored in the fragmented montage, through the apparently separate and independent shots. This aesthetic recalls certain Buñuel films—for example, the enigmatic style and the juxtaposition of apparently disconnected shots that follow a discontinuous narrative thread, as, for example, in his short film *Un Chien andalou* (*An Andalusian Dog*, 1929), but also the intrusion of dreams, as in *Los Olvidados* (*The Young and the Damned*, 1950). This fragmented expressive form reflects the experience of a man who returns to his home village decomposed, in pieces. Gerima explains the intermittent structure of his montage as follows:

> When I talk about memory, my memory is afflicted also by my experience of the diaspora. It's ruptured, like lightning ruptures. I couldn't be at peace in Ethiopia having experienced all these journeys. So, my writing is ruptured constantly, or intercepted, by these experiences.[64]

The last twenty minutes of the film take place in the village, back in the film's present day, as if to loop the loop, for *Teza* is based on the reconstruction of the past in order to imagine a new future. Finally, Anberber reconstructs his path by reassembling the different shreds of his past; he thus becomes the sum of all the "sheets of past." Thus, like Kongo in *Juju Factory*, or El Hadj in *L'Afrance*, Anberber can begin his current life again and advance towards the future. He embraces simplicity and replaces the former village schoolteacher. His way of teaching will be revolutionary, in the sense that he abandons mechanical, repetitive instruction and takes an interest in the pupils, with whom he strikes up a real dialogue. With them, he enters a new human relationship. In this scene, the children are filmed in close-up; we see their faces. In the previous scenes with the other teacher, they were framed from behind, in a group long shot, impersonally. This attitude is also represented by the bicycle (a simple but efficient means of transport that evokes freedom and hope) that the other teacher left him, but which Anberber shares with the pupils, playing together. Metta Sáma and Greg Thomas qualify this sequence as "touching."[65] In *Rage,* towards the epilogue, the young man, gratified by the production of his album, crosses the streets of London on a bike to distribute them. These two films seem to indicate that equilibrium is to be found again in sobriety.

Anberber will finally live with Azanu, a marginal figure like him. Azanu is often filmed on the edge of the image, which corresponds to her social position, or alone in the frame, as was seen in shot 54. Just before, her face was framed next to that of Anberber's mother, Tadfe (shot 40), the two women looking in the same direction (towards Anberber's house). Their almost superimposed faces may suggest that Azanu is the young double of Anberber's mother; moreover, the young woman is wearing a traditional dress that is very similar to Tadfe's. The camera then singles out Azanu, who remains alone on the screen, which suggests that her destiny will be linked to that of the protagonist, in a kind of opening to the future (Azanu) that comes from the past (the mother). Azanu also represents Cassandra, Anberber's girlfriend in Germany, forced to have an abortion because he did not want a child, and who then disappears without a trace. "The fact is Cassandra is really Azanu and vice versa. She's everywhere. The marginalized are everywhere. Unless you choose only to see dominant society and to forget the people on the edges," says Gerima.[66] Anberber and Azanu will have a son, whose birth ends the film. A synthesis of the recomposed character Anberber, the child bears the past within him. He will be named Tesfaye in memory of the friend. Moreover, this name, which signifies "hope," is an opening to the future. At the end of the film, Anberber's voice-over evokes the legend of the dragon and a world to come over images of children, of the sun rising in the sky, and of the fire's brightly burning flames.

In conclusion, it can be said that *Teza* represents a *paraphrase* of part of the filmmaker's reality, not just in content, but also in its aesthetic form. Different elements of his experience are found reorganized and reformulated in the fictional world of *Teza*. Gerima indeed confirms: "The two levels, the personal level and the general level, naturally wove together from the start, effortlessly."[67] Like that of Anberber, the filmmaker's path is a constant quest to reconstruct the self and identity after life's psychological and physical fractures. As Gerima confirms: "I made few films, but it's all about the idea of reconstructing one's identity from the fragmented self. . . . So, I start always from myself."[68]

The aesthetics and style draw both on Ethiopian oral tradition (for example, the spiral narrative structure, which advances through the enigmas that Anberber must (re)solve) and on the diasporic experience. Traces of this are found in the fragmented montage, as the filmmaker explains, but also in the use of jazz (which comes from African American culture) and Western film techniques, such as the shot/reverse shot, that are different to the medium and group shots typical of the first films made by African filmmakers.

In Guise of a Conclusion

Filmmakers' Trajectories and Artistic Creation

The films' analysis has demonstrated two hypotheses formulated at the outset: firstly, that the fictional worlds created by the filmmakers evoke their own realities. Next, that the filmmakers' paths—and thus their films—are affected by particularly scarring personal and collective experiences.

The black diasporic filmmakers are confronted—as has been stated here—with the need to recompose fragmented identities after the fractures arising from history and migration. Such a process forces them to take into account the complexity and cultural plurality that is their own. Indeed, their position at the intersection of different heritages, societies, and cultures affords them a particular viewpoint: one that is mobile, decentered, and multifocal. Nonetheless, beyond certain shared traits (the intersectionality of being African, of having migrated to traditionally white societies, and thus perceiving themselves as black), each portrays his or her own vision, forged in their own histories in all their uniqueness.

They construct fictional universes that, consciously or not, express their worlds. In this sense, their films—as has been shown—are *paraphrases* of their worlds, in the sense that Jean-Pierre Esquenazi defines. Indeed, the creation of these fictional worlds surpasses them. The Congolese filmmaker Mweze Ngangura put it in these terms: "I think that the works we make are always in relationship to ourselves, our lives, even if we are not always aware of it"[1] It is precisely the fact that a filmmaker can be surpassed by his or her work that gives us access to it, and means we can be moved by it, without knowing the maker's biographical story.

It is striking to note the degree to which their fictions embrace plurality, ambivalence, wanderings, memory, identity transformations and reconstructions, both in content (the plot) and form (the narrative). Complexity and becoming are omnipresent, and I have demonstrated many ways in which they are portrayed.

Plurality and Complexity

Multiple cultures, languages, spaces, temporalities, and points of view inhabit the five films analyzed. This plurality reflects the filmmakers' multicultural thinking and multidimensional visions, which never stop at a monolithic or simplistic history. They deconstruct the banality of stereotypes to construct other ways of looking; they thereby take a stance and pose a critical gaze on the world around them. Without accepting them blindly, they constantly question the values assumed to be universal by different cultures. Theirs, in general, is an approach to the world founded on the embracing of complexity, the plurality of possibilities—in other words, the very opposite of radicalization.

Geographic Diversity

The plurality of geographic spaces is translated into many journeys between different countries and cultures. The narrative of *Notre étrangère,* for example, constantly journeys back and forth between Paris and Bobo-Dioulasso. In *Juju Factory,* it is by carrying out research to write a history of Congo that the protagonist finds his place in Belgium. In *L'Afrance,* Senegal is present in the memories of Paris-based El Hadj and through inserts included here and there in the montage. *Teza's* story is set in Germany and Ethiopia, but also between the city and rural spaces. This geographic and cultural plurality has always been present, right from Sembène Ousmane's first feature film, *La Noire de . . . (Black Girl,* 1966), set in Antibes and Dakar. It is also present in more contemporary works, such as *Pièces d'identités (Identity Pieces,* Mweze Ngangure, 1998) set in Belgium and the DRC; *Clando* (Jean-Marie Teno, 1996) set in Cameroon and Germany; *Des étoiles* (*Under the Starry Sky,* Dyana Gaye, 2013) set in Italy, the United States, and Senegal; and *Morbayassa* (Cheick Fantamady Camara, 2015) set in Senegal and France. Finally, Dani Kouyaté's latest film, *Medan vi Lever* (*While We Live,* 2016), is set in Gambia and Sweden.

This errantry, which is a cultural errantry too, does not take the form of the road movie, however. Depending on the contexts they traverse, the protagonists are confronted with different perceptions of themselves. Rather than the journey itself, or the action, it is emotional situations that are foregrounded, and their transformations and interior movements.

A Plurality of Languages and Points of View

The characters are also faced with a multitude of cultures and languages: for example, French and Wolof in *L'Afrance;* French and Jula in *Notre étrangère;* and Amharic, English, and German in *Teza.* This plurilingualism has been present from the very start of these cinemas and continues today. It is found in many early and recent films, such as *Xala* and *Faat Kiné* (Sembène, 1975 and 1999), *Le Monologue de la muette* (*The Silent Monologue,* Kahdy Sylla, 2008), *Tey* (Alain Gomis, 2012), *Saint-Louis Blues* (Dyana Gaye, 2009), all of which are in Wolof and French; *Daratt* (Mahamet Saleh Haroun, 2006), which is in Arabic and French; in *Kinshasa Palace,* in which, in addition to French, we hear Portuguese, Tshiluba, English, and Khmer; or Wolof, French, Italian, and English in *Des étoiles* (Dyana Gaye, 2013). In *Keïta: The Heritage of the Griot* (Jula/French), the bilingualism is overdetermined and comes to represent the hierarchization of languages and cultures and the conflict between traditional heritages and the culture imposed by the (post)colonial order.

But the films analyzed are not only spoken in several languages; they are polyphonic too in the sense that they deploy a great variety of often discordant narrators and subjectivities. They are populated with characters who all have their own visions. As it follows them, the camera reveals a great variety of perspectives and different truths. In *Rage,* this diversity of viewpoints is not only explicitly enunciated, it is also rendered so by the camera movements and by a remarkable play of shadows and light. The women in *Notre étrangère* each reveal their own relation to the world, to cultural belonging, and to maternity. In both *Juju Factory* and *L'Afrance,* the discussions between the characters, whose positions are well entrenched, are extremely animated and illustrate different possible conceptions of the same issue. In *Juju Factory,* Kongo clearly says, referring to his novel: "It's a story between reality and *several* realities." He takes complexity as the basis of his sensible experience.

Complex, Evolving Characters

The characters are thus not Manichean, nor are they monolithic, and even less static. They have complex personalities, forged and forged again in the discontinuity of their trajectories.

For Amy (*Notre étrangère*) and Rage (*Rage*), this complexity is firstly manifest visibly, due to their biological biracialism. But they are at the same time the bearers of a cultural plurality that takes them obstinately in search of a new synthesis and personal equilibrium, beyond that of their place in society. El Hadj (*L'Afrance*) and Anberber (*Teza*) embody this complexity through their interior dilemmas. In *Juju Factory,* Kongo expresses it through the multiplicity of roles he takes on (protagonist, writer, narrator) and between which he splits himself.

In *Rage* we also are witness to a series of doublings, but of another kind. The protagonist is lit by two types of light; he occupies different positions in the apartment—in addition to the two shadows that his form projects on the wall. *L'Afrance* shows the protagonist at different moments of his life. Moreover, in his memories, El Hadj sees himself as a child. This is taken even further in *Teza*. Here, the main character is doubled in the coalescence of Anberber child and adult, who appear simultaneously on the screen in "crystal-images," as Deleuze describes them.[2] This displacement of perspective allows the characters to imagine a different future from the one that seemed inexorably set out for them.

At times, the complexity is taken to a second degree, in the sense that certain characters are formed by the fusion of two (that is, Rage and Marcus, Anberber and his mother, Amy and her mother). Finally, the complexity culminates in the "global character" composed of the indissoluble multiplicity of those in a narrative, out of their fragmented subjectivities. These beings are destined to mobility: a physical, symbolic, and interior mobility. In a resolute quest to recompose their identities, they produce a double movement—that is, both a rooting and an opening.

In this movement, the center is constantly displaced, and with it, the perspective from which we see. Physical displacement can thus engender a perceptive, cognitive, and ontological decentering. It generates new gazes capable of seeing differently. It is this decentering that diasporic filmmakers constantly operate.

Like their characters, the filmmakers adopt an unstable point of view rooted in unconventional positions, at the interstices of cultures. It is the fact of always being a bit "elsewhere" in relation to the places they find themselves that is the force of their gaze. As Maria Silvia Bazzoli notes, this is a nomadic one, which turns from Africa to Europe, and from Europe to Africa, weaving together crisscrossing paths between "here" and "there"—paths that are situated both "inside" and "outside" different cultures.[3] It may be added too that the "there" of the past can become the "here" of the present, and vice versa. Filming from an original, decentered angle thus changes perspectives and makes it possible to challenge the norm, producing innovative enunciations that offer other possible epistemological structures.

Indeed, the filmmakers studied here constantly question territorial and cultural rootings. They constantly operate *reterritorializations* and generate new imaginaries, following a deterritorialization, to borrow Gilles Deleuze and Félix Guattari's term.[4] Physical deterritorialization corresponds to an attitude freed of conventions, which allows for a reterritorialization that is more in conformity with desires, and for the invention of new, innovative forms. This is a decontextualization of an ensemble of relations, a kind of declassification that liberates from conventional usages and thereby generates a creative moment. Deterritorialization allows a distance, making it possible to see things in different lights and to shift the horizon.

Moreover, by operating a change of perspective that brings the margin to the center, these filmmakers home in on differences and give a sample of visions that break with the uniformity with which we are generally confronted in Western cinema, notably when it comes to black or African characters. It is the same when it comes to their continent.

This is a way of avoiding the risk that all minorities be relegated to the same homogeneous group, whose only characteristic would be to stand out from the center—as if a single monolithic center were opposed to an equally rigid margin. It has been seen here through the characters' disparate positions and contrasting tendencies that this is clearly not the case, even if they belong to the same community (the Congolese in Brussels, London's black community, Africans in Paris, and so on). This treatment allows us to grasp each character in both their collective belonging and individual specificity, and to follow their evolution.

After Fractures, Reconstitution

Internal Transformations

Marked by ruptures, fragmentation, and by the intolerableness of their current condition, the characters here are moved to operate an internal revolution. Before reconstructing themselves, they pass through antechambers, places of passing and connection. Mariam's hostel, the compound yard or hotel for Amy (*Notre étrangère*), El Hadj's shower (*L'Afrance*), Mussolini Mountain (*Teza*), Marcus's apartment (*Rage*), the Tervuren Museum (*Juju Factory*) are examples of the poetics of transformation being put into play.

These internal transformations are painful. The psychological scars and fractures are sometimes manifest through corporal scars. El Hadj's scar is an example of this, like some of his physical reactions shown in close-up and extreme close-up (we see his body tremble, sweat; we see him vomit, as if to exorcise the unbearable). Similarly, Anberber in *Teza*—who, to save his life and that of his friends, is forced to abandon his Marxist ideals and his faith in the revolution—vomits, disgusted with himself. The physical signs evoke internal situations. Not only is Anberber's amputated body symbolic of his "torn" self, but, shown repeatedly, the amputation of his leg echoes his trauma-induced amnesia. His amnesia recalls that of Ezra, the eponymous protagonist of Newton I. Akuaka's film. In other films, characters are voiceless (Nassara in *Daratt*;[5] Onitcha, the protagonist's sister, in *Ezra*; Aïcha, the protagonist's sister in *The Absence*). This is also suggested in the impossibility of speaking a local language, like Abdallah in *Heremakono*, or Amy in *Notre étrangère*).

The characters are often initially trapped. They must escape the impasse of their present condition and change their way of seeing (themselves) to find new paths. It is precisely a problem or an impossibility that triggers movement and transformation. Thus, in a kind of renaissance of new possibilities, unexpected paths to the future open.

El Hadj's Renaissance (*L'Afrance*)

The example of El Hadj is emblematic. He is first of all paralyzed by his obsession with returning to Senegal, which is translated on the screen by the fact that he is shut in his room or in his shower, which play the role of mental prisons, and throughout the first shot by the vision of his lost, staring face to one side of the frame. He is later forced to abandon his project, to die to himself and accept what he has become.

This is the only way he will be able to let his true nature blossom and realize his dreams, including in France. Faithful to his promise "not to let himself be eaten by this country," he will nonetheless not be forced to leave it. Almost in a trance, beside himself, his vision blurred and deformed, he shouts at a friend who has come looking for him a meaningful "I fuck the El Hadj you know." It is thus in acts that he accepts his transformation. The trip he later makes back to Senegal to tell his family he has decided to remain in France shows that he is not forced to cut himself off from his roots. He embraces them, he unites the different components of his being, and he includes his past in his future. Just before leaving for Dakar, Miriam cuts his hair and shaves him, in a kind of rite of passage towards a new life that opens before him. The scene that expresses his personal revolution takes place just after he pulls back from the brink of suicide. This uncompleted extreme act represents the death of his former dreams and the renaissance of El Hadj. Alain Gomis thus reverses the destiny of Samba Diallo, the hero of the novel *Ambiguous Adventure* from which *L'Afrance* takes its inspiration, and offers a different perspective, proposing a synthesis rather than a conflict between cultures.

Anberber and the New World (*Teza*)

In *Teza,* Anberber is also stuck, his memory lost. He is mutilated, holed up in his solitude, haunted by nightmares, remote from the other villagers, and isolated and fragmented by the camera. He will only be able to reconcile and rebuild himself after agreeing to take part in a ritual: that of being sprayed with holy water. He will not abandon his dream of contributing to his country's development, but will transform it, putting it into action in the sobriety of a refound equilibrium. After having fought for grand ideals, he will abandon his dogmatic faith in Marxism and call himself into question. He will find his way in the simplicity of his village. As a schoolteacher, he will instruct the new generations and contribute to creating a new people. The birth of his child becomes an allegory, highlighted by the legend of the dragon that he narrates in voice-over:

> Childhood legend says we are descended from dragons. The youngsters hiding from war in the cave also say that the dragon watches over them. The dragon will give birth to them as her own children. They will have their own language. They will create the world destined for them. And in that new world, they will not have a word for murder or killing. . . . Azanu and I named our child Tesfaye. And our

hope will be brought up by the dragon, with the rest of its children in the cave, as it prepares them all to emerge and create their new society.[6]

It is revealing that the film ends on a (re)birth, thereby reinforcing the almost cyclical form of the narrative.

El Hadj and Anberber are initially animated by the same desire to return to their home countries and to contribute to bringing about change. At first, we see the former's solitude in France, and the latter's in his village in Ethiopia. Ultimately, it is, however, in these two places—in which they were initially lost—that they will remain to make their contribution to transforming society. It is no longer a question of a destiny one is subject to, but a chosen and willingly embraced path.

Rage's Revolution (*Rage*)

Rage also initially appears blocked. He cannot get his music—his way of expressing himself—heard, and thus cannot truly exist. He is torn between his two cultural belongings and goes through different moments of crisis. He is troubled by the play about biculturality, then argues fiercely with his friends about the question of identity. A female friend reproaches him for not truly being himself. At that point, the music changes and we hear "Your Revolution," by the African American Sarah Jones, in the background, as if to point out that Rage must still carry out his internal revolution. This song, which calls for self-respect, also suggests that it is the foundations that need to be changed to create a more egalitarian society. At the height of his identity crisis, Rage breaks down in tears in the intimacy of his room, and bitterly voices the fundamental question "What the fuck am I?" In voicing the issue, he liberates himself. Until this point, he is filmed in confined places (in his car; in Marcus's apartment; in narrow, oppressive corridors; between supermarket shelves; behind bars). The exterior night scenes are set in dimly lit streets. After this crisis, contrastingly, he is filmed in broad daylight (the rays of the sun shining into his car) and in open spaces like the balcony of Marcus's new apartment (the medium long shot gives the impression of air and of opening to a new horizon). He is finally capable of composing his music. His rap—a manifestation of his individual self—becomes a collective expression, the voice of the voiceless, of those who are invisible or misrepresented in the dominant imagination and mainstream media. His songs may be seen as a form of resistance, proposing alternatives to his present reality. This is a mise-en-abyme of what cinema represents for Aduaka. In a scene near the end of the film, Rage looks at himself in the car rearview mirror—a quintessentially intimate space that is highly present throughout the film. This image recalls another similar, yet not identical one at the start of the narrative. Rage's expression has changed, something in him has transformed, and he now seems serene and calmer. He has found his way of expressing himself and a new way of seeing (himself). As has already been shown, this was also the case with Amy's mother in Sarah Bouyain's film.

Amy: Embracing Biracialism (*Notre étrangère*)

After her intercontinental odyssey, Amy is transformed. In Bobo-Dioulasso, she is confronted with a perception of herself that is quite different to that in Paris. She is like a foreigner there, different to everyone else, even to her family members. At first, she is seen to be detached from the Burkinabè context, shut in her own world, in interstitial waiting spaces: the yards, cars, hotel room. She is often positioned on thresholds and in front of open, half-open, or closed doors. This is a poetics of constrained vision. Thresholds and limits can separate, create caesuras and incommunicability, but they can also be crossed, surpassed, to enter other worlds. Thanks to her obstinate resistance, Amy finally manages to reconcile herself and embrace her dual culture. At this point, she is symbolically dressed in an African print top and European trousers.

Kongo: Reclaiming History (*Juju Factory*)

In *Juju Factory,* Kongo is totally incapable of writing the book that his publisher expects of him (a kind of tourist guide, destined to highlight the exoticism of the Matonge district). The publisher demands that Kongo forget his origins, a part of his history, that he forget the colonial past that his novel references. To exist, he needs to find another way to speak out. He must confront the past. Thanks to its inclusion of history, Kongo's novel becomes a collective expression for Belgium's minority Congolese community. For Kongo, decentering and re-centering do not take the form of a long journey; he simply needs to make the trip to the Tervuren cemetery.

Aesthetics of Reconstruction

Even though their endings bear seeds of hope, *L'Afrance, Teza, Rage, Notre étrangère,* and *Juju Factory* do not offer fixed happy endings. Each film and its individual structure (the doublings, multiplication of viewpoints, and changes of rhythm induced by the camera movements in *Rage;* weaving memory into the present in *Teza* and *Juju Factory;* the parallel editing in *L'Afrance* and *Notre étrangère*) offers an opening to new possibilities. By taking "flexible and composite inheritances" into account,[7] by remodeling them in the present, they engender the original and unexpected that can arise from cultural blending.

Taking place discontinuously, this painful reconstruction is generally portrayed through fragmented montage, nonlinear narratives, and by a confluence of narrative styles. The neologism of the title *L'Afrance* demonstrates the inability of a single language to express a cultural complexity that surpasses it. To express the becoming and cultural complexity specific to them, then, these filmmakers have had to find adequate film forms. To translate certain realities, a language has to be invented and enriched with new signifiers, giving it new connotations and the inflexion of its own *accent.*[8]

Each filmmaker thus invents the style best adapted to expressing his or her complex and plural universe. In *Rage,* the hand-held camera follows the rap movement with a varied, sometimes fast, sometimes slowed rhythm, or with rapid shots alternating with sequence shots. Inspired by the world of underground music, Newton I. Aduaka achieves a specific narrative intensity that unveils the intimate world and evolution of his characters. In *Notre étrangère,* the lengthy shots and slow rhythm reveal the hiatus between Amy and the Burkinabè context. Moreover, the shots—which already suffice unto themselves—are juxtaposed to alternately show the mother's and the daughter's lives. The narrative of *L'Afrance* is structured around the to-ing and fro-ing between different moments of the protagonist's life, to the point that it is sometimes impossible to distinguish the flashbacks from the flash-forwards. *Juju Factory,* as has been seen, is a paradigm of stylistic syncretism. Documentary or report-like scenes, archive sounds and images, or an extract of a documentary are woven into this fiction in which black-and-white scenes are mixed (at times superimposed) with color ones. The ensemble is woven together (the narrative shots, temporalities, roles), as in the Congolese *Kasala* tradition. The spiral structure of *Teza*—typical of the Ethiopian art of oral narration in which Haile Gerima grew up—well illustrates the interior and psychological collapse of

Anberber, who must take twisting and turning paths to return to himself, to the new individual he has become. The fragmented shots in which past and present, virtual and real overlap clearly highlight the interdependence of the experiences of yesteryear and of the present day. Haile Gerima indeed comments: "To me, the first encounter with the structure is when you take each of the segments and you play with them. Then, you regroup all the segments and you look at them."[9] *Teza's* jarring montage also reflects his migratory experience, which provokes ruptures in his memory.

Films such as *Rage, Juju Factory, Notre étrangère, L'Afrance,* and *Teza,* which personalize film language, may be described as "minor" as defined by Deleuze and Guattari, and as "accented" as defined by Hamid Naficy.

Minor Films, Accented Cinema

The concept of *minor literature,* which Gilles Deleuze and Félix Guattari formulated regarding the works of Kafka, can in part be transposed to the films discussed here. The authors define a *minor literature* as "not the literature of a minor language but the literature a minority makes in a major language."[10] Kafka, "a Czech Jew [who] writes in German," uses a decontextualized language that he reinvents and enriches from his own experiences, as the filmmakers do. They indeed adopt narrative forms and film styles capable of representing their worlds, with syncretic aesthetics that are derived from the juxtaposition of different narratives.

The concept of minor literature evokes that of *accented cinema* that Hamid Naficy develops in his book *An Accented Cinema: Exilic and Diasporic Filmmaking.* The films in question here meet several characteristics described by Naficy: they are at the same time local and global, not monolithic, and are multilingual and polyphonic. They thus defy the authority of classical realism's omniscient narrator, letting a multitude of subjectivities and contingent truths be expressed. They pose a critical gaze on values taken for granted in their societies of origin and adoption. It is interesting to note that Naficy himself develops his theory from Deleuze and Guattari's analyses. He stresses that, through the subversion of narrative conventions that modify the role of spectators, and through a critical juxtaposition of language, cultures, and different worlds, the accented style offers an alternative to dominant cinema. Naficy asserts: "For these reasons, accented cinema is not only a minority cinema but also a minor cinema, in the way that Deleuze and Guattari have defined the concept."[11] Speaking a language with one's own accent indeed signifies appropriating and deterritorializing it in a creative becoming, giving rise to a textual richness and narrative innovations that are found in these mises-en-scène.

The minor character that Hamid Naficy refers to is not a value judgment, nor is it pejoratively connoted. It must indeed first be noted that for Deleuze and Guattari, the conceptual major/minor pair does not correspond just to something quantitative, but evokes the relationship between a normative dominant state and subgroups: the minorities that stand out from the norm. If the majority is standardized by its dominant status, minorities—precisely because they are distinct from it—can be distinguished in their plurality. The embraced minoritarian state can be seen as an exercise in transgression. By deviating from the dominant model, a minority can put its virtual becoming into act, its creative, revolutionary potential, in a logic of transformation and inventiveness. Moreover, minor films are able to enter the interstices of society that remain inaccessible to major cinema.

The films selected here illustrate this well, as their directors assume the subjectivity of the gaze that they train on situations they are familiar with from the inside, but which they are also able to evoke with a certain distance. In this critically distant subjective speaking-out, they deconstruct the norm that has historically erased diverse subjectivities in the name of a so-called universal vision of the world. It is thus a question not of losing one's identity by assimilating into a dominant culture, but rather of contributing one's knowledge, artistic personality, and own style, which are an enrichment.

According to Deleuze and Guattari, the intensive use of a language, which expresses interior tensions, makes invention and flexibility possible, and it is in this that minor literatures can become revolutionary. The films here express their auteurs' artistic creativity and point of view. That is where their interest lies.

Other characteristics of minor literatures highlighted by Deleuze and Guattari are particularly relevant here. In the minor, everything becomes political. In a major literature, the public and private spaces remain distinct and separate, whereas in a minor literature, this frontier disappears: "Because it exists in a narrow space, every individual matter is immediately plugged into the political."[12]

Deleuze makes the same remark concerning modern political cinema, in which the frontiers between private and public are abolished and in which "the private affair merges with the social—or political—immediate."[13] For Deleuze, modern political cinema resides in the impossibility of bearing the intolerable.[14] To illustrate this, he takes the example of Black American Cinema shot in the ghettos. Rather than reversing the negative image of black people, this cinema "multiplies types"[15] and characters, and creates emotional states through visions and pure sounds, thereby inventing a new expressive form. The filmmakers of the L.A. Group that Haile Gerima belonged to learned filmmaking together; then each developed their own style and created their own cinematic universe. But they remained united by the fact that their struggle involved the medium itself, as Haile Gerima stresses.[16] The members of this group adapted technique to suit their needs. They deterritorialized the dominant cinema, not only because they took their cameras to new territories, but also and above all because they looked for forms that moved away from Hollywood codes. Accordingly, they constituted a "minority" in Los Angeles.

Political Films

Today, the films of the African diaspora are very often political. But they are so in ways that are different from the works of the African pioneers. The latter—militants animated by an anti-imperialist, anticolonial fervor—were reinforced by a collective political awareness. The expression of their sociopolitical commitment generally went hand in hand with an aesthetic close to social realism and its linear narratives. Today, in contrast, participation in collective struggle is less manifest, and individualities tend to predominate. The contemporary diasporic filmmakers look beyond the nation and situate their filmic discourse in the turbulent "cross flows" of globalization.[17] Political challenges play out in a cultural combat. Without neglecting the role of history and memory, they foreground their artistic gazes, are more attentive to media representations, and propose alternative visions. That is the political reach of these contemporary films. This is linked to representation—a central question that subverts the dominant logics and equilibriums through a (re)negotiation of cultures, gazes, and their hierarchies.

In the films studied, the intimate erupts into the narrative and the private mixes with the public, the narrative threads crossing. And, as Edouard Glissant states in *Caribbean Discourse,* "this inner self is inseparable from the future evolution of his community."[18] A rooting in personal history is indispensable because, looking more closely, this echoes other histories, hence the social and political dimension. For these minorities, it is a matter of challenging the current system and ways of life, for they cannot continue to live under the cultural domination to which they are subjected. The anger of the auteurs discussed here, like that of Rage, is thus transformed into a creative force and source of artistic inspiration.

Individual Histories, Collective History

Through the singular experience of the characters, part of collective history enters the fictions. That may be in the form of a protagonist's personal thoughts, as is the case with Kongo, Anberber, or El Hadj. In *L'Afrance,* shut in the confined space of his shower, El Hadj relives his incarceration. He has committed no crime; he just forgets to renew his residency permit. His incarceration becomes that of all migrants who risk finding themselves in the same situation, on the margins of society. Thus, the condition of the colonized yesterday and that of the immigrant today bear the same feeling of the intolerableness.

In *Juju Factory,* Kongo enters the realm of the political and collective from the moment he seeks his people's history in the Tervuren cemetery. Here, the colonial past takes a central, more explicit place, whereas in *Teza* and *L'Afrance,* the question is only touched upon. However, these three films draw on historical documents and existing memorials. That is another way of integrating the historical and political into the fictional realm.

For *Teza*'s protagonist, colonization is both a personal, family experience and a collective burden. Anberber and the commemorative monument on Mount Mussolini form a unity in which the individual and collective fuse. Personal and collective history weave together indelibly.

Along with the films in this corpus, another remarkable example is *Kinshasa Palace* (Zeka Laplaine, 2006). In this fiction, we follow the vicissitudes of a family (that of the filmmaker) dispersed across three continents. Between the uprooting and wounds, it is the history of a country—the Democratic Republic of Congo—and its colonial past that is recounted.

The rereadings of the past that these films propose is not animated by a nostalgic pleasure, nor by the fact that the filmmakers are trapped in history and unable to free themselves from it. The driving force is the need to understand the present and to advance towards the future. These films traverse different temporalities. It is up to the spectator to piece together the plot, whose elements are given to them unchronologically. Haile Gerima, Alain Gomis, Balufu Bakupa-Kanyinda, and Zeka Laplaine thus challenge linear narration and a single point of view. In the fictions analyzed, everything takes on a collective value—which is not the same as being a spokesperson for the community, a role that none of the filmmakers here takes on. Thanks to a personal questioning before contemporary realities, and while telling completely singular stories, these fictions broach the human, the universal. But, as has been clearly shown, they do so via a completely different route to that of a vertically imposed norm.

It is through this imbrication of personal (hi)stories and collective history, of the private and the public, that the African diasporic films of the 2000s are political works. They become necessary and urgent ways of speaking out that break the wall of silence or the hypocrisy that, today still, often invisibilize (migrant) Africans, or shut them in stereotypical and reductive representations. They give voice to uncodified words: words it is no longer possible to silence; words that are capable of opening new ontological and hermeneutic perspectives and of enriching imaginations.

Revolutionary Films in Their Own Right

Newton I. Aduaka, Sarah Bouyain, Haile Gerima, Alain Gomis, and Balufu Bakupa-Kanyinda achieve a remarkable narrative intensity that goes hand in hand with a great sobriety of cinematic language. The films analyzed reveal a sober cinema, without special effects, using few technical means (cranes, jibs, camera dollies) and often nonprofessional actors. These films are the result of highly divergent production conditions, which range from the independent production of *Rage* to the tricontinental coproduction of *Teza,* via the low-budget *Juju Factory.* They are set in natural décors better suited to their storylines and the adventures of their characters, who, as already stated, can be qualified as intercessors (in Deleuzian terms) or mediators (according to Kate Hamburger) between the fictional and real worlds.

These neither spectacular nor sensational styles prove themselves to be most effective. It is through the assemblage of different fragments, the succession of constructions and reconstructions, the nonlinear narratives, that these works express complexity and plurality. Their characters manage to change the set course of events and to open other paths. They do so with a simplicity that seems within the reach of all; they embody neither heroes, nor social types, but ordinary humans.

Rage, Juju Factory, Notre étrangère, L'Afrance, and *Teza,* like so many other African diasporic films, can be described as revolutionary in the dual sense that, based on actual contexts, they testify to a profound epistemological upheaval and that they envisage a different future, made possible in each individual case through self-reconstruction.

It is noteworthy that all of these works are born out of the convergence of theoretical reflection (artistic, social, political) and absolutely singular lives. By conjointly mobilizing their personal experiences and social preoccupations, a certain number of filmmakers raise questions that interpellate the contemporary world. They center their preoccupations about crucial (and often silenced) subjects such as colonial history and its consequences, contemporary politics, the place of minorities in our societies, freedom of expression, and the potential of cultural blending, thereby opening new possibilities. By subverting the hierarchy of gazes, they propose other truths, while also opening new paths to artistic creation.

I have indeed demonstrated how, far from being secondary to artistic experimentation, the urgency of speaking out is on the contrary inseparable from it, for the composite styles and synthetic aesthetics of these filmmakers are the very expression of their worlds. These are made up of original gazes and become a form of resistance to dominant representations and logics.

Through their ontological and hermeneutic decentering, the plurality of their visions, and the polyphony of their narrations, these films enable a surpassing of dominant thought and invite us all to take responsibility for our choices. They place the spectator in the assuredly uncomfortable position of no longer being able to watch without reacting, of no longer feigning ignorance, of no longer shutting their eyes to injustice, of having also to take a position themselves.

Notes

Introduction: Contemporary African Diasporic Films

1. This refers to Gayatri C. Spivak's concept of "epistemic violence" described in her essay "Can the Subaltern Speak?" [in Cary Nelson and Lawrence Grossberg (eds.), *Marxism and the Interpretation of Culture,* Basingstoke, Maximillian Education, 1988, pp. 217–313, 280]. See also Gayatri C. Spivak, *A Critique of Postcolonial Reason: Toward a History of a Vanishing Present,* Cambridge (MA), Harvard University Press, 1999.

2. John Akomfrah, *in* Daniela Ricci, *Imaginaires en exil. Cinq cinéastes d'Afrique se racontent* (*Creation in Exile: Five Filmmakers in Conversation*), documentary, 53 min., HD, France, 2013. With Newton I. Aduaka, John Akomfrah, Haile Gerima, Dani Kouyaté, Jean Odoutan.

3. The term refers to Kimberlé Crenshaw's concept, introduced in "Mapping the Margins: Intersectionality, Identity Politics, and Violence against Women of Color," *Stanford Law Review,* vol. 43, no. 6, 1991, pp. 1241–1299. First used to describe the situation of African American women in the United States, the term may more widely designate the condition of those simultaneously subjected to several forms of domination or discrimination in society.

4. Sheila J. Petty, *Contact Zones: Memory, Origin and Discourse in Black Diasporic Cinema,* Detroit, Wayne State University Press, 2008, p. 6.

5. I prefer "transcontinental" to the more frequently used term "transnational," as the concept of nation is not sufficiently meaningful when it comes to the African continent. Born out of the colonial divisions and artificial borders imposed by the European countries at the Berlin Conference in 1885, today's nations do not reflect Africa's cultures.

6. Mary Louise Pratt, "Arts of the Contact Zone," *Profession*, no. 91, 1991, pp. 33–40.

7. Gaston Kaboré, "Regard singulier, auteur singulier," in Médias France Intercontinents, *Cinémas africains d'aujourd'hui. Guide des cinématographies d'Afrique*, Paris, Karthala/RFI, 2007, p. 16. Unless otherwise stated, all quotations are translated by Melissa Thackway. In this event, the original French is given thus: [chaque cinéaste "fait des films à partir de ce qu'il est."]

8. For further information, see, for example, Beti Ellerson, *Sisters of the Screen: Women of Africa on Film, Video and Television*, Trenton (NJ), Africa World Press, 2000. See also Ellerson's blog *African Women in Cinema*.

9. Angèle Diabang Brener is currently working on her first fiction feature film, inspired by Mariama Ba's novel *Une si longue lettre* (*So Long a Letter*).

10. Soussaba Cissé's first feature film was released in 2013: *N'gunu N'gunu Kan* (*Rumors of War*), Mali, 114 min. Since the original French publication of this book, the following women filmmakers have also released feature-length fictions: Ramatou Keita, *Zin'naarya* (2016); Wanuri Kahiu, *Rafiki* (2018); Rungano Nyoni, *I Am Not a Witch* (2018); Apolline Traoré, *Desrances* (2019), *Frontières* (2017), *Moi, Zaphira* (2013).

11. Although Guadeloupean, Sarah Maldoror is often considered an African filmmaker by virtue of her personal and professional commitment to the liberation struggles of the African continent, and particularly to those of Angola and Algeria.

12. In its themes and aesthetics, *Des Étoiles* (*Under the Starry Sky*) (Dyana Gaye, France/ Senegal, 2013) could have legitimately been part of this selection. It offers a diasporic vision of contemporary Senegal, errancy, and self-quest through the intertwining yet never-meeting paths of its three protagonists from New York, Dakar, to Turin. This alternating narrative lightly and poetically illustrates the ruptures arising from the migratory experience, the reconstructions, and the reinventions of the future.

13. Jean-Marie Schaeffer, *Pourquoi la fiction?*, Paris, Seuil, 1999, p. 218. ["une modélisation de l'univers réel."]

14. *Ibid.*, p. 182.

15. Jean-Pierre Esquenazi, *La Vérité de la fiction. Comment peut-on croire que les récits de fiction nous parlent sérieusement de la réalité?* [Fiction's Truth: How Can We Believe That Fiction Narratives Talk Seriously about Reality?], Paris, Lavoisier, 2009.

16. Esquenazi, *La Vérité de la fiction*, p. 10.

17. Interview with Newton Aduaka, Paris, January 2011.

18. Balufu Bakupa-Kanyinda, "Africa's Own Mirror Leaves It Invisible," *in* Manthia Diawara, *African Film: New Forms of Aesthetics and Politics*, Berlin, Prestel, 2010, pp. 217–225, 223.

19. Kate Hamburger, *Logique des genres littéraires*, Paris, Seuil, 1986, p. 30, cited in Esquenazi, *La Vérité de la fiction*, p. 129.

20. Gilles Deleuze, *The Time-Image*, trans. Hugh Tomlinson and Robert Galeta, Minneapolis, University of Minnesota Press, 1989, p. 152.

21. Alain Gomis, in Daniela Ricci, "Incontro con Alain Gomis, dopo la proiezione del film *Aujourd'hui*, al Festival Internazionale di Contis 2012" [online], *Melisandra*, July 2012, www.melisandra.org/wordpress/wp-content/uploads/2012/07/Incontro-con-Alain-Gomis.pdf.

22. Schaeffer, *Pourquoi la fiction?*, p. 223.

23. For part of the interviews with the filmmakers (edited together with extracts of their films), see Ricci, *Imaginaires en exil* (*Creation in Exile*).

Chapter 1. The Question of Identity

1. Bernard Lahire, *L'Homme pluriel. Les ressorts de l'action*, Paris, Nathan, 1998.

2. Amadou Hampâté Bâ, *Aspects de la civilisation africaine. Personne, culture, religion*, Paris, Présence Africaine, 2000 [1972].

3. Amin Maalouf, *In the Name of Identity: Violence and the Need to Belong*, trans. Barbara Bray, London, Penguin Books, 2000, p. 18.

4. Norbert Elias, *La Société des individus*, trans. Jeanne Etoré, Paris, Fayard, 1991 (written in 1939).

5. Édouard Glissant, *Introduction à une poétique du divers*, Paris, Gallimard, 1996 [1995], p. 31. [La "racine, mais allant à la rencontre des autres racines, alors ce qui devient important n'est pas tellement un prétendu absolu de chaque racine, mais le mode, la manière dont elle entre en contact avec d'autres racines: la Relation."]

6. Sheila J. Petty, *Contact Zones: Memory, Origin and Discourse in Black Diasporic Cinema*, Detroit, Wayne State University Press, 2008, p. 56.

7. Clifford Geertz, *The Interpretation of Cultures*, New York, Basic Books, 1973, p. 49.

8. Pierre Sorlin, "Quelqu'un à qui parler," *in* Jean-Pierre Esquenazi (ed.), *Politique des auteurs et théories de cinéma*, Paris, L'Harmattan, coll. "Champs Visuels," 2003, p. 162. ["L'auteur parle de la place qu'il occupe dans le monde."]

9. Daniela Ricci, *Imaginaires en exil. Cinq cinéastes d'Afrique se racontent* (*Creation in Exile: Five Filmmakers in Conversation*), documentary, 53 min., HD, France, 2013.

10. Dani Kouyaté, *Joseph Ki-Zerbo. Identités/Identité pour l'Afrique,* documentary, Burkina Faso, 2005, 52 min. ["C'est à partir du moment où [les autres] ont décidé, en profitant de leur supériorité militaire, de faire des Noirs des esclaves, que le mépris a commencé et que les Noirs sont entrés dans cette dynamique, cette dialectique consistant à se mépriser soi-même. À partir de cet instant-là, les choses ont basculé."]

11. This vision sadly still exists. One only need cite the "Discours de Dakar" (26 July 2007), in which the French president Nicolas Sarkozy stated: "Africa's tragedy is that Africans have not sufficiently entered history." ["Le drame de l'Afrique, c'est que l'homme africain n'est pas assez entré dans l'Histoire."]

12. Léopold Sédar Senghor, "Ce que l'homme noir apporte," in Jean Verdier (ed.), *L'Homme de couleur,* Paris, Librairie Plon, 1939, pp. 291–313, 295.

13. Mweze Dieudonné Ngangura, *Pièces d'identités,* Belgium/DRC, 1998.

14. Sembène Ousmane, *Emitai,* Senegal, 1971.

15. Med Hondo, *Sarraounia,* Burkina Faso/France, 1986.

16. Kwaw Ansah, *Heritage Africa!,* Ghana, 1989.

17. Jean-Marie Teno, *Afrique, je te plumerai . . . ,* France/Cameroon, 1992.

18. Haile Gerima, *Sankofa,* Germany/Burkina Faso/Ethiopia/USA, 1993.

19. Dani Kouyaté, *Keïta! L'héritage du griot,* France/Burkina Faso, 1995.

20. Aimé Césaire, *Notebook of a Return to the Native Land,* trans. Clayton Eshleman and Annette Smith, Middletown (CT), Wesleyan University Press, 2001, p. 23. [First edition: *Cahier d'un retour au pays natal,* Paris, Présence Africaine, 1956.]

21. Petty, *Contact Zones,* p. 1.

22. James Clifford, "Diaspora," *Cultural Anthropology,* vol. 9, no. 3, August 1994, pp. 302–328, cited in Petty, *Contact Zones,* p. 6.

23. Jean-Pierre Esquenazi, *Hitchcock et l'aventure de Vertigo. L'invention à Hollywood,* Paris, CNRS Éditions, 2001, p. 24. ["Les problèmes du milieu ne sont pas ressentis par des individus différents de la même façon. Appréhender les milieux comme la source d'invention ne veut pas dire méconnaître la particularité humaine."]

24. Christine Chivallon, "La Notion de diaspora appliquée au monde noir des Amériques: l'historicité d'un concept," *Africultures,* "Diaspora: identité plurielle" (special edition), no. 72, 2008, pp. 18–35.

25. *Ibid.,* p. 28. ["instable, précaire, aventureuse, fluide, amorphe . . ."]

26. For further information, see Jean Bernabé, Patrick Chamoiseau, and Raphaël Confiant, *Éloge de la créolité,* Paris, Gallimard, coll. "Hors série Littérature," 1993 (written in 1989).

27. Stuart Hall, "Cultural Identity and Diaspora," *in* Patrick Williams and Laura Crisman (eds.), *Colonial Discourse and Post-Colonial Theory: A Reader,* London,

Harvester-Wheatsheaf, 1994, pp. 227–237, 235. First published in *Framework,* no. 36, 1989, pp. 68–81.

28. Paul Gilroy, *The Black Atlantic: Modernity and Double-Consciousness,* London, Verso, 1993.

29. Cited by Chivallon, "La Notion de diaspora," p. 33.

30. Stuart Hall, "Introduction: Who Needs Identity?," *in* Stuart Hall and Paul Du Gay (eds.), *Questions of Cultural Identity,* London, Sage, 1996, pp. 1–17, 2.

31. *Ibid.,* p. 3.

32. Haile Gerima, at the Q&A after the screening of his film *Bush Mama,* Washington, DC, Smithsonian Institution, 7 November 2015.

33. Q&A, Pero (Milan), 23 May 2006. ["Je me suis posé la question de ce que signifie être Noir dès que je suis arrivé en Europe."]

34. Cinéclub Q&A, hosted by Catherine Ruelle, Musée Dapper, Paris, 28 February 2010. ["En Russie, pour la première fois je me suis senti l'Autre, l'Étranger, le Noir."]

35. Pap Ndiaye, *La Condition noire. Essai sur une minorité française,* Paris, Gallimard, coll. "Folio actuel," 2009 [Calmann-Lévy, 2008].

36. Jean-Louis Sagot-Duvauroux, *On ne naît pas Noir, on le devient,* Paris, Éditions Albin Michel, 2004, p. 10. ["Noir est une couleur presque partout synonyme de position subalterne."]

37. For more on the question, see "L'insoutenable invisibilité des Noirs en France" (The Unbearable Invisibility of Black People in France), a collective article published in la Guilde's (the African Guild of Filmmakers and Producers) first newsletter in March 2003. The signatories notably included Balufu Bakupa-Kanyinda, Serge Issa Coelo, Mahamat Saleh Haroun, Mama Keita, Zeka Laplaine, Fanta Regina Nacro, Jean-Marie Teno, and François Woukoache. See also Sylvie Chalaye, *Nègres en images,* Paris, L'Harmattan, 2002; Sylvie Chalaye, "Acteurs noirs" [online], *Africultures,* 1 April 2000, http://www.africultures.com/php/?nav=article&no=1310.

38. Olivier Barlet, "Entretien avec Jose [Zeka] Laplaine" [online], *Africultures,* 30 August 2002, http://www.africultures.com/php/index.php?nav=article&no=2487. ["Sur un scénario, quand on ne spécifie pas 'Noir,' le rôle est forcément pour un Blanc."]

39. Interview, Paris, August 2010. ["J'avais envie de raconter des histoires qui n'étaient pas racontées, de montrer des gens qu'on ne voyait pas."]

40. https://www.dani-kouyate.com, my emphasis. ["Française *mais* Noire, libre mais descendante d'esclave."]

41. Edward W. Saïd, *Orientalism,* New York, Pantheon Books, 1978.

42. V. Y. Mudimbe, *The Invention of Africa: Philosophy and the Order of Knowledge,* Bloomington, Indiana University Press, 1988.

43. Axel Honneth, *Lotta per il riconoscimento. Proposte per un'etica del conflitto,* Milan, Il saggiatore, 2002.

44. Axel Honneth, "Reconnaissance et justice" [online], *Le passant,* no. 38, January–February 2002, http://www.passant-ordinaire.org/revue/38-349.asp#. [Les "conditions de reconnaissance mutuelle dans lesquelles la formation de l'identité personnelle et, ce faisant, l'épanouissement individuel, pourront se réaliser."]

45. Charles Taylor, "Multiculturalism and the Politics of Recognition," Princeton (NJ), Princeton University Press, 1992, p. 25.

46. Hall, "Cultural Identity and Diaspora," p. 225.

Chapter 2. Cinematographic Representations: Representations and Their Consequences

1. Stuart Hall, "Cultural Identity and Diaspora," *in* Patrick Williams and Laura Chrisman (eds.), *Colonial Discourse and Post-Colonial Theory: A Reader,* London, Harvester-Wheatsheaf, 1994, p. 222.

2. Férid Boughedir, *Caméra d'Afrique,* documentary, Tunisia, 1983. ["On ne peut pas défendre sa dignité, quand on ne se voit pas sur les écrans. . . . Si l'Africain ne se regarde pas en images, il est dominé, il est aliéné."]

3. Gaston Kaboré, "L'image de soi, un besoin vital," in Fédération panafricaine des cinéastes (Fepaci), *L'Afrique et le centenaire du cinéma,* Paris, Présence Africaine, 1995, p. 21. ["Tout individu a un besoin vital de son propre reflet, de sa propre image, car une part importante de l'équation de l'existence se fonde sur la capacité à établir un dialogue avec cette image, pour la questionner, pour se confronter à elle."]

4. Franz Fanon, *Black Skin, White Masks,* trans. Charles Lam Markmann, London, Pluto Press, 2008, p. 114.

5. *Ibid.,* p. 113.

6. *Ibid.,* p. 113.

7. Robert Stam and Ella Shohat, "Film Theory and Spectatorship in the Age of the 'Post,'" *in* Christine Gledhill and Linda Williams (eds.), *Reinventing Film Studies,* London, Arnold, 2000, pp. 381–401, 386.

8. Françoise Pfaff, *Twenty-five Black African Filmmakers: A Critical Study, with Filmography and Bio-bibliography,* Westport (CT), Greenwood Press, 1988, p. 138.

9. Melvin Van Peebles and Jérôme Beauchez, "La Fierté noire en images: une infra-politique du film" [online], *Cultures & Conflits,* no. 89, Spring 2013, http://conflits.revues.org/18674#quotation.

10. Daniela Ricci, *Imaginaires en exil. Cinq cinéastes d'Afrique se racontent* (*Creation in Exile: Five Filmmakers in Conversation*), documentary, 53 min., HD, France, 2013.

11. Adichie Chimamanda, "The Danger of a Single Story: Chimamanda Adichie on TED.com" [online], July 2009, http://www.ted.com/talks/chimamanda_adichie_the_danger_of_a_single_story.html.

12. Nwachukwu Frank Ukadike, *Black African Cinema,* Berkeley, University of California Press, 1994, p. 35.

13. Paulin Soumanou Vieyra, *Le Cinéma africain. Des origines à 1973,* Paris, Présence Africaine, 1975, p. 16. ["toujours à la gloire des colonisateurs et de leurs entreprises."]

14. A certain number of works explore representations of Africans in colonial films, and iconography of black people in general. For example, see Youssef El Ftouh and Manuel Pinto, "L'Afrique dans les images coloniales," *in* Catherine Ruelle et al. (eds.), *Afriques 50. Singularités d'un cinéma pluriel,* Paris, L'Harmattan, coll. "Images plurielles," 2005. See also Jean Rouch, *Situations et tendances actuelles du cinéma africain,* a report written for UNESCO, 23 August 1961; Guy Gauthier and Philippe Esnault, "Le cinéma colonial," *Revue du cinéma,* no. 394, May 1984; Raymond Lefèvre, "Le cinéma colonial," *Images et Colonies,* exhibition catalog and conference minutes, Paris, Association Connaissance de l'histoire de l'Afrique contemporaine (ACHAC)/Bibliothèque de documentation internationale contemporaine (BDIC), 1993; Nicolas Bancel and Pascal Blanchard, "De l'indigène à l'immigré, images, messages et réalités," Paris, Gallimard, coll. "Découverte Gallimard," no. 345, 1998 (and "De l'indigène à l'immigré, images, messages et réalités," *Hommes et Migrations,* "L'Héritage colonial, un trou de mémoire" (dossier), no. 1228, 2000); Catherine Coquery-Vidrovitch, "Le Postulat de la supériorité blanche et de l'infériorité noire," *in* Marc Ferro (ed.), *Le Livre noir du colonialisme,* Paris, Robert Laffont, 2002; Jean-Claude Yrzoala Meda, "Le Cinéma colonial: les conditions de son développement," *Écrans d'Afrique,* no. 9–10, 1994; Odile Goerg, *Fantômas sous les tropiques. Aller au cinéma en Afrique coloniale,* Paris, Vendémiaire, coll. "Empires," 2015; Francis Ramirez and Christian Rolot, *Histoire du cinéma colonial au Zaïre, au Rwanda et au Burundi,* Annales, série IN-18, Sciences historiques no. 7, Tervuren, Musée royal de l'Afrique centrale, 1985; Dina Sherzer, *Cinema, Colonialism, Postcolonialism,* Austin, University of Texas, 1995; Rosallen Smyth, "The Development of British Colonial Film Policy, 1927–1939," *Journal of African History,* vol. 20, no. 3, 1979.

    I have not discussed German colonial cinema here, as it was less pervasive. The Germans began producing their colonial films in 1912–1913, but they were most often shot on African sets in Berlin-based studios. Travel and expedition films mainly remained the fruit of private initiatives. For further information, see Wolfgang Fuhrmann, *Imperial*

Projections: Screening the German Colonies, New York, Berghahn Books, 2015.

15. For more on the question, see the works of Guido Convents: *Afrique? Quel cinéma! Un siècle de propagande coloniale et de cinéma africain,* Antwerp, Éditions EPO, 2003; *Images et démocratie. Les Congolais face au cinéma et à l'audiovisuel,* Afrika Film Festival, Leuven, 2005; and *Image & paix: les Rwandais et les Burundais face au cinéma et à l'audiovisuel,* Afrika Film Festival, Leuven, 2008. See also Ramirez and Rolot, *Histoire du cinéma colonial.*

16. Manthia Diawara, *African Cinema: Politics and Culture,* Bloomington, Indiana University Press, 1992, p. 12.

17. Pierre Haffner, "Entretien avec le père Alexandre Van den Heuvel, pionnier d'un 'cinéma missionnaire' au Congo," *in* Ruelle et al., *Afriques 50.*

18. Rouch, *Situations et tendances actuelles,* p. 23. ["d'une naïveté et d'un paternalisme désarmants. L'Africain y est toujours représenté comme un grand enfant, auquel on doit tout apprendre."]

19. For further information, see "Towards a Third Cinema" (original title: "Hacia un tercer cine"), the manifesto written by directors Octavio Getino and Fernando Solanas, published for the first time in Spanish, French, English, and Italian in the journal *Tricontinental* in 1969.

20. Clyde Taylor, "Film Reborn in Mozambique: Interview with Pedro Pimenta," *Jump Cut,* no. 28, 1983, p. 31.

21. *Ibid.*, p. 30.

22. For further information, see Mino Argentieri, *L'occhio del regime. Informazione e propaganda nel cinema del fascismo,* Florence, Vallecchi, 1979; Gian Piero Brunetta and Jean A. Gili, *L'ora d'Africa del cinema italiano 1911–1989,* Rovereto, Materiali di lavoro— Rivista di studi storici, 1990; Alessandra Speciale, "Le Rêve africain du cinéma italien," Écrans d'Afrique, no. 9–10, 1994.

    Italian colonial cinema was the object of the retrospective *Faccetta nera: il cinema coloniale italiano,* held in Rome 6–12 April 2006 and which was presented as "a journey in imaginations of the time, from 1909 to 1942, *from exoticism to propaganda*" (my emphasis).

23. About a dozen feature films in total, according to Maria Coletti (*Facetta Nera* retrospective brochure).

24. Maria Coletti, "Fantasmi d'Africa, dal muto al sonoro. Facce, faccette e *blackface," in* Leonardo de Francesci (ed.), *L'Africa in Italia. Per una controstoria postcoloniale del cinema italiano,* Rome, Aracne, 2013.

25. This overview of British colonial cinema draws on several sources, notably the chapter

"The Historical Background of Colonial African Instructional Cinema," *in* Femi
Okiremuete Shaka, *Modernity and the African Cinema,* Trenton (NJ), Africa World Press,
2004. Also see Manthia Diawara, "Sub-Saharan African Film Production: Technological
Paternalism," *Jump Cut,* no. 32, 1987, pp. 61–65; and his book *African Cinema.* I have also
drawn on the site http://www.colonialfilm.org.uk.

26. Diawara, *African Cinema,* p. 4.

27. Leslie Allen Notcutt and George Chitty Latham, *The African and the Cinema,* London,
Edinburgh House Press, 1937.

28. Yrzoala Meda, "Le Cinéma colonial," p. 86. ["présentés comme des hordes sauvages
s'entretuant et se dévorant entre eux. Ainsi, les conquêtes coloniales étaient présentées
sous un aspect humaniste; elles devenaient des œuvres de pacification de ces peuples."]

29. *Catalogue Films ethnographiques sur l'Afrique noire,* Bruges, Les presses Saint-Augustin,
1967, preface by Jean Rouch, p. 22. ["Ce règlement, pratiquement jamais appliqué aux
cinéastes français, servait de prétexte au refus d'autorisation de tournage signifié aux
jeunes Africains jugés trop turbulents par l'administration coloniale."]

One of the first French directors to fall foul of the Laval Decree was René Vautier
when shooting *Afrique 50* in Ivory Coast. Considered one of the first French anticolonial
films, it was censored in France from 1950 to 1990, and only broadcast on French
television for the first time in 2003.

Chapter 3. African Cinema: New Perspectives

1. "Masterclass with Gaston Kaboré: Cannes Film Festival 2007" [online], hosted by
Jean-Pierre Garcia, director of the Amiens Festival international du film, organized
at the Cinémas du Sud Pavillion by the French Ministry of Foreign Affairs, 20 June
2007, *Africultures,* http://africultures.com/masterclass-with-gaston-kabore-6656/.
["Pendant ma maîtrise d'histoire [en France] j'ai remarqué que l'Afrique était racontée
en permanence par des anthropologues, des ethnologues, des sociologues . . . presque
exclusivement non africains. Où était la part d'investigation de l'Afrique sur elle-même?
J'ai décidé d'analyser la façon dont l'Afrique était représentée au-delà des mots, en
images. . . . Il fallait qu'en tant qu'Africain, et moi en tant qu'historien, on puisse changer
ce regard sur l'Afrique car il était porteur de beaucoup de malentendus. . . . C'était un
regard unilatéral.]

2. Françoise Pfaff, À *l'écoute du cinéma sénégalais,* Paris, L'Harmattan, coll. "Images
plurielles," 2010, p. 9. ["Longtemps consommateurs d'images venues d'ailleurs."]

3. Victor Bachy, "Survol sur le cinéma noir," *in* Centre d'Étude sur la Communication

en Afrique (Cesca), *Camera nigra. Les discours du film africain,* Brussels/Paris, Ocic-L'Harmattan, coll. "Cinémedia. Cinémas d'Afrique noire," 1984. ["Le cinéma importé [restait] encore dominant."]

4. Olivier Barlet, *Contemporary African Cinema,* trans. Melissa Thackway, East Lansing, Michigan State University Press, 2016, p. 40.

5. Ella Shohat and Robert Stam, *Unthinking Eurocentrism: Multiculturalism and the Media,* New York, Routledge, 1994, p. 343.

6. Melissa Thackway, *Africa Shoots Back: Alternative Perspectives in Sub-Saharan Francophone African Film,* Bloomington, Indiana University Press, 2003.

7. Bill Ashcroft, Gareth Griffiths, and Helen Tiffin, *The Empire Writes Back: Theory and Practice in Post-Colonial Literature,* New York, Routledge, 1989.

8. Olivier Barlet, "Entretien avec Zeka Laplaine" [online], *Africultures,* 10 October 2003, http://www.africultures.com/php/?nav=article&no=3071. [une "volonté manifestée non pas d'inverser forcément les choses, mais de montrer une autre réalité."]

9. It is important to specify "political," for even if the fiftieth anniversary of Independence was recently celebrated, the question remains whether certain African countries are, today, truly independent. In economic terms, the answer is ambivalent, particularly in terms of film production.

10. Ousmane Sembène, "Continuons à travailler sans relâche . . . ," *in* Catherine Ruelle et al. (eds.), *Afriques 50. Singularités d'un cinéma pluriel,* Paris, L'Harmattan, coll. "Images plurielles," 2005, p. 13. ["chaque fois qu'un des nôtres mettait un film en boîte, c'était une victoire pour nous tous."]

   A certain confusion exists concerning Sembène's first name and surname. In accordance with his wish, I shall call him Sembène Ousmane here. Ousmane is his first name, and Sembène his surname. As the colonial administration inverted surnames and first names, Ousmane Sembène decided to take "Sembène Ousmane" as his pen name for as long as "colonial ideology distills its poison" (Thierno I. Dia, "L'Aîné des Anciens," foreword, *Africultures,* "Sembène Ousmane (1923–2007)" (dossier), no. 76, 2008, p. 11).

11. For further information, see María Roof, "African and Latin American Cinemas: Contexts and Contacts," *in* Françoise Pfaff, *Focus on African Films,* Bloomington, Indiana University Press, 2004, pp. 241–270.

12. Barlet, *Contemporary African Cinema,* p. 109.

13. This is a 20-minute fiction film, shot in Paris—due to the Laval Decree—by the Groupe africain de cinéma (a collective set up by the Benin-born, Senegalese national Paulin Soumanou Vieyra, Senegalese Mamadou Sarr and Jacques Mélo Kane, and by Robert Caristan from French Guyana).

14. Alexie Tcheuyap, *Postnationalist African Cinemas,* New York, Manchester University Press, 2011, p. 19.

15. Giuseppe Gariazzo, *Breve storia del cinema africano,* Turin, Lindau, 2001.

16. Claire Diao, "Le 32ᵉ Festival du Film de Femmes de Créteil rend hommage à Safi Faye" [online], *Africultures,* 7 April 2010, http://www.africultures.com/php/?nav=article&no=9413.

17. Olivier Barlet, "Cinquante ans de cinéma africain en cinq décennies," *Africamania* press kit, Paris, 17 January–17 March 2008. ["un manifeste surréaliste et prophétique."]

18. For further information, see Michel Amarger, *Djibril Diop Mambéty ou l'ivresse irrépressible de l'image,* Paris, ATM-MTM, 2000; Anny Wynchank, *Djibril Diop Mambéty, ou le voyage du voyant,* Ivry-sur-Seine, Éditions A3, 2003; Julie Ledru, *Djibril Diop Mambéty: un autre cinéaste d'Afrique Noire,* film studies master's dissertation, Université de Paris 3, Paris, 1999; Sada Niang, *Djibril Diop Mambéty: un cinéaste à contre-courant,* Paris, L'Harmattan, 2002; Nar Sene, *Djibril Diop Mambéty. La caméra au bout . . . du nez,* Paris, L'Harmattan, coll. "La bibliothèque d'Africultures," 2001; or the works of Thierno Ibrahima Dia.

19. "The Algiers Charter on African Cinema, 1975," in Imruh Bakari and Mbye Cham (eds.), *African Experiences of Cinema,* London, British Film Institute, 1996, p. 26.

20. *Ibid.,* p. 25.

21. Tcheuyap, *Postnationalist African Cinemas,* p. 4.

22. *Ibid.,* p. 5.

23. *Ibid.,* p. 6.

24. Claire Andrade-Watkins, "Portuguese African Cinema: Historical and Contemporary Perspectives, 1969–1993," *in* Michel T. Martin (ed.), *Cinemas of the Black Diaspora: Diversity, Dependency and Oppositionality,* Detroit, Wayne State University Press, 1995, p. 189.

25. The UAC was a subsidiary of the French company UGC, which had taken over the SECMA (Sosiété d'Exploitation Cinématographique Africaine) and (Compagnie Africaine Cinématographique Industrielle et Commerciale). UGC had the monopoly on distribution in the Francophone African countries. See Barlet, *Contemporary African Cinema,* p. 112.

26. Férid Boughedir, "Cinémas nationaux et politiques cinématographiques en Afrique noire: Du rêve Sud-Sud à la défense de la diversité culturelle," *in* Ruelle et al. (eds.), *Afriques 50,* p. 165.

27. Barlet, *Contemporary African Cinema,* p. 113.

28. Pfaff, À l'écoute du cinéma sénégalais, p. 23. [le "cinéma statique et politique [des]

prédécesseurs" / "dire les choses autrement."]

29. Élisabeth Lequeret, *Le Cinéma africain: un continent à la recherche de son propre regard*, Paris, Cahiers du cinéma, coll. "Les petits cahiers," Scérén-CNDP, 2003, p. 64.

30. As Thierno Ibrahima Dia writes, this was a record for an African film, the previous record being held by Youssef Chahine's *Destiny*, with 619,669 entries. The significance of this for sub-Saharan Africa is all the clearer when one considers that *Yeelen* totaled 341,700 entries in France in 1987, and Sissako's previous film, *Bamako*, 207,137 (http://www.imagesfrancophones.org).

31. Best Film, Best Director, Best Editing, Best Cinematography, Best Original Screenplay, Best Sound, Best Music.

32. This statement was relayed and cited by many filmmakers and critics. See, for example, Carlos Pardo, "Du cinéma africain à son dernier 'Cri du cœur,' entretien d'Ouedraogo: 'La force de continuer,'" *Libération*, 8 April 1995. Also see Abel Kouvouama, Abdulaye Gueye, Anne Piriou, and Anne-Catherine Wagner, *Figures croisées d'intellectuels. Trajectoires, modes d'action, production*, Paris, Karthala, 2007; Boris Boubacar Diop, "Identité africaine et mondialisation," *Africultures*, no. 41, 2001.

33. *Trois Couleurs*, "Interview avec Xavier Dolan" [online], 28 September 2010, http://www.mk2.com/troiscouleurs/index.php?post/2010/09/28/Interview-Xavier-Dolan. ["J'espère simplement que je serai jugé de façon impitoyable, sans que l'âge constitue un argument contre la maladresse. J'espère que l'épithète 'jeune' devant 'réalisateur' ne confinera pas mes films à un rayon limité de premières œuvres 'courageuses.' Je veux que mon cinéma soit le moins étiqueté possible, qu'on parle de mes films comme de bons ou de mauvais films, mais jamais comme d'un 'bon film pour un réalisateur de 20 ans.'"]

34. *Living in Bondage* (Chris Obi-Rapu, produced by Kenneth Nnebue, Nigeria, 1992, 120 min.).

35. For further information on Nollywood productions—the second film industry in the world after Bollywood, according to a UNESCO study published on 5 May 2009—see the works of Pierre Barrot, and notably *Nollywood: The Video Phenomenon in Nigeria*, Bloomington, Indiana University Press, 2009. See also the chapter "Nollywood: Popular Cinema and the New Social Imaginary," *in* Manthia Diawara, *African Film: New Forms of Aesthetics and Politics*, Berlin, Prestel, 2010; and the works edited and published by Jonathan Haynes.

36. See, for example, Mathias Krings and Onookome Okome (eds.), *Global Nollywood: The Transnational Dimension of an African Video Film Industry*, Bloomington, Indiana University Press, 2013.

37. Nwachukwu Frank Ukadike, *Questioning African Cinema: Conversations with Filmmakers*,

Minneapolis, University of Minnesota Press, 2002, p. 136.

38. The film was coproduced by British Film Institute of London (BFI), Kola Case Production, Framework International (Zimbabwe), and MGI International (France), with funding from the Fonds Sud Cinéma Unesco, the Rockefeller Foundation, the Hubert Bals Fund, and the European Union. *Le Complot d'Aristote* was part of a series commissioned by the BFI for the centenary of cinema, which included works by Martin Scorsese, Stephen Frears, Bernardo Bertolucci, and Jean-Luc Godard.

39. "Le Blog de Jean-Pierre Bekolo. Le cinéma peut-il nous aider à accoucher d'un nouveau monde?," http://jeanpierrebekolo.blogspot.fr.

40. Olivier Barlet, "*Les Saignantes* de Jean-Pierre Bekolo" [online], *Africultures,* 8 August 2005, http://www.africultures.com/php/?nav=article&no=3943.

41. Tcheuyap, *Postnationalist African Cinemas,* p. 12.

42. Jude Akudinobi, "Nationalism, African Cinema, and the Frames of Scrutiny," *Research in African Literature,* no. 32, 2001, pp. 123–142, 125, cited by Tcheuyap, *Postnationalist African Cinemas.*

43. Mbye Cham, "Le Cinéma africain: continuité et rupture," *in* Ruelle et al. (eds.), *Afriques 50,* p. 181. [une "prise en compte de l'hybridité raciale et culturelle en tant que direction du futur (opposée à un nationalisme narcissique et essentialiste, racial, ethnique et culturel)."]

44. Olivier Barlet, "Nouvelles écritures francophones des cinéastes afro-européens," *Cinémas: revue d'études cinématographiques,* vol. 11, no. 1, 2000, pp. 113–132, 114. ["Un nouveau cinéma apparaît à l'orée du siècle, annoncé par des films comme *La Vie sur terre* du Mauritanien Abderrahmane Sissako (1998) ou *Bye Bye Africa* du Tchadien Mahamat Saleh Haroun (1999), emblématiques d'une nouvelle écriture capable de prendre des risques dans la forme comme dans le fond, de poser des questions sans réponses, d'explorer l'humain sans concession."]

45. The same setup—which is also found in *Chronicle of a Disappearance* (Elia Suleiman, Palestine, 1996)—is also deployed by Jean-Marie Teno, but this time in a documentary, in *Vacances au pays* (*Trip to the Country,* 2000). Jean Odoutan uses a similar approach in his fiction film *Pim Pim Tché* (2016), shot in Benin. In it, he plays his own role, namely, the organizer of the Quintessence International Film Festival in Ouidah.

46. Barlet, *Contemporary African Cinema,* p. 116.

47. Olivier Barlet, "Du cinéma métis, au cinéma nomade," *Africultures,* "Métissages: un alibi culturel?" (dossier), no. 62, 2005. ["cinéma nomade / cinéma métis."]

48. Barlet, *Contemporary African Cinema,* p. 116.

49. Teshome H. Gabriel, "Thoughts on Nomadic Aesthetics and Black Independent

Cinema: Traces of a Journey," *in* Russell Ferguson (ed.), *Out There: Marginalization and Contemporary Cultures,* Cambridge (MA), MIT Press, 1990, pp. 395–410. This article is also available online: http://www.teshomegabriel.net.

50. Quoted by Barlet, *Contemporary African Cinema,* p. 13.

51. Iain Chambers, *Migrancy, Culture, Identity,* London, Routledge, 1994, p. 2.

52. Sheila J. Petty, *Contact Zones: Memory, Origin and Discourse in Black Diasporic Cinema,* Detroit, Wayne State University Press, 2008, p. 1.

53. Serge Gruzinski, *La Pensée métisse,* Paris, Fayard, 1999. Published in English as *The Mestizo Mind,* New York, Routledge, 2002.

54. Selasi Taiye, "Bye-Bye Babar" [online], LIP Magazine, 3 March 2005, thelip.robertsharp. co.uk/?p=76.

55. Jean-Paul Sartre, *Black Orpheus,* trans. John McCombie (1951), *in Massachusetts Review,* vol. 6, no. 1, Autumn 1965, p. 49. First published as *Orphée Noir,* preface to Léopold Sédar Senghor, *Anthologie de la nouvelle poésie nègre et malgache de langue française,* Paris, PUF, 1948, p. xli.

56. Jonathan Rutherford, "The Third Space: Interview with Homi K. Bhabha," in Ders. (Hg), *Identity: Community, Culture, Difference,* London, Lawrence and Wishart, 1990, pp. 207–221, 211.

57. Petty, *Contact Zones,* p. 6.

58. Interview, Paris, August 2011. ["Ce qui est parfois difficile, quand on est cinéaste et africain—c'est la situation à laquelle je suis confrontée—, est que, quand le public vient voir un film qu'on lui a présenté comme africain, il cherche une vérité sociologique, une valeur d'exemple, il ne regarde pas le travail du cinéaste et, ça, c'est assez pénible." / "Je pense que personne ne fait du cinéma africain, les gens sont ce qu'ils sont et font les films qu'ils font, ensuite ce sont les autres derrière qui vont classer les films dans le *cinéma africain.*"]

59. David Murphy and Patrick Williams, *Postcolonial African Cinema: Ten Directors,* New York, Manchester University Press, 2007, p. 19.

60. Olivier Barlet, "L'Exception africaine," *Africultures,* "Cinéma: l'exception africaine," (dossier), no. 45, 2002, p. 5.

61. Olivier Barlet, "African Filmmakers' New Strategies" [online], *Africultures,* 30 September 2001, http://africultures.com/african-filmmakers-new-strategies-5505.

62. Balufu Bakupa-Kanyinda, "Africa's Own Mirror Leaves It Invisible," *in* Diawara, *African Film,* p. 223.

63. Hans Robert Jauss, *Pour une esthétique de la réception,* Paris, Gallimard, coll. "Tel," 1990, p. 49 ["horizon d'attente"].

64. Raphaëlle Moine, *Les Genres au cinéma,* Paris, Armand Colin, 2005 [Nathan, 2002], p. 85 ["attentes génériques"].

65. Imunga Ivanga, "Au Sud, des cinémas," *in* Ruelle et al. (eds.), *Afriques 50,* p. 175. ["Lorsque des propositions nouvelles surgissent, il n'est pas rare d'entendre: 'ce n'est pas africain!' [on peut ainsi voir] le Sud se transporter dans le Nord, ce qui ajoute à la confusion de ceux qui prônent l'authenticité . . . que penser d'un Alain Gomis qui fait *L'Afrance?* D'un Zeka Laplaine avec son *Paris XY?* . . . les définitions initiales sont vite dépassées par les envies des créateurs; leurs statuts ne peuvent être enserrés dans un carcan."]

66. Tcheuyap, *Postnationalist African Cinemas,* p. 230.

67. David Murphy, "Africans Filming Africa: Questioning Theories of an Authentic African Cinema," *in* Elizabeth Ezra and Terry Rowden (eds.), *Transnational Cinema and the Film Reader,* New York, Routledge, 2006, pp. 27–38.

68. Achille Mbembe, "Afropolitanisme" [online], *Africultures,* 26 December 2005, http://www.africultures.com/php/?nav=article&no=4248. [des "réponses nouvelles à la question de savoir 'qui est Africain' et qui ne l'est pas."]

69. Chambers, *Migrancy, Culture, Identity,* p. 74.

70. Isabelle Boni-Claverie, "L'Avenir fantôme," *in* Ruelle et al. (eds.), *Afriques 50,* p. 267. ["Mes films sont-ils africains? En tout cas, moi je le suis. Mais d'une Afrique contemporaine, cosmopolite et décomplexée, qui se souvient de ses traditions mais n'a plus besoin de s'y réfugier pour se croire une identité."]

71. Barlet, "Nouvelles écritures francophones," p. 117. ["Ils témoignent ainsi de nouvelles formes d'africanité, métissées, fluides, en évolution, exprimées par chacun avec ses propres expériences et ressentis, refusant de se laisser enfermer dans les concepts figés d'identité ou d'authenticité, récusant ainsi les discours communautaristes, culturalistes ou essentialistes idéalisant les valeurs culturelles."]

72. Achille Mbembe, "À propos des écritures africaines de soi," *Politique africaine,* no. 77, 2000, pp. 16–43. ["au-delà d'une appartenance territoriale."]

73. For more on the notion of "contact zones," see Mary Louise Pratt, Imperial Eyes: Travel Writing and Transculturation, London, Routledge, 1992; Mary Louise Pratt, "Arts of the Contact Zone," *Profession,* no. 91, 1991, pp. 33–40.

74. Tcheuyap, *Postnationalist African Cinemas,* pp. 29–30.

75. *Ibid.,* p. 18.

76. Kenneth H. Harrow, *Postcolonial African Cinema: From Political Engagement to Postmodernism,* Bloomington, Indiana University Press, 2007.

77. Tcheuyap, *Postnationalist African Cinemas,* p. 28.

78. Pierre Sorlin, *Sociologie du cinéma,* Paris, Aubier, 1977, p. 121 ["milieux du cinéma"].

79. Jean-Pierre Esquenazi, "Éléments de sociologie du film," *Cinémas*, vol. 17, no. 2–3, 2007, pp. 117–141, 141.

80. *Ibid.*, p. 117.

81. Pfaff, À l'écoute du cinéma Sénégalais, p. 10 ["la tradition du cinéaste homme-orchestre qui s'essouffle à écrire, produire et distribuer ses films"].

82. Daniela Ricci, *Imaginaires en exil. Cinq cinéastes d'Afrique se racontent* (*Creation in Exile: Five Filmmakers in Conversation*), documentary, 53 min., HD, France, 2013.

83. Lequeret, "Le Cinéma africain: un continent," pp. 9–10. ["Si les réalisateurs n'aiment pas employer le mot de censure, le fait est qu'ils sont plus dépendants que jamais du verdict de quelques lecteurs de scénarios. Ainsi a-t-on pu, çà et là, entendre parler de tel script réécrit de façon à 'étoffer le rôle des colons' ou d'incitations diverses tendant à 'alléger' un scénario politique pour le tirer vers la comédie ou à adoucir un sujet un peu sulfureux. . . . Preuve que la censure demeure. Simplement, elle est intériorisée et souvent anticipée par les cinéastes eux-mêmes: économique, et non plus politique."]

84. June Givanni (ed.), *Symbolic Narratives/African Cinema: Audiences, Theory and the Moving Image*, London, British Film Institute, 2001, p. 149.

85. *Africultures*, "Cinéma: l'exception africaine."

86. Olivier Barlet, *Les Cinémas d'Afrique noire. Le regard en question,* Paris, L'Harmattan, coll. "Images plurielles," 1996, p. 134. ["Soutenir l'expression d'une communauté minoritaire revient à en admettre l'existence, et donc un droit à la différence. Cela supposerait qu'il faille accepter une mutation de notre propre identité enrichie de l'expérience de l'Autre et de la confrontation des cultures. C'est notamment à cela que nous invite le cinéma noir."]

87. Barlet, "*Les Saignantes* de Jean-Pierre Bekolo." ["Ces commissions donnent par pitié avec des arguments qui n'ont plus rien à voir avec le cinéma."]

88. Accessed 27 November 2012.

89. It annually allocates 1.3 million euros (shared between cinema and television)—in other words, far less that the average budget of a single French feature film. This body indeed allocates to a feature film on average 100,000 € in production funding, and 15,000 € to help complete a work.

90. Production grants were a maximum of 152,000 €, and completion funds a maximum of 46,000 € per film.

91. Barlet, "Entretien avec Zeka Laplaine."

92. Interview, Paris, June 2010. ["Après avoir terminé un film, d'habitude, nous sommes financièrement ruinés."]

93. Esquenazi, "Éléments de sociologie du film," p. 129. ["la vie d'un film ne s'arrête pas à sa

production. Sa 'vraie vie' aurait-on envie de dire, celle qui en fait une œuvre filmique, commence avec son appropriation par des spectateurs."]

94. The Evolving African Film Culture Conference, 10–11 November 2012, University of Westminster, London.

95. This documentary portrays the daily workings of a neighborhood video parlor in Ouagadougou, which screens all kinds of mainly foreign films. In it, Teno analyzes the complex questions and contradictions concerning the place of cinema in Africa.

96. Olivier Barlet, "Entretien avec Mama Keita," *Africultures*, "Cinéma: l'exception africaine." ["Jusqu'à maintenant, le cinéma africain est fait par des cinéastes africains, mais pas à destination des Africains. Je ne professe pas que c'est une obligation pour un cinéaste africain de le faire 'pour son peuple': ce n'est pas comme ça que je fonctionne. Mais je note qu'à l'inverse, le cinéma était fait pour un certain public, à destination de certaines commissions, de certains festivals ou certaines sélections, et que c'était donc un cinéma réducteur."]

97. Tahar Cheriaa, Écrans d'abondance ou cinémas de libération en Afrique, *Tunis*/Tripoli, *Satpec*/El-Khayala, 1978. ["qui tient la distribution tient le cinéma."]

Chapter 4. Introduction to the Socio-Aesthetic Analysis of African Diasporic Film

1. Edward Branigan, "Quand y a-t-il caméra?," *in* Jean-Pierre Esquenazi and Bruno Pequignot (eds.), *Penser, cadrer: le projet du cadre,* Paris, L'Harmattan, coll. "Champs Visuels," no. 12–13, 1999, pp. 19–31.

2. Edward Branigan, *Point of View in Cinema: A Theory of Narration and Subjectivity in Classical Films,* New York, Mouton de Gruyter, 1984.

3. On the question of the mind, see also Jean-Pierre Esquenazi, *Le Film Noir. Histoire et significations d'un genre populaire subversif,* Paris, CNRS Éditions, 2012, p. 223.

4. Laurent Jullier, *L'Analyse des séquences,* Paris, Armand Colin, coll. "Cinéma," 2009 (3rd ed.) [Nathan/Vuef, 2001].

5. *Ibid.,* pp. 9–10, original emphasis. ["fermer les yeux sur les *consignes externes* (hors du film), pour se concentrer sur les *consignes internes* (fournies par le seul 'texte filmique')."]

6. *Ibid.,* p. 10. ["la pure analyse interne même est une chimère."]

7. *Ibid.,* p. 145. [ceci "passe à côté d'un certain nombre de richesses du film.]

8. *Ibid.*, p. 145. ["une prudente mixité interne/externe."]

9. Noël Burch and Geneviève Sellier, *La Drôle de Guerre des sexes du cinéma français: 1930–1956,* Paris, Armand Colin, 2005 [Nathan, 1996].

10. Gianni Rondolino and Mario Tomasi, *Manuale del film. Linguaggio, racconti, analisi,* Turin, Utet Università, 2007 [1995], p. 267. ["nel cinema, come in ogni produzione significante, non c'é contenuto indipendente dalla forma nella quale viene espresso."]

Chapter 5. To Each Their Own Truth: *Rage,* by Newton I. Aduaka

1. Newton I. Aduaka, *Rage,* United Kingdom, 1999, fiction, 93 min., 35 mm. Production: Granite Filmworks Ltd (Newton Aduaka and Maria Elena L'Abbate); image: Carlos Arango; editing: Marcela Cuneo.

2. *Musique Info,* 5 July 2002.

3. *Le Monde,* 6 July 2002.

4. Newton I. Aduaka, "Rage au poing," *Vibrations,* no. 42, March 2002. [Translated back into English from the published French translation of Aduaka's words.]

5. Newton I. Aduaka, *Untold,* no. 11, March–April 2000.

6. *Film Review,* February 2001. Furthermore, Aduaka was later listed as one of the fiftieth greatest living African artists at www.cinelite.fr.

7. *Rage* won several awards, including the Best First Film Award at the Ouagadougou Pan-African Film and Television Festival (FESPACO) in 2001, the Best Director and Best First Film Awards at the Los Angeles Pan-African Film Festival in 2001, the Youth Award at the Vues d'Afrique Festival in Montreal in 2001, and the Office catholique international du cinéma et l'audio-visuel (OCIC) Grand Prix at the Amiens Film Festival.

8. Newton I. Aduaka, "Rage against the Machine," *Black Filmmaker,* vol. 4, no. 12, 2001, p. 28.

9. *Ibid.*

10. *Ibid.*

11. Certain similarities can also be found between *Rage* and *La Haine,* two films that take inspiration from the real. The two filmmakers were not in contact, however, *Rage*'s screenplay having been written in London in 1994, before the release of *La Haine* in France in 1995. One can imagine, however, that both Kassovitz and Aduaka were influenced by Martin Scorsese's cinema, but also by the independent American cinema of Cassavetes or Spike Lee (for example, *Do the Right Thing*).

12. Granit Films, "Director's Notes" [online], http://www.granitfilms.com/english/rage.

13. Aduaka, "Rage against the Machine," pp. 27–28.

14. Granit Films, "Director's Notes."

15. Aduaka worked as sound engineer on a number of documentaries and notably on the fiction feature *Quartier Mozart,* by Jean-Pierre Bekolo (Cameroon, 1992). The latter won the Best Sound Award at the FESPACO.

16. Granit Films, "Director's Notes."

17. Julien David, *Télérama,* 6 to 12 July 2002.

18. To this end, he set up the production company Granite Filmworks in 1997. This first film won many major international awards, including the Best Short Film Award at the Milan African Film Festival in 1998 and at the FESPACO in 1999, giving Aduaka international recognition. It was also selected in the Forum section at Cannes in 1998.

19. After seceding from Nigeria, Biafra only existed as a country for three years, from 1967 to 1970.

20. *Ezra* won a considerable number of international awards, including the Golden Stallion Award at FESPACO 2007, the Golden Unicorn at the Durban Film Festival, the Jury Awards and the Best Director Awards at Amiens and Zanzibar, the Public Award Tarifa, the United Nations Award for Peace and Tolerance at the Granada Festival, the Special Jury Award at Milan. It was in official competition at the Sundance Film Festival, and during the International Critics' Week at Cannes.

21. *Funeral* was selected at the Directors' Fortnight at Cannes in 2002.

22. http://www.africultures.com. For further information, see www.granitfilms.com, or Granit Films's presentation page on *Africultures.com,* http://www.africultures.com/php/index.php?nav=structure&no=5752&texte_recherche=granit.

23. Granit Films, *"One Man's Show,* http://www.granitfilms.com/rage. ["Émile a 50 ans, l'âge de son pays de naissance, le Cameroun. S'il est né à l'heure de l'indépendance, il doit maintenant réussir sa propre décolonisation, intime et psychologique."]

24. Marcus refers to the Black Panthers, which takes us to another context: that of the United States at the end of the 1960s. This citation, which broadens the spatial and temporal context, is characteristic of Newton Aduaka's work, which seeks to portray human drama. The racism, oppression, and both individual and collective liberation struggles belong to different contexts and different eras. While firmly rooted in a specific milieu, *Rage* thus at the same time reflects a more general human condition.

25. Although Rage dreams of an AK-47, he does not really want to use it; it is simply the representation of the paroxysm of his anger, which he has not yet learned to channel. In the film, the only weapon seen is a pistol in Rage's hands, which his friends—not realizing it is a toy—tell him to get rid of. Appearances are often deceptive!

26. John Cassavetes, "Derrière la caméra," *Cahiers du cinéma,* no. 119, May 1961, pp. 1–7.

27. Aduaka, "Rage au poing."

28. Granit Films, "Director's Notes."

29. In this sense, it would be interesting to analyze *Rage* in the light of Paul Gilroy's study of British musical subcultures, even if that is beyond the scope of this present work.

30. The rap of the Burundi-born, French-based Franco-Rwandan rapper Gaël Faye clearly demonstrates this. For further information, see his interview with Anne Bocandé, "Afri' Festival: Belleville Citoyenne Gaël Faye rappe l'exil et le métissage. Entretien avec Gaël Faye" [online], *Africultures,* 8 June 2012, http://www.africultures.com/php/?nav=article&no=10813.

31. These include DJ Vadim, Mark B, Linton Kwesi Johnson, and Al'Tariq.

Chapter 6. Between Fiction and Experience: *Juju Factory,* by Balufu Bakupa-Kanyinda

1. Balufu Bakupa-Kanyinda, *Juju Factory,* France/Belgium/DRC, 2007, fiction, 97 min., Coproduction Akangbe Productions (France), BlackStarLine (Belgium), Canal+ Horizons (France), Dipanda Yo! (Congo). Director of photography and camera: Olivier Pulinckx; sound operator and camera: Balufu Bakupa-Kanyinda; editor: Sébastien Touta; shooting format: DV, cinema distribution format: 35 mm.

    Juju Factory won an array of international awards in 2007, including the Best Film Awards at the Innsbruck International Film Festival, Zanzibar International Film Festival, Kenya International Film Festival, Festival d'Apt, and the Festival Écrans noirs in Yaoundé. Carole Karemera (Béatrice), won the Best Actress Award at the Bari Festival del Cinema Africano in Italy.

2. After his assassination, Patrice Lumumba's body was dissolved in acid and he thus has no tomb. This was all the more terrible for the Congolese, who would have liked to pay homage to their leader in a dignified way, especially considering that in DRC, as in other African countries, specific rites must be carried out when burying the dead, who go to join the world of the ancestors. If these rituals are not respected, the deceased may come back to haunt the living.

3. His name brings to mind those of Joseph Désiré Kabila and Joseph Désiré Mobutu (the birthname of Mobutu Sese Soko). These two Congolese presidents are infamous for their despotism.

4. In the credits, the director thanks the "anonymous and occasional extras."

5. Balufu Bakupa-Kanyinda, "Africa's Own Mirror Leaves It Invisible," *in* Manthia Diawara, *African Film: New Forms of Aesthetics and Politics: Filmmakers in Conversation,* London, Prestel, 2010, pp. 217–225, 217.

6. Christine Sitchet, "La Structure narrative est à la base de tout." Interview with Balufu Bakupa-Kanyinda [online], *Africultures,* 12 May 2001, http://africultures.com/la-structure-narrative-est-a-la-base-de-tout-8951. [ne pas "soigner les corps mais les

esprits."]

7. Bakupa-Kanyinda, "Africa's Own Mirror," p. 218.

8. Africine.org, "Fiche biographique de Bakupa-Kanyinda" [online], http://www.africine.org.

9. In the documentary *Balufu Bakupa-Kanyinda. Le poète, le penseur,* by Issaka Compaoré, 2010. ["Je suis assez libre dans ma tête, parce que je ne suis pas le produit d'une [seule] école."]

10. *Ibid.* ["Balufu Bakupa-Kanyinda vient du Congo, mais je crois pouvoir dire, sans me tromper, qu'il vient un peu de partout."]

11. Olivier Barlet, "Le *conflit créatif* d'un artiste en exil. Entretien avec Balufu Bakupa-Kanyinda," *Africultures,* "Migrations intimes" (dossier), no. 68, 2006.

12. Avtar Brah, *Cartographies of Diaspora: Contesting Identities,* New York, Routledge, 1996.

13. His writings include the 1979–1981 travel journal *Les Visages de la mort au Shaba,* Lumumbashi, Centre culturel français, 1981; the play *Si tu es Afrique . . . ,* Brussels, Centre culturel d'Auderghem, 1984; *Les Routes du Sud: l'image du Noir dans le Cinéma français,* Festival d'Amiens catalog, 1986; *Not Guilty—Riot in L.A. 1992,* poems, Los Angeles, Nu-Art, 1992; "Une si longue mémoire," *Présence Africaine,* Paris, 1998; "Filming in Africa: Challenging Stereotypes," *UN Chronicle: The Magazine of the United Nations,* New York, 2003.

14. Bakupa-Kanyinda, "Africa's Own Mirror," p. 219.

15. Balufu Bakupa-Kanyinda, *Zaire 1885–1985: cent ans de regards belges,* Brussels, CEC, 1985.

16. Captain Thomas Sankara was an anti-imperialist, anticolonialist revolutionary. After becoming president in 1983, it was he who, in 1984, gave Upper Volta its current name, by combining a More word and a Bambara word: Burkina Faso, or "the Land of Upright People." He is famous for his attempt to set up a participative democracy. His policies focused on women's emancipation, and on tackling corruption, desertification, malnutrition and the spread of illnesses, and illiteracy. Famous for his integrity, Sankara was one of the rare presidents to put himself on the same level as his people. Assassinated during a coup d'état on 15 October 1987, he remains a reference for young Burkinabès, and Africans in general.

Thomas Sankara was close to the filmmakers, many of whom remember him with nostalgia. Some claim that during the two FESPACO festivals where Sankara was present, a veritable Pan-African spirit reigned. After his death, the FESPACO became more "Francophone."

17. Bakupa-Kanyinda, "Africa's Own Mirror," p. 222.

18. Balufu Bakupa-Kanyinda, *Dix mille ans de cinéma,* 13 min., 16 mm, coproduction France/DRC, between Dipanda Yo!, the production company that the filmmaker had just set

up in Kinshasa, and Myriapodus Films in Paris, a production company run by Stéphan Oriach, and which backed him on several films. In the documentary, Bakupa-Kanyinda questions, among others, Djibril Diop Mambéty, David Achkar, Moussa Sène Absa, Mambaye Coulibaly, Idrissa Ouédraogo, and Mansour Sora Wade.

19. Balufu Bakupa-Kanyinda, "Djibril Diop Mambéty: tribut cinématographique à Colobane," *in* Catherine Ruelle et al. (eds.), *Afriques 50. Singularités d'un cinéma pluriel,* Paris, L'Harmattan, coll. "Images plurielles," 2005, p. 277.

20. In *Juju Factory,* Bakupa-Kanyinda pays homage to the late Guinean filmmaker David Achkar. In a conversation with Béatrice, Bibi, the publisher's wife, cites the Guinean poet William Sassine, incorrectly attributing his words to David Achkar before immediately being corrected by Béatrice.

21. Shot on 16 mm, it was funded by Channel Four, GB and backed by the Thomas Sankara Memorial Fund, Washington. It was coproduced by Dipanda Yo! and Myriapodus. Haile Gerima also participated in the film (see http://www.africultures.com), and his wife, Shirikiana Aina, shot some of the images. The film is constructed out of archive photos and testimonies by those close to Sankara.

22. 1999, 26 min., 16 mm, coproduction France/DRC.

23. Balufu Bakupa-Kanyinda, *Le Damier, Papa National oyé!,* 40 min., 35 mm, coproduction France/DRC/Gabon. This film won several major international awards, including a Mention by the Jury at FESPACO 1997; the Agence de coopération culturelle et technique (ACCT) Francophonie Award; the Reel Black Talent Award in Toronto in 1997; the Festival de Villeurbanne Grand Prix in 1997; the Centre national de la cinématographie (CNC) Quality Award, France, 1998; the Best Screenplay Lutin and the Best Music Lutin, France, 1998; and the Best Short Film Award at the Namur International Francophone Film Festival, 1998. Balufu Bakupa-Kanyinda was elected Best Emerging Artist and obtained the National Black Programming Award in Philadelphia in 1998. Despite all these awards, the film was never released in France. It was distributed by ArtMattan Productions in the USA and by Cinénomada in Spain.

    In 1999, Balufu Bakupa-Kanyinda made two other 35 mm short films: *Article 15 bis,* 15 min.; and *Watt,* 19 min. (France/DRC).

24. "I detest the colonial borders," he said to Olivier Barlet (Olivier Barlet, "Entretien avec Balufu Bakupa-Kanyinda, Paris, avril 1997" [online], *Africultures,* 30 August 2002, http://www.africultures.com/php/index.php?nav=article&no=2475. ["J'ai horreur des frontières coloniales."]

25. Balufu Bakupa-Kanyinda, *Afr@digital,* documentary, 52 min., DRC/France 2002.

26. Olivier Barlet, "Entretien avec Balufu Bakupa-Kanyinda. Berlin, février 2000" [online],

Africultures, 30 August 2002, http://africultures.com/entretien-dolivier-barlet-avec-balufu-bakupa-kanyinda-2476. ["en créant toujours, à l'intérieur de la sphère narrative, cette tresse qui paraît être une déstructuration, mais qui devient une structuration, parce qu'elle est voulue ainsi."]

27. During a debate moderated by Catherine Ruelle at the screening of *Juju Factory,* Musée Dapper, Paris, 23 March 2012. ["J'ai travaillé dans 35 pays africains, je connais les problèmes de production dans ce continent, tous les jours je suis confronté à des complexes d'infériorité. . . . Notre rôle d'artistes est aussi de donner confiance aux jeunes, il y a énormément de créativité en Afrique, parfois elle ne ressort pas parce que les outils professionnels manquent."]

28. Olivier Barlet, *Contemporary African Cinema,* trans. Melissa Thackway, East Lansing, Michigan State University Press, 2016, p. 63.

29. Barlet, "Le *conflit créatif* d'un artiste en exil." ["Un film comme *Juju Factory* ne pouvait être financé par eux [les "maîtres" qui subventionnent]. Pourquoi? Parce qu'un film réalisé par un Africain dans un décor européen n'est éligible à aucun financement européen. On finance l'Africain pour qu'il filme la misère de chez lui, les histoires de son village, son puits d'eau, tiens!"]

30. Jean-Marie Mollo Olinga, "Nous ne sommes pas allés dans les guichets traditionnels. Entretien de Jean-Marie Mollo Olinga avec Balufu Bakupa-Kanyinda, cinéaste" [online], *Africine.org,* 30 August 2008, http://www.africine.org/?menu=art&no=8049. *Juju Factory* received funding from the Belgian nonprofit association Artspheres, and from the Région Bruxelles-Capitale.

31. This 16-minute film is a DRC/Algerian coproduction. In 2009, the second Algiers Pan-African Cultural Festival took place. The first was held forty years earlier in 1969, the year in which this short film is set.

32. It is interesting to note that in the same *L'Afrique vue par . . .* project, Mama Keita's short film, *One More Vote for Obama,* was also inspired by the American political climate at the time of the election of the first black president in the history of the United States.

33. The Tshokwe people are present in Angola and Congo.

34. A Congolese people famous for their widespread ritualistic use of masks.

35. Tervuren is a Dutch-speaking municipality next to the capital.

36. *Juju Factory* remains a fiction, from which one does not expect historical exactitude. In reality, the Congolese exhibited in Brussels died of the cold, as Dutch speakers can read on the plaque, not from the heat.

37. In the credits, we learn that it is a photo of the 1897 Universal Exhibition belonging to the museum's collection.

38. Known for her role in the Dardenne Brothers' *L'enfant* (*The Child*).

39. Olivier Barlet, "*Juju Factory:* une plongée déjantée dans le quartier congolais de Bruxelles," *Africultures,* "Migrations intimes" (dossier), no. 68, 2006, pp. 38–39, 39. ["Le film ose des incartades dans le reportage documentaire pour capter en écho les rapports des habitants avec leur quartier."]

40. Bakupa-Kanyinda, "Africa's Own Mirror," pp. 217–218.

41. Balufu Bakupa-Kanyinda, "*Juju Factory:* Director's Statement" [online], *Africiné.org* http://www.africine.org/?menu=film&no=973&rech=1.

42. Olivier Barlet, "Le Développement est une diplomatie qui n'a rien à voir avec la qualité. Entretien avec Balufu Bakupa-Kanyinda à propos de *Juju Factory*" [online], *Africultures,* 14 August 2006, http://africultures.com/le-developpement-est-une-diplomatie-qui-na-rien-a-voir-avec-la-qualite-4558. ["Une fois de plus, nous retrouvons la structure tissée et décalée du kasala : la vie de Kongo Congo et la vie autour de lui, son histoire et son imagination forment les eaux du même fleuve, qui produit son livre Juju Factory."]

43. Olivier Barlet, "Nouvelles écritures francophones des cinéastes afro-européens," *Cinémas: revue d'études cinématographiques,* vol. 11, no. 1, 2000, pp. 113–132, 124.

44. *Ibid.*, p. 32. ["Il y a dans la perception de notre écrivain un ensemble de regards construits par une multitude d'expériences et de rencontres de personnages de la vie. L'écriture de Kongo porte en effet 'son' regard sur la société qu'il côtoie, en partant de son environnement personnel."]

45. *Ibid.*, p. 36. ["Cette vie [celle de Kongo] ressemble à celle de la plupart de mes amis, écrivains, poètes, dramaturges et acteurs."]

46. The street plaques are also bilingual—for example, Avenue (*laan*) Congo/Kongo—and denote a linguistic plurality. Moreover, in a film shot mainly in French, people in the street speak a Congolese language, whereas Bibi, the publisher's wife, reads a book in English.

47. Hamid Naficy, *An Accented Cinema: Exilic and Diasporic Filmmaking,* Princeton (NJ), Princeton University Press, 2001.

48. Barlet, "Le développement est une diplomatie." ["Dans le point de vue de *Juju Factory,* l'exil belge des Congolais est une question brûlante qui torture encore la face sombre de la politique belge, qui assassina Lumumba et créa Mobutu.]

49. This documentary is part of the "Political Assassinations" collection, by Michell Noll. In this disturbing extract, Gérard Soete, a Belgian officer in Katanga in the colonial era, joyfully explains in macabre detail how he did away with Lumumba's body the day after his execution.

50. For further information, see Arthur Conan Doyle, *The Crime of the Congo,* in *Collected*

Works of Sir Arthur Conan Doyle, Cambridge, Cambridge Scholars Publishing, 2009 [1909]; or Adam Hochschild, *King Leopold's Ghost,* Boston (MA), Mariner Books, 1998.

51. In his documentary *Afrique, je te plumerai . . . ,* France/Cameroon, 1992.

52. Associated with rituals, masks are used, for example, to cure certain illnesses, to ward off death, to punish, or to bless. They are also associated with birth rituals, circumcision, the inauguration of chiefs, or funerals.

53. Moreover, this character tells the story of Karamoko, a great hunter who chased away all the lions. As he tells the story, shots of Brussels, of Kongo writing, of Béatrice at the library, of the statue of Léopold II, and of the masks at the museum are seen. The storyteller ends his tale: "Until lions have their own storytellers, all the hunting tales will glorify the hunter." This proverb is cited in various films, for example in *Keïta! L'héritage du griot (Keita! Voice of the Griot*), by Dani Kouyaté (1995). This proverb, which broadens our vision of the plurality of truths, also questions the point of view from which a story, or history, is told. On this point, also see the documentary *Le Point de vue du lion (The Lion's View*), by Didier Awadi (Senegal, 2011).

54. This recalls the documentary *Les Statues meurent aussi (Statues Also Die*) (Chris Marker and Alain Resnais, 1953), which poses this question, and which was censored in France for eight years. The two directors began with the observation that, in Paris, African art was housed in the Musée de l'Homme (Museum of Mankind), whereas Ancient Greek or Egyptian art was housed in the Louvre. They pointed not only to the lack of consideration for African art, but also and above all to the way in which the specificities of certain civilizations are destroyed by the exotic and commercial desires of another people that views these objects for what they are not.

55. Barlet, "Le *conflit créatif* d'un artiste en exil," p. 36. ["Comme Kongo Congo, je ne suis que le maillon d'une chaîne. J'appartiens à l'histoire des miens et à mon histoire individuelle. Le vécu dont il s'agit ici est celui de l'exil. L'histoire de cet exil est politique."]

Chapter 7. In-Between Places: *Notre étrangère,* by Sarah Bouyain

1. Sarah Bouyain, *Notre étrangère (The Place in Between*), Burkina Faso/France, 2010, fiction, 35 mm, 86 min. A Franco-Burkinabè coproduction: Athénaïse (Sophie Salbot) in France and Abissia Productions (Sekou Traoré) in Burkina Faso. Screenplay: Sarah Bouyain, in collaboration with Gaëlle Macé; image: Nicolas Gaurin; sound: Marianne Roussy, Cécile Chagnaud, Thierry Delor; editing: Valérie Loiseleux, Pascale Chavance; music: Sylvain Chauveau.

This production was the fruit of a long-term collaboration. Sophie Salbot had indeed already produced Sarah Bouyain's first documentary, *Les enfants du Blanc* (*The White Man's Children*), with the production company Les Films de la Plaine, producer of several of Idrissa Ouédraogo's films, including *Le Cri du cœur* (*The Heart's Cry*), on which Bouyain was assistant camerawoman. *Notre étrangère* was screened in many festivals. At the FESPACO 2011, it won the European Union Award and the Oumarou Ganda Award for Best First Film.

2. Calmel played Chouchou in Jean-Pierre Bekolo's *Les Saignantes* (*The Bloodletters*), 2004.

3. Assita in *The Promise,* by the Dardenne Brothers, 1996.

4. In the first sequence, a lone black woman in jeans (Mariam) crosses an overpass at nightfall, in silence, with no accompanying music. From the surroundings and the lights, we can tell this is a European town. Mariam is on her way to work. She cleans an empty building that the staff has already left. In the following scene in which she is still alone, she pushes her cleaning trolley down a long corridor lit by spots of light coming from the empty offices, accentuating her solitude. The camera does not follow her but remains static as she moves in and out of the frame, her head sometimes cut.

5. Napoko in *Delwendé,* by Pierre Yaméogo, 2005.

6. Claire Diao, "Entretien avec Sarah Bouyain" [online], *Afrik.com,* 1 February 2011, https://www.afrik.com/notre-etrangere-eloge-de-la-femme-et-de-l-acculturation.

7. Interview, Paris, August 2011.

8. Meanwhile, she continued working as a television camerawoman.

9. The first version dates back to 2003; the shoot took place in 2009, the film was completed in 2010, and was released in cinemas in France on 2 February 2011, distributed by Colifilms, and on DVD in October 2011 by Albares Productions (Source: Cineuropa, entretien avec Sarah Bouyain, Journées des auteurs à Venise, 2010).

10. Interview, Paris, August 2011.

11. The title was apparently *Mon dioula à moi* (*My Own Jula*). Sarah Bouyain, "Quel avenir pour mon Afrique passée. Du fantasme à la réalité, de la pensée à l'action . . . ," *Africultures,* "Penser l'Afrique: des objets de pensée aux sujets pensants," no. 82, 2010, pp. 145–151, 149.

12. *Ibid.,* p. 151. ["une langue contient aussi une vision du monde."]

13. Sarah Bouyain, *Métisse Façon,* La chambre d'échos, Paris, 2003.

14. *Les enfants du Blanc,* documentary, produced by Athénaïse (France), Stalker Films (Switzerland), Pyramide Films (Burkina Faso), 2000, 60 min. See the presentation of the film on Sarah Bouyain's website, "Les enfants du Blanc" [online], http://www.sarahbouyain.fr/sarahbouyain/Les_enfants_du_Blanc.html.

15. Interview, Paris, August 2011. ["C'était assez personnel, parce que d'une certaine façon, je

confrontais le métissage de ma grand-mère avec le mien."]

16. Olivier Barlet, "*Notre étrangère,* de Sarah Bouyain" [online], *Africultures,* 2 February 2011, http://www.africultures.com/php/?nav=article&no=9928. My emphasis. ["dans toute son œuvre tant littéraire que cinématographique, Sarah Bouyain prend *son* métissage comme sujet."]

17. The Franco-Chadian filmmaker Serge Issa Coelo, contrastingly, has shot most of his films (documentary and fiction) in Chad, focusing more on the country's domestic sociopolitical questions than identity-based issues.

18. On the platform of a Paris suburb station, Mariam does not board the train with her friend; she remains like a passive spectator watching the train of her life pass by. We see her to the left of the screen, in semi-profile, still, looking in the direction of the movement of the train as it pulls off (to the right); in the middle of the frame, the line of the platform delimits both an empty space and the gap between her and the train (her life) passing by. Cutting straight to the following scene, we see Amy in a tailor's shop in Burkina Faso.

19. This echoes the spartan hotel room where Amy ends up in the final image of this extract.

20. Barlet, "*Notre étrangère,* de Sarah Bouyain." ["C'est donc du point de vue d'Amy que [la cinéaste] se situe ici."]

21. This shot recalls *Heremakono* (*Waiting for Happiness*), by Abderrahmane Sissako (2002). Before leaving for Europe, Malian Abdallah goes to visit his mother in Mauritania. He cannot speak Hassaniya, and in his maternal town, in this *heremakono,* this fishing village tucked between the desert and the sea, he is a foreigner. (*Heremakono* is a Malian term meaning "waiting for happiness.") This is how temporary places are referred to, a stage in which people earn a little money before emigrating, a sort of pre-voyage in which one is already elsewhere. In one of the opening scenes, we see Abdallah arriving from abroad, in a collective taxi with other men, sitting in the middle, not speaking. The other passengers remain silent too.

22. Radio France International (RFI), *Cinéma d'aujourd'hui, Cinéma sans frontières,* radio program, 5 February 2011. ["À travers le voyage d'Amy j'ai voulu montrer ce que moi, je ressens à chaque fois que je viens au Burkina, où je suis désignée comme une Blanche, comme étrangère, alors que c'est un pays que je considère comme étant le mien." / "Pour moi c'était important de planter dès le début du film que mon regard était européen. Bien que je sois métisse, mon regard dans ce film est plus européen qu'africain."]

23. Luc Dardenne, *Au dos de nos images, 1991–2005,* Paris, Editions du Seuil, 2005, p. 20. ["Ne pas faire dire aux personnages ce qu'ils ne peuvent pas dire. Ils ne peuvent pas sortir de leur situation pour la dire avec des mots."] Certain shots of *Notre étrangère* have the same

tension as in the Dardenne Brothers' work. Assita Ouédraogo, (Mariam, the mother), who was also in *The Promise,* conserves the characteristics of a Dardennian character, who seeks to exist through self-will.

24. Bouyain, "Quel avenir pour mon Afrique passée," p. 150. ["Je définissais alors le sujet central comme étant la langue en tant qu'objet affectif. Une langue, lorsqu'on la parle vous rapproche intellectuellement de ceux qui la parlent, mais aussi physiquement, dans le sens où l'on met dans sa propre bouche des sonorités jusque-là étrangères et qui deviennent les vôtres."]

25. Diao, "Entretien avec Sarah Bouyain." ["Lorsque j'ai perdu mon père en 2000, j'ai eu l'impression que la seule façon de prouver que j'étais burkinabè—au-delà de ma pièce d'identité—c'était de parler cette langue."] The journalist, who is also of dual French-Burkinabè heritage, begins her article thus: "What is interraciality if not the constant quest for one's dual culture?" ["Qu'est-ce que le métissage si ce n'est la quête constante de sa double culture?"]

26. Bouyain, "Quel avenir pour mon Afrique passée," p. 145. ["Coincée dans la cour familiale à Bobo Dioulasso" / "incapable d'affronter les *toubabou,* que [lui] lançaient les enfants lorsqu'[elle] mettai[t] le nez dehors."] *Toubabou,* and other variations of it, is a term used in various Francophone West African regions to designate white people.

27. *Ibid.,* p. 151 (original emphasis).

28. *Ibid.,* p. 147. ["J'ai le sentiment que ce que j'ai essayé d'explorer dans mon travail, c'est la distance qui existe entre le Burkina réel, passé et présent, et le Burkina qui m'a été transmis à travers les récits de mon père et de ma grand-mère. (Il n'est pas étonnant alors que la plupart de mes histoires se situent à Bobo Dioulasso, ville on ne peut plus nostalgique.)"]

29. *Ibid.,* pp. 145 and 147. ["je garde de ces vacances le souvenir d'un ennui profond et d'une grande solitude, en total décalage avec les récits passionnants que mon père me faisait de son enfance."]

30. Michel Amarger, "Entretien avec Sarah Bouyain" [online], 2 February 2011, http://www.sarahbouyain.fr/sarahbouyain/entretien.html. ["J'ai le souvenir d'être assise, qu'il ne s'y passait rien, que rien ne bougeait, même si j'ai aussi beaucoup parlé avec ma grand-mère. J'en ai une sensation très statique.]

31. *Ibid.* ["Je n'avais pas conscience que c'était un film qui empruntait autant d'éléments à ma vie et à celle de ma famille.]

32. Diao, "Entretien avec Sarah Bouyain." ["Quant à Dorylia Calmel [Amy], je l'avais rencontrée à l'époque où le personnage que j'avais écrit n'était pas métis mais noir. La productrice m'a un jour fait remarquer qu'elle faisait métisse et m'a demandé si ça n'allait

pas semer le trouble. Finalement, à trois ou quatre mois du tournage, j'ai décidé que le personnage serait métis parce que cela me paraissait plus juste. La raison de ma réticence est que je ne voulais pas que ce soit trop proche de mon histoire."]

33. *Ibid.* ["Il y a eu un tournant au moment de l'écriture du film. Depuis le début, j'étais persuadée de faire un film sur l'identité et la langue. Un jour, ma productrice m'appelle et me dit: "Bon, écoute Sarah, il faut absolument réécrire ta note d'intention parce que ton film tourne surtout autour de la maternité." J'ai mis un jour ou deux à me remettre de ce choc et admettre l'évidence. Donc oui, mon film parle de maternité."]

34. *Écrans d'Afrique*, no. 11, 1st trimester 1995, p. 18. ["Je me situe à la frontière de deux continents; . . . j'ai de ce fait un regard particulier qui n'appartient ni à l'un, ni à l'autre des deux continents . . . il est certain qu'en tant que femme, je ne peux écrire autrement qu'avec ma sensibilité féminine."] Clément Tapsoba reported Sarah Bouyain's words in the "Nouveaux visages" ("New Faces") column at the time when she was an assistant director.

35. RFI, *Cinéma d'aujourd'hui, Cinéma sans frontières.* ["Quand elle est en France, son esprit est occupé par l'Afrique et quand elle est en Afrique, elle se rend compte à quel point elle est française, c'est un constant chassé-croisé mental qui s'opère dans sa tête et dans la tête de beaucoup de gens qui vivent comme ça, dans une condition de double appartenance."]

36. Like Sarah Bouyain, Claude Haffner has a complex, multiple identity. She was born to a French father (the film historian Pierre Haffner) in the Democratic Republic of Congo (then-Zaire), before moving to France at the age of five. She returned to DRC twenty years later, with the intention of making a documentary about the complex Congolese political situation. But once there, her personal history caught up with her; like Sarah Bouyain, she does not speak her mother tongue—Lingala—and she also felt an outsider in her Congolese family. During the shoot, she improvised a conversation about her identity and her belonging with her cousins, who were almost strangers to her. This scene, also shot in the yard of the family compound, became central in the documentary. It was during this exchange that Claude Haffner realized the richness of her dual culture. Beti Ellerson, "Interview with Claude Haffner: *Black Here, White There / Footprints of My Other*" [online], http://africanwomenincinema.blogspot.fr/2012/03/claude-haffner-black-here-white-there.html.

37. Like Sarah Bouyain, Isabelle Boni-Claverie also writes. For further information, see http://www.boniclaverie.com.

38. For the inspiration for the title, see http://www.sarahbouyain.fr.

39. Bouyain, "Quel avenir pour mon Afrique passée," p. 145.

40. Interview, Paris, August 2011. ["pour ne pas avoir une affiche avec le sempiternel fond rouge. Le distributeur voulait détourner l'image du film pour l'étiqueter 'cinéma africain,' au motif que si le film n'entrait pas dans une case, il n'attirerait pas les gens; ce qui est paradoxal, dans la mesure où le *cinéma africain* ne marche pas vraiment!"]

41. The inspiration for the title, http://www.sarahbouyain.fr. ["Appartenir à deux cultures. ... Naviguer entre deux familles séparées par tant de distance qu'elle soit géographique, culturelle ... séparées par l'héritage de la colonisation, parfois, on se sent contraint de choisir entre ses deux pays. Doit-on choisir entre deux parents?"]

42. Bouyain, cited by Emmanuel Sama, "*Notre étrangère* de Sarah Bouyain (France/Burkina Faso). Les déchirures du métissage" [online], *Africine.org,* 23 April 2011, http://www. africine.org/?menu=art&no=10083. ["Tout au long de ma vie je ne cesserai de naviguer et d'osciller dans l'entre-deux, je serai toujours une étrangère dans chacun des deux pays. Mais je ne le vis pas mal en définitive. La double culture est aussi une richesse, par l'inconfort qu'elle génère."]

Chapter 8. Interior/Exterior Worlds: *L'Afrance,* by Alain Gomis

1. Alain Gomis, *L'Afrance,* France/Senegal, 2001, fiction, 35 mm, 90 min., Mille et Une Productions (Anne Cécile Berthomeau and Édouard Mauriat). Image: Pierre Stoeber; first assistant: Ivan Rousseau; sound: Erwan Kerzanet; editing: Fabrice Rouaud; sound editing: Raphaël Sohier; sound mix: Fabrice Conesa Alcoléa; script: Sophie Audier; music: Patrice Gomis. Adaptation and dialogues: Alain Gomis, Pierre Schoeller, Marc Wels, Xavier Christiaens, Nathalie Stragier. With the participation of the CNC, the Fonds d'Action Sociale (FAS), and the association Théâtre et Cinéma en Île-de-France (Thécif).

2. A landmark novel written by Senegal's Cheik Hamidou Kane in the 1950s during the colonial era and published for the first time in 1961 (Julliard). It tells the story of a Senegalese Fulani, Samba Diallo, who, after having been educated by a strict master at the Quranic school, is sent to "the new school"—that is, the French school—but only after great debates in his community. He later continues his studies in France. The "ambiguity" of the adventure lies in the difficulty of finding a synthesis between the two schools: on the one hand the wisdom of Fulani culture, the ancient heritage of generations of Diallobé, and on the other, the modern, Cartesian education of the colonizers. In Paris, Samba Diallo is torn between two cultures. He decides to abide by his father's request and return to Senegal, but he gets killed by a madman for having stopped practicing his religion. In *L'Afrance,* El Hadj tells Miriam the story of *Ambiguous Adventure,* but in his version of it, Samba Diallo kills himself. Indeed, most critics have

seen a kind of suicide, a desired death, in Samba Diallo's ambiguous demise.

3. Interview, Paris, August 2010.

4. Granit Films, "Tourbillons," http://www.granitfilms.com/tourbillons. [Ousmane "sent qu'il vit les derniers instants où il est encore capable de prendre la décision de rentrer au Sénégal. Mais n'est-il pas déjà trop tard?"]

5. Interview, Paris, August 2010. ["*À* un moment, j'ai failli ne pas le faire mais à la fin, ça s'est bien passé. De toute manière, ils auraient dû me tuer pour que ce film ne se fasse pas."]

6. *Ibid.* ["J'ai appris le système des chaînes de télévision, qui ne financent pas des films comme celui-ci à cause du sujet (insuffisamment commercial) ou à cause du *cast* (trop Noir). Les *films africains* ne marchent pas, me disait-on; ce qui est vrai mais je crois que ça ne dépend pas du fait d'être Noir ou Blanc. Le problème se pose quand on sort d'une narration commerciale, homologuée et rassurante."]

7. Gomis's trusty actor Mbengue has only featured in Gomis's films for the time being. In France, he was nominated in the Best Actor of the Year category for the Michel Simon Award in 2002.

8. Samir Guesmi is a recognized actor in France, and writer and director of the short film *C'est dimanche!* (*It's Sunday,* 2007), which also focuses on the question of migration, but from a different angle. Here, through the vicissitudes of the young Ibrahim and his father, the film confronts two generations of Algerians in France.

9. Djibril Diop Mambéty, "Djibril, prince et poète du cinéma africain," *Écrans d'Afrique,* no. 24, 1998. ["Faire du cinéma n'est pas une chose difficile. Lorsque tu fermes les yeux, tu vois l'obscurité; mais si tu les fermes encore plus fort, tu commences à voir de petites étoiles. Certaines d'entre elles sont des personnes, d'autres des animaux, des chevaux, des oiseaux. Maintenant, si tu leur dis comment bouger, où aller, quand s'arrêter, quand tomber, tu as un scénario. Une fois fini, tu peux ouvrir les yeux: le film est fait."]

10. Olivier Barlet, "Petite lumière d'Alain Gomis (a review)" [online], *Africultures,* 7 March 2003, http://www.africultures.com/php/?nav=article&no=2799. [Il "franchit encore un pas dans son écriture de l'entre-deux, un pas convaincant et magnifique."]

11. Michaël Morera was the winner of the first regional French competition for screenplays on memories of immigration, *Notre histoire vraie,* organized by the nonprofit association Gindou cinéma (2004–2005). The film won the Short Film Award at the Besançon Lumières d'Afrique Festival in 2007 (http://www.africine.org).

12. Granit Films, "Andalucia," http://www.granitfilms.com/andalucia. ["Yacine est né en France. Yacine est né étranger."]

13. Axel Zeppenfeld, "Extase," *Les cahiers du cinéma,* no. 632, March 2008. ["accompagne l'extase de son héros."]

14. Granit Films, http://www.granitfilms.com. [des "thèmes liés à des questions identitaires, au sens large du terme."]

15. *Tey* was coproduced by Granit Films, Maia Cinema, Agora Film (in France), and Cinekap (in Senegal). Selected at the Berlin and Venice Film Festivals, it won a number of prestigious awards, including the Grand Prize at the Festival of African, Asian and Latin American Cinema 2012, the Public Award at the Carthage Film Festival in 2012, and the FESPACO Golden Stallion in 2013.

16. *Tey/Aujourd'hui* brochure published by the Groupement national des cinémas de recherche and by Jour 2 Fête. ["interroge l'identité et la déconstruction du récit."]

17. Saul Williams first made his reputation as an actor in the film *Slam* by Marc Levin (1998), which won the Golden Camera Award at Cannes in 1998 and the Grand Jury Prize at the Sundance Film Festival the same year. It is not by chance that Gomis chose a foreigner to play the main part in *Tey*, as the character returns to Senegal like an outsider.

18. BQHL Éditions.

19. In addition to the two films that Raoul Peck devoted entirely to him, the figure of Patrice Lumumba is often evoked. He is present in the fiction *Juju Factory*. He is also present in two of Sembène Ousmane's films: *La Noire de . . .* (*Black Girl*, 1966), in the room of one of Diouana's friends, and among the portraits in Faat Kiné's house (*Faat Kiné*, 1999).

20. Granit Films, "L'Afrance," http://www.granitfilms.com/lafrance. ["L'Afrance, c'est ce monde où l'on ne vit que sur un pied, en transit, en planifiant sans cesse le Retour."]

21. A little later in the film, we see El Hadj photocopy this photo and hear him explain as the image comes out of the machine: "Look. Lumumba, he knows it's over, that he's soon going to be executed, but do you see his expression? He knows he is right." Contrastingly, in another scene when El Hadj's Dakar memories play on the screen, it is a photo of the footballer Michel Platini, who was famous at the time of his childhood, that we see on the wall of his room in Senegal.

22. While the protagonist is in a different position, this same contrast is found with Isaach de Bankolé in Frieder Schlaich's *Otomo* (1999). The same impression of solitude in an indifferent or hostile European context (Germany, in *Otomo*) is conveyed.

23. The words read here in fact combine several passages of the book about when, after attending Quranic school, the young Samba Diallo is sent to the new French school.

24. The filmmaker's statement, Granit Films, "L'Afrance." ["un être humain pris dans les tourbillons de ses contradictions."]

25. *Ibid.* ["ce monde mental, mélange de souvenirs et d'espérances, ces bouts d'Afrique reconstitués en France. C'est ce tout et ce rien dans lequel vit El Hadj, le personnage principal, au début du film, dans lequel le temps et l'espace n'existent pas, où tout est

possible, où tout est rêvé. Où le pays natal vit dans la mémoire et dans les projets, tuant le véritable présent, et dilatant les frontières."]

26. On 28 September 1958, the French were asked by the de Gaulle government and under the presidency of René Coty to reach a verdict on the constitution of the Fifth Republic by referendum. The question of the creation of a French Community was also posed. For the African colonies, that meant agreeing to form a community with France rather than independence. Sékou Touré's Guinea voted "no" and thus gained independence on 2 October 1958.

27. Not only is El Hadj a Muslim name, but El-Hajj (other spellings include Hajji and Alhaji) is also an honorary title given to those who have completed the *Hajj* (pilgrimage) to Mecca.

28. Interview, Paris, August 2010. ["L'idée d'être étranger à son propre pays m'était très proche, à un double titre. C'est ce sentiment, cette douleur qui anime El Hadji: ce dont il a peur, c'est de devenir étranger chez lui, au Sénégal. Moi je suis étranger en France et étranger au Sénégal, ma condition de métis est celle-ci, c'est à la fois une qualité et un défaut."]

29. Clap Noir, "*L'Afrance* d'Alain Gomis" (film file) [online], *Clap Noir*, 2006, http://www.clapnoir.org/spip.php?article106. ["J'ai grandi en entendant mon père planifier notre retour *pour bientôt*. J'ai vu des cousins venir faire leurs études *pour cinq ans*. Et, bien qu'étant né ici d'une mère française, je sais le mal que j'ai à affirmer: *Ici, c'est chez moi*. El Hadj, le personnage principal du film, rejoint alors nos préoccupations. Celles de mon père qui ne dit plus qu'un jour il rentrera, mais qui se demande où il sera enterré. Les miennes, en devant affronter un espace-temps, sans fuir en se reposant sur un ailleurs. Et sans doute, celles de tous."]

30. Interview, Paris, August 2010. ["Dans ce film, je me souviens d'une femme qui disait que dans sa famille, ils ne réparaient rien, par exemple, quand un robinet se cassait . . . parce qu'ils savaient qu'ils allaient rentrer."]

31. This recalls the opening of *La Vie sur terre* (*Life on Earth*, Abderrahmane Sissako, 1999). At the very start of his film, Abderrahmane Sissako portrays the protagonist (played by him) returning to Mali, his birth country, where he feels an outsider. He receives a letter from his father. It is full of excerpts from Aimé Césaire's *Notebook of a Return to the Native Land*. In *Teza*, as shall be seen later, a radio also occupies an important place in Anberber's life on his return to his village in Ethiopia after a long absence. In *Teza*, he does not listen to recorded cassettes, however, but to the news of Ethiopia and the rest of the world (or especially of the socialist countries) on a radio that Anberber holds tightly to his ear during his long moments of solitude and isolation in the village. In

Moolaadé (Sembène Ousmane, 2004), the radios, which symbolize the subversive values of modernity according to the male leaders of the village, are burned on a big bonfire. Finally on the role of radio, the short comedy *La Radio* (Armand Brice Tchikamen and Fidèle Koffi, Ivory Coast, 2012, 15 min.) also comes to mind, in which an elderly man tries to get his radio fixed because it only broadcasts bad news.

32. Interview, Paris, August 2010. ["Si j'avais pu mettre la caméra dans son corps, je l'aurais fait, j'avais vraiment envie d'entrer dedans. Je voulais qu'on soit lui, qu'on passe par son esprit et son corps, il y a des réactions qui passent aussi par la peau."]

33. Interview, Paris, August 2010.

34. Granit Films, "L'Afrance." ["Celle des étrangers, celle qui se trouve dans les centres de rétentions, comme à Paris, sous les pieds des milliers de touristes qui visitent tous les jours le Quartier latin.]

35. *Ibid.* ["Il me semblait important que la fiction aborde des lieux et des populations si peu représentés dans le pays dans lequel je suis né, ma volonté profonde était de faire un film sur l'Homme."]

36. Interview, Paris, August 2010. ["Un de mes proches a eu des problèmes de papiers. J'avais été le voir au centre de rétention. C'était une expérience très forte: moi, je suis de nationalité française, lui non. Du coup, bien que comme moi, il n'ait jamais commis un crime, il était en prison. Cela a à voir avec l'exclusion. Je suis métis et tu te demandes sans cesse à qui tu rassembles, à quoi tu appartiens."]

37. Granit Films, "L'Afrance" (synopsis). ["le souvenir de l'homme qu'il était, l'image de l'homme qu'il espérait incarner, et le constat de l'homme qu'il se sent devenir."]

38. *Ibid.* ["Je ne voulais pas faire un film sur un Noir au pays des Blancs, mais justement sur quelqu'un qui puisse aussi dire: 'J'en ai marre d'être Black, je suis Sénégalais.'"]

39. *Ibid.*

40. It is also interesting to point out that Gomis wrote *L'Afrance* when he was a student, like his protagonist.

Chapter 9. Worlds in Construction and the Intellectual's Return: *Teza*, by Haile Gerima

1. Haile Gerima, *Teza,* Ethiopia/Germany/France, 2008, 140 min. Production: Negodgwad Production (Haile Gerima), Pandora Film Produktion (Karl Baumgartner), in coproduction with Unlimited, Westdeutscher Rundfunk; coproducers: Marie-Michèle Cattelain, Philippe Avril; associate producers: Joachim von Mengershausen, Salome Gerima. Ethiopian production: Pedro Pimenta, Yemane Demissie (also first assistant);

German production: Johannes Rexin, Sasha Verhey. Image: Mario Masini; sound: Umbe Adan, Stephan Konken; editing: Haile Gerima, Loren Hankin; sound editing: Martin Langenbach; music: Vijay Iyer and Jorga Mesfin. Format: S-16mm and HD (blown up into 35 mm). Funded by Filminstung NRW/WDR ARTE, Filmförderung, Hamburg-Schleswig-Holstein, Hubert Bals Fund, Fonds Sud Cinéma, French Ministry of Culture and Communication, CNC, French Ministry of Foreign Affairs, Fonds Images Afrique, European Union (European Development Fund), Communauté urbaine de Strasbourg, Région Alsace. For a further study of this film, a rich bibliography is available in the journal *Black Camera,* vol. 4, no. 2, 2013, pp. 144–162, an edition in part devoted to *Teza.*

2. In Greek mythology, Cassandra is gifted with being able to see the future, but no one heeds the terrible misfortunes that she predicts.

3. Teodross, Tesfaye and Gaby's son, will find his way of fighting racism through poetry, just as the biracial youth Rage does with rap in Newton Aduaka's film. Like Rage, he feels misunderstood by his white mother and finds solace in Anberber, who, returning to Germany ten years later, reconnects with the now teenage youth. Teodross will remain fatherless without realizing so, however, as Anberber does not find the courage to announce Tesfaye's violent death to the family.

4. *The Journal of the University Film and Video Association,* Spring 1983, p. 60, *in* Françoise Pfaff, *Twenty-five Black African Filmmakers: A Critical Study,* Westport (CT), Greenwood Press, 1988, p. 137. That was how Hassouna Mansouri also described him in "Haile Gerima: Cinema of Disillusion: Interview with Haile Gerima" [online], *Africine.org,* http://www.africine.org/?menu=art&no=8492. For Haile Gerima's bio-filmography, see Françoise Pfaff's above-cited *Twenty-five Black African Filmmakers* and her more recent *Focus on African Films,* Bloomington, Indiana University Press, 2004. Both were published before the release of *Teza.*

5. Interview, Washington, April 2011.

6. See Françoise Pfaff, *Twenty-Five Black African Filmmakers,* p. 138.

7. Larry Rohter, "For Filmmaker, Ethiopia's Struggle Is His Own," *New York Times,* 29 March 2010.

8. Pfaff, *Twenty-five Black African Filmmakers,* p. 139.

9. Nwachukwu Frank Ukadike, *Questioning African Cinema: Conversations with Filmmakers,* Minneapolis, University of Minnesota Press, 2002, p. 256.

10. *Le Monde,* 7 July 1984, cited by Pfaff, *Twenty-five Black African Filmmakers,* p. 146.

11. Françoise Pfaff, "From Africa to the Americas: Interviews with Haile Gerima (1976–2001)," *in* Pfaff (ed.), *Focus on African Films,* p. 206.

12. Daniela Ricci, *Imaginaires en exil. Cinq cinéastes d'Afrique se racontent (Creation in Exile:*

Five Filmmakers in Conversation), documentary, 53 min., HD, France, 2013.

13. During this period, his film culture was enriched by the works of Vittorio De Sica, Luis Buñuel, Fernando Solanas, Humberto Solas, Tomás Gutierrez Alea, and Jorge Sanjines (Pfaff, *Twenty-five Black African Filmmakers,* p. 140).

14. Ricci, *Imaginaires en exil.*

15. Yann Lardeau, "Cinémas des racines, histoires du ghetto," *Cahiers du cinéma,* no. 340, October 1982. ["Quand une partie des cinéastes américains s'attachent à renouer le passé, à chercher les racines d'un continent, d'une terre, d'une culture, d'une langue, dont ils ont été arrachés et qui tient place pour eux du mythe fondateur, Haile Gerima regarde l'empire avec ses yeux d'Africain. C'est pourquoi, si on a tendance à le placer en tête de file du *Roots Mouvement,* il semble à l'opposé, mû par le mouvement inverse de porter la lutte culturelle du Tiers-Monde, comme les deux faces d'un même territoire culturel. La culture africaine est restée en Amérique, il y a un continent noir qui se prolonge en Amérique, comme il y a une Europe anglo-saxonne qui s'y continue. Il y a un colonialisme intérieur à l'Amérique, comme il y a un assujettissement du Tiers-Monde aux valeurs sociales et à la puissance économique de l'impérialisme occidental. . . . Le cinéma intégré à une culture africaine-américaine ne peut pas se contenter seulement d'un changement des contenus. . . . Le langage cinématographique lui-même, le montage, le rapport du son et de l'image doivent être repensés et remodelés au contact de la culture africaine-américaine."]

16. *Ibid.* [une "lutte inhérente à un mouvement de libération culturelle."]

17. Pfaff, *Twenty-five Black African Filmmakers,* p. 140.

18. It is on these words, taken from the letters of George Jackson, that the film ends. Jackson was one of the leaders of the Black Panther Party.

19. Greg Thomas, "Close-up: Dragons! George Jackson in the Cinema with Haile Gerima— from Watts Films to *Teza," Black Camera: An International Film Journal,* vol. 4, no. 2, 2013, pp. 55–83, 62.

20. In fact, the DVD of *Bush Mama* also contains *Child of Resistance* and *Hour Glass* in the bonuses, without this being mentioned on the cover. The DVD is produced by Gerima's company, Mypheduh Films.

21. Lardeau, "Cinémas des racines, histoires du ghetto." ["un repère dans le cinéma noir américain."]

22. Ricci, *Imaginaires en exil.*

23. *Harvest: 3000 Years* was shot on 16 mm, in two weeks, with a budget of 2,000 dollars. The editing took a whole year, however, and the film was released in 1976. It was then blown up into 35 mm for theatrical release in Ethiopia.

24. Rohter, "For Filmmaker, Ethiopia's Struggle Is His Own."

25. *Ibid.*

26. Greg Thomas, "On *Teza,* Cinema, and American Empire: An Interview with Haile Gerima," *Black Camera,* vol. 4, no. 2, 2013, p. 88.

27. To make the film, Gerima set up Positive Production, a nonprofit collective aiming to distribute independent films. He later set up a production and distribution company, Mypheduh, in order to safeguard his intellectual freedom. It is interesting to note that *Mypheduh* means "sacred shield" in Geez, one of Ethiopia's languages. Mypheduh also distributes the films of other African American filmmakers.

28. The film's budget was 100,000 dollars. The images were credited to Augustin A. Cubano, Elliot Davis, and Charles Burnett.

29. The image is credited to Augustino Cubano. In Pan-African spirit, *Sankofa* was coproduced by Ghana, Burkina Faso, the USA, and Germany. It was a collective work, in which members of the African American community participated. The American poster of *Teza* deliberately states, "A film by Haile Gerima and the Makers of *Sankofa.*" For more on *Sankofa,* see Sheila J. Petty, "Africa and the Middle Passage: Recoupment of Origin in *Sankofa,*" in *Contact Zones: Memory, Origin and Discourse in Black Diasporic Cinema,* Detroit, Wayne State University Press, 2008. Also see Mark A. Reid, "Black Independent Film: Haile Gerima's *Sankofa,*" *in* Mark A. Reid (ed.), *Black Lenses, Black Voices: African American Film Now,* Lanham (MD), Rowman & Littlefield Publishers, 2005.

30. The DVD of *Sankofa* continues to be sold around the world. At the time of writing, no French version of the film was available.

31. Savrina Chinien, "Le cinematografies della diaspora africana: un'arte impegnata?," *in* Vanessa Lanari, Fabrizio Colombo, and Stefano Gaiga (eds.), *Camera Africa. Classici, noir, nollywood e la nuova generazione del cinema delle Afriche,* Verona, Cierre Edizioni, Sequenze, 2011, p. 61. ["metonimia per designare secoli di orrori . . . un modo di rivedere la storia raccontata esclusivamente attraverso il patrimonio degli stereotipi coloniali."]

32. Olivier Barlet, "*Amistad* de Steven Spielberg. Toujours la vieille rengaine!" [online], *Africultures,* 1 March 1998, http://www.africultures.com/php/?nav=article&no=320. ["Le Noir ne parle ainsi que par une traduction simultanée orchestrée par la générosité du Blanc. À la fin du film, une scène lacrymogène fait dire au Noir *thank you* et le Blanc réussit à sortir aussi une expression africaine."]

33. Pfaff, *Focus on African Films,* p. 210.

34. Ricci, *Imaginaires en exil.*

35. The subject of *Teza* had inhabited Gerima for over ten years but came back to him during a trip to Ethiopia for the funeral of his sister, to whom the film is dedicated.

36. These include the Jury Award and the UNICEF Award at the Mostra del Cinema in Venice, 2008; the Golden Stallion Award at the FESPACO 2009; and five awards at the Carthage Film Festival (JCC) in 2008 (Best Film, Best Screenplay, Best Image, Best Supporting Actor, Best Music).

37. Hassouna Mansouri, *L'Image confisquée: le cinéma du Sud, ce cinéma (de) subalterne,* Depuis le Sud, Amsterdam, 2010, p. 119.

38. The film remained in Ethiopian cinemas for approximately a year. In France, the film was not a success, due to poor promotion. The distributor (Atlantis), which had already poorly handled the distribution of *Ezra* and *Il va pleuvoir sur Conakry,* is untraceable today.

39. Casting Aron Arete (Anberber) came about after meeting in a restaurant in Los Angeles: "I was in a bar with his father, Aron entered, I looked at him, I looked at him, and I looked at him. He was a bit too young, but I nonetheless saw him again and he became Anberber," Gerima recounts. An English-speaker, Arete learned Amharic for the shoot. Takelech Beyene (Tadfe, Anberber's mother) had never acted either. She went to an orphanage school run by Italian missionaries with the director's mother. Gerima recounts: "It was hard persuading her to be in the film, but she was incredible." It was also Abeye Tedla's first time on the screen (Tesfaye), which did not stop him from winning the Best Supporting Actor Award at the Carthage Film Festival in 2008. (Source: Carthage Film Festival, 2008, press conference).

40. All quotes are taken from the film's English subtitles.

41. A kind of crêpe that is a staple of Ethiopian cuisine.

42. Gilles Deleuze, *The Time-Image,* trans. Hugh Tomlinson and Robert Galeta, Minneapolis, University of Minnesota Press, 1989.

43. The film is dedicated to Gerima's mother and sister, but also "To all the Black people who have been beaten and killed just for being Black, and to countless young Ethiopians, who were killed for daring to bring sincere change in Ethiopia."

44. Deleuze, *The Time-Image,* p. 48.

45. *Ibid.,* p. 54.

46. *Ibid.,* p. 55.

47. *Ibid.,* p. 50.

48. *Ibid.,* p. 50.

49. *Ibid.,* p. 50.

50. *Ibid.,* p. 50.

51. Olivier Barlet, "*Teza* de Haïlé Gerima" [online], *Africultures,* 26 February 2009, http://www.africultures.com/php/index.php?nav=article&no=8417. ["Un puzzle rythmé de

chants, d'orage, de feu, d'enluminures traditionnelles, de voiles, de souvenirs d'enfance, d'accident, le tout entremêlé par une caméra mouvante et une puissante musique. Tout le film est déjà là mais nous ne le savons pas: l'ancrage culturel, l'enfance, la mémoire, le traumatisme, l'exorcisme."]

52. Deleuze, *The Image-Time,* p. 99.
53. *Ibid.*, p. 99.
54. *Ibid.*, p. 99.
55. *Ibid.*, p. 68.
56. *Ibid.*, p. 80.
57. *Ibid.*, p. 78.
58. *Ibid.*, p. 23.
59. Mansouri, "Haile Gerima, ou le cinéma de la désillusion," *L'image confisquée,* p. 115. [Translated back to English from the French translation/publication of Gerima's original words.]
60. Deleuze, *The Time-Image,* p. 12.
61. Mansouri, "Haile Gerima," p. 115.
62. Deleuze, *The Time-Image,* p. 3.
63. *Ibid.*, p. 70.
64. Thomas, "On *Teza,* Cinema, and American Empire," p. 99.
65. Metta Sáma and Greg Thomas, "Close-up Gallery: *Teza,*" *Black Camera: An International Film Journal,* vol. 4, 2013, pp. 106–133, 111.
66. Mansouri, "Haile Gerima," p. 121.
67. Italian press kit (Editions Ripley). ["I due piani, quello personale e quello generale, si intrecciavano naturalmente sin dall'inizio, senza dover fare alcuno sforzo."]
68. Ricci, *Imaginaires en exil.*

In Guise of a Conclusion

1. Gabriel Rosenthal, *Cinematografías de Africa. Un encuentro con sus protagonistas,* documentary, 59 min., Spain, Casa Africa, 2010.
2. Gilles Deleuze, *The Time-Image,* trans. Hugh Tomlinson and Robert Galeta, Minneapolis, University of Minnesota Press, 1989, p. 69.
3. Maria Silvia Bazzoli, "Spaesementi della storia. Odisee per un puzzle del cinema arabo-mediorientale," *in* Mohamed Challouf, Giuseppe Gariazzo, and Alessandra Speciale (eds.), *Un posto sulla terra. Cinema per (r)esistere,* Milan, Editrice Il Castoro, 2002, p. 33.
4. Gilles Deleuze and Félix Guattari, *L'Anti-Œdipe. Capitalisme et schizophrénie 1,* Paris, Les

Éditions de Minuit, 1972.

5. Mahamat Saleh Haroun, 2006.

6. To further this analysis, see Greg Thomas, "Close-up: Dragons! George Jackson in the Cinema with Haile Gerima—from Watts Films to *Teza*," *Black Camera: An International Film Journal,* vol. 4, no. 2, 2013, pp. 55–83 (and in particular pp. 70 and 78).

7. Iain Chambers, *Migrancy, Culture, Identity,* London, Routledge, 1994, p. 102.

8. Hamid Naficy, *An Accented Cinema: Exilic and Diasporic Filmmaking,* Princeton (NJ), Princeton University Press, 2001.

9. Hassouna Mansouri, "Haile Gerima, ou le cinéma de la désillusion," *L'image confisquée: le cinéma du Sud, ce cinéma (de) subalterne,* Amsterdam, Depuis le Sud, 2010, pp. 113–114.

10. Gilles Deleuze and Félix Guattari, "What Is a Minor Literature?," trans. Robert Brinkley, *Mississippi Review,* vol. 11, no. 3, Winter/Spring 1983, p. 16.

11. Naficy, *An Accented Cinema,* p. 26.

12. Deleuze and Guattari, "What Is a Minor Literature?," p. 16.

13. Deleuze, *The Time-Image,* p. 218.

14. *Ibid.,* p. 222.

15. *Ibid.,* p. 220.

16. *Ibid.,* p. 220.

17. Alexie Tcheuyap, *Postnationalist African Cinemas,* New York, Manchester University Press, 2011, p. 12.

18. Edouard Glissant, *Caribbean Discourse,* trans. J. Michael Dash, Charlottesville, Caraf Books, University Press of Virginia, 1989, p. 236. The original French cited by Olivier Barlet, "Nouvelles écritures francophones des cinéastes afro-européens," *Cinémas: revue d'études cinématographiques,* vol. 11, no. 1, 2000, pp. 113–132, 119.

Bibliography

Film Analysis

ALTMAN Rick (ed.). *Sound Theory, Sound Practice*. London, Routledge, 1992.

AUMONT Jacques, BERGALA Alain, MARIE Michel, VERNET Marc. *Esthétique du film*. Paris, Nathan, 1983.

AUMONT Jacques, MARIE Michel. *L'Analyse des films*. Paris, Armand Colin, coll. "Cinéma," 2008 [Nathan, 1998].

BELLOUR Raymond. *L'Analyse du film*. Paris, Éditions Albatros, 1979.

BOURGET Jean-Louis. *Hollywood, la norme et la marge*. Paris, Nathan, 1998.

BURCH Noël, SELLIER Geneviève. *La Drôle de Guerre des sexes du cinéma français: 1930–1956*. Paris, Armand Colin, 2005 [Nathan, 1996].

ESQUENAZI Jean-Pierre, PEQUIGNOT Bruno (eds.). *Penser, cadrer: le projet du cadre*. Paris, L'Harmattan, coll. "Champs Visuels," no. 12–13, 1999.

JULLIER Laurent. *L'Analyse des séquences*. Paris, Armand Colin, coll. "Cinéma," 2009 (3rd ed.) [Nathan/Vuef, 2001].

JULLIER Laurent. *L'Écran post-moderne, un cinéma de l'allusion et du feu d'artifice*. Paris, L'Harmattan, 1997.

RONDOLINO Gianni, TOMASI Mario. *Manuale del film. Linguaggio, racconti, analisi*. Turin, Utet Università, 2007 [1995].

Discourse Analysis

ADAM Jean-Michel. *Le Récit.* Paris, PUF, coll. "Que sais-je?," 1999 [1984].

BARTHES Roland, BOOTH Wayne C., HAMON Philippe, KAYSER William. *Poétique du récit.* Paris, Seuil, 1977.

DELEUZE Gilles, GUATTARI Félix. *Kafka. Pour une littérature mineure.* Paris, Les Éditions de Minuit, 1975 ("What Is a Minor Literature?," trans. Robert Brinkley, *Mississippi Review,* vol. 11, no. 3, Winter/Spring 1983, pp. 13–33.

FUCHS Catherine. *La Paraphrase.* Paris, PUF, 1982.

GENETTE Gérard. *Fiction et diction.* Paris, Seuil, 1991.

HAMBURGER Kate. *Logiques des genres littéraires.* Paris, Seuil, 1986.

PAVEL Thomas. *Univers de la fiction.* Paris, Seuil, 1988.

RICŒUR Paul. *Du texte à l'action. Essais d'herméneutique II.* Paris, Seuil, 1986.

———. *Temps et récit.* Paris, Seuil, 1982 (vol. 1), 1984 (vol. 2), 1985 (vol. 3).

SCHAEFFER Jean-Marie. *Pourquoi la fiction?* Paris, Seuil, 1999.

Cinema and Film Sociology

BARNIER Martin, MOINE Raphaëlle (eds.). *France/Hollywood. Échanges cinématographiques et identités.* Paris, L'Harmattan, coll. "Champs Visuels," 2002.

BAZIN André. *Qu'est ce que c'est le cinéma?* Paris, Éditions du Cerf, 1975.

BRANIGAN Edward. *Point of View in Cinema: A Theory of Narration and Subjectivity in Classical Films.* New York, Mouton de Gruyter, 1984.

CASETTI Francesco. *Dentro lo sguardo. Il film e il suo spettatore.* Milan, Bompiani, 1986.

CHALLOUF Mohamed, GARIAZZO Giuseppe, SPECIALE Alessandra (eds.). *Un posto sulla terra. Cinema per (r)esistere.* Milan, Editrice Il Castoro, 2002.

DELEUZE Gilles. *L'Image-temps.* Paris, Les Éditions de Minuit, 1985 (*The Time-Image,* trans. Hugh Tomlinson and Robert Galeta, Minneapolis, University of Minnesota Press, 1989).

ESQUENAZI Jean-Pierre. *Godard et la société française des années 1960.* Paris, Armand Colin, 2004.

———. *Hitchcock et l'aventure de Vertigo. L'invention à Hollywood.* Paris, CNRS Éditions, 2001.

———. *La Vérité de la fiction. Comment peut-on croire que les récits de fiction nous parlent sérieusement de la réalité?* Paris, Lavoisier, 2009.

———. *Le Film Noir. Histoire et significations d'un genre populaire subversif.* Paris, CNRS Éditions, 2012.

ESQUENAZI Jean-Pierre (ed.). *Cinéma contemporain, état des lieux.* Paris, L'Harmattan, 2002.

GLEDHILL Christine, WILLIAMS Linda (eds.). *Reinventing Film Studies.* London, Arnold 2000.

HJORTH Melte, PETRIE Duncan (eds.). *The Cinema of Small Nations*. Bloomington, Indiana University Press, 2007.

JOST François. *L'Œil-caméra. Entre film et roman*. Lyon, PUL, 1987.

MOINE Raphaëlle. *Les Genres au cinéma*. Paris, Armand Colin, 2005 [Nathan, 2002].

ODIN Roger. *De la fiction*. Brussels, De Boeck Université, 2000.

ROBERTSON Patrick. *I record del cinema. Enciclopedia dei fatti, delle curiosità e dei primati del cinema mondiale, dall'epoca del muto ad oggi*. Rome, Gremese, 2004.

SORLIN Pierre. *Sociologie du cinéma*. Paris, Aubier, 1977.

———. "Quelqu'un à qui parler." *In* Jean-Pierre Esquenazi (ed.), *Politique des auteurs et théories de cinéma*, p. 162. Paris, L'Harmattan, coll. "Champs Visuels," 2003.

Sociology of Works and Audiences

BAXANDALL Michael. *Formes de l'intention*. Nîmes, Éditions Jacqueline Chambon, 1991.

BECKER Howard S. *Les Mondes de l'art*. Paris, Flammarion, 1987.

BENGOZHI Jean-Pierre. *Le Cinéma entre l'art et l'argent*. Paris, L'Harmattan, coll. "Logiques sociales," 1989.

ESQUENAZI Jean-Pierre. *Sociologie des publics*. Paris, La Découverte, 2003.

———. *Sociologies des œuvres. De la production à l'interprétation*. Paris, Armand Colin, 2007.

JAUSS Hans Robert. *Pour une esthétique de la réception*. Paris, Gallimard, coll. "Tel," 1990.

RANCIER Jacques. *Le Spectateur émancipé*. Paris, La Fabrique Éditions, 2008.

African Cinema, Colonial Cinema

AA. VV. *Caméra Nigra. Le discours du film africain*. Brussels/Paris, Cesca/OCIC/L'Harmattan, 1983.

AA. VV. *Cinémas africains d'aujourd'hui. Guide des cinématographies d'Afrique*. Paris, Karthala/RFI, 2007.

AA. VV. "Cinémas d'Afrique." *Notre Librairie. Revue de littérature du Sud*, no. 149. Paris, L'Harmattan, 2002.

AA. VV. *Dictionnaire du cinéma africain*. Vol. 1. Paris, L'Association des Trois Mondes/Karthala, 1991.

AA. VV. Fepaci. *L'Afrique et le centenaire du cinéma*. Paris, Présence Africaine, 1995.

AA. VV. *Le Cinéma d'Afrique*. Paris, L'Association de Trois Mondes/Fespaco/Karthala, 2000.

ARGENTIERI Mino. *L'occhio del regime. Informazione e propaganda nel cinema del fascismo*. Florence, Vallecchi, 1979.

ARMES Roy. *African Filmmaking: North and South of the Sahara.* Bloomington, Indiana
  University Press, 2006.

———. *Dictionnaire des cinéastes africains des long-métrages.* Paris, Karthala, 2008.

BACHY Victor. *Pour une histoire du cinéma africain.* Brussels, OCIC, 1987.

BAKARI Imruh, CHAM Mbye (eds.). *African Experiences of Cinema.* London, British Film
  Institute, 1996.

BARLET Olivier. *Les Cinémas d'Afrique des années 2000, Perspectives critiques.* Paris,
  L'Harmattan, coll. "Images plurielles," 2012 (*Contemporary African Cinema,* trans. Melissa
  Thackway, East Lansing, Michigan State University Press, 2016).

———. *Les Cinémas d'Afrique noire. Le regard en question.* Paris, L'Harmattan, coll. "Images
  plurielles," 1996.

BARROT Pierre. *Nollywood. Le phénomène vidéo au Nigeria.* Paris, L'Harmattan, coll. "Images
  plurielles," 2005.

———. *Nollywood: The Video Phenomenon in Nigeria.* Bloomington, Indiana University Press,
  2009.

BEKOLO Jean-Pierre Obama. *Africa for the Future. Sortir un nouveau monde du cinéma.*
  Yaoundé, Dagan, 2009.

BENALI Abdelkader. *Le Cinéma colonial au Maghreb. L'imaginaire en trompe-l'œil.* Preface by
  Benjamin Stora. Paris, Éditions du Cerf, coll. "7Art," 1998.

BOUGHEDIR Férid. *Le Cinéma africain de A à Z.* Brussels, OCIC, 1987.

BRAHIMI Denise. *Cinémas d'Afrique francophone et du Maghreb.* Paris, Nathan, 1997.

BRUNETTA Gian Piero, GILI Jean A. *L'ora d'Africa del cinema italiano 1911–1989.* Rovereto,
  Materiali di lavoro—Rivista di studi storici, 1990.

CARRIERI Giuseppe. *Le voci del silenzio. Scene dal cinema dei cantastorie africani.* Milan, Bietti
  Heterotopia, 2011.

CHERIAA Tahar. Écrans d'abondance ou cinémas de libération en Afrique. *Tunis*/Tripoli,
  Satpec/El-Khayala, 1978.

COLETTI Maria, DE FRANCESCHI Leonardo. *Souleymane Cissé con gli occhi dell'eternità.* Turin,
  Kaplan, 2010.

CONVENTS Guido. *Afrique? Quel cinéma! Un siècle de propagande coloniale et de cinéma
  africain.* Antwerp, Éditions EPO, 2003.

———. *Images et démocratie. Les Congolais face au cinéma et à l'audiovisuel.* Leuven, Afrika
  Film Festival, Leuven, 2005.

———. *Images et paix: les Rwandais et les Burundais face au cinéma et à l'audiovisuel.* Leuven,
  Afrika Film Festival, Leuven, 2008.

DIAWARA Manthia. *African Cinema: Politics and Culture.* Bloomington, Indiana University

Press, 1992.

———. *African Film: New Forms of Aesthetics and Politics.* London, Prestel, 2010.

ELLERSON Beti. *Sisters of the Screen: Women of Africa on Film, Video and Television.* Trenton (NJ), Africa World Press, 2000.

FRINDETHIE K. Martial. *Francophone African Cinema: History, Culture, Politics and Theory.* Jefferson (NC), McFarland, 2009.

FUHRMANN Wolfgang. *Imperial Projections: Screening the German Colonies.* New York, Berghahn Books, 2015.

GARDIES André. *Cinémas d'Afrique noire francophone. L'espace miroir.* Paris, L'Harmattan, 1989.

GARDIES André, HAFFNER Pierre. *Regard sur le cinéma négro-africain.* Brussels, OCIC, 1987.

GARIAZZO Giuseppe. *Breve storia del cinema africano.* Turin, Lindau, 2001.

———. *Poetiche del cinema africano.* Turin, Lindau, 1998.

GIVANNI June (ed.). *Symbolic Narratives/African Cinema: Audiences, Theory and the Moving Image.* London, British Film Institute, 2001.

GOERG Odile. *Fantômas sous les tropiques. Aller au cinéma en Afrique coloniale.* Paris, Vendémiaire, coll. "Empires," 2015.

GUGLER Josef. *African Film: Reimagining a Continent.* Bloomington, Indiana University Press, 2003.

HAYNES Jonathan (ed.). *Nigerian Video Films.* Athens (OH), Ohio University Center for International Studies, 2000.

HAFFNER Pierre. *Essai sur les fondements du cinéma africain.* Abidjan, Les Nouvelles Éditions Africaines, 1978.

HARROW Kenneth W. *Postcolonial African Cinema: From Political Engagement to Postmodernism.* Bloomington, Indiana University Press, 2007.

———. *Trash! African Cinema from Below.* Bloomington, Indiana University Press, 2013.

HENNEBELLE Guy, RUELLE Catherine. *Cinéastes d'Afrique noire.* Paris, Corlet, coll. "CinémAction," no. 3, 1978.

KANE Momar Désiré. *Marginalité et errance dans la littérature et le cinéma africains francophones.* Paris, L'Harmattan, coll. "Images plurielles," 2004.

KRINGS Mathias, OKOME Onookome (eds.). *Global Nollywood: The Transnational Dimensions of an African Video Film Industry.* Bloomington, Indiana University Press, 2013.

LANARI Vanessa (ed.), COLOMBO Fabrizio, GAIGA Stefano (collab.). *Camera Africa. Classici, noir, nollywood e la nuova generazione del cinema delle Afriche.* Verona, Cierre Edizioni, Sequenze, 2011.

LAROUCHE Michel (ed.). *Films d'Afrique.* Montreal, Guernica, 1991.

LELIÈVRE Samuel (ed.). *Les Cinémas africains, une oasis dans le désert.* Paris, Corlet, coll.

"CinémAction," no. 106, 2003.

LEQUERET Élisabeth. *Le Cinéma africain: un continent à la recherche de son propre regard.* Paris, Cahiers du cinéma, coll. "Les petits cahiers," Scérén-CNDP, 2003.

MALKNUS Lizbeth, ARMES Roy. *Arab and African Film-Making.* London, Zed Books, 1991.

MANSOURI Hassouna. *De l'identité, ou "Pour une certaine tendance du cinéma africain."* Tunis, Éditions Sahar, 1996.

———. *L'Image confisquée: le cinéma du Sud, ce cinéma (de) subalterne.* Amsterdam, Depuis le Sud, 2010.

MURPHY David, WILLIAMS Patrick. *Postcolonial African Cinema: Ten Directors.* New York, Manchester University Press, 2007.

NOTCUTT Leslie Allen, LATHAM George Chitty. *The African and the Cinema.* London, Edinburgh House Press, 1937.

OUEDRAOGO Jean. *Cinéma et littérature du Burkina Faso. De la singularité à l'universalité.* Ouagadougou, Éditions Sankofa & Gurli, 2005.

OUEDRAOGO Jean (ed.). *Figuration et mémoire dans les cinémas africains.* Paris, L'Harmattan, coll. "Images plurielles," 2010.

PFAFF Françoise. *À l'écoute du cinéma sénégalais.* Paris, L'Harmattan, coll. "Images plurielles," 2010.

———. *The Cinema of Ousmane Sembène. A Pioneer in African Films.* Westport (CT), Greenwood Press, 1984.

———. *Twenty-five Black African Filmmakers: A Critical Study, with Filmography and Bio-bibliography.* Westport (CT), Greenwood Press, 1988.

PFAFF Françoise (ed.). *Focus on African Films.* Bloomington, Indiana University Press, 2004.

PRABHU Anjali. *Contemporary Cinema of Africa and the Diaspora.* Chichester, Wiley-Blackwell, 2014.

PREDAL René. *Jean Rouch, un griot gaulois.* Paris, Corlet, coll. "CinémAction," no. 17, 1982.

RAMIREZ Francis, ROLOT Christian. *Histoire du cinéma colonial au Zaïre, au Rwanda et au Burundi.* Annales, série IN-18, Sciences Historiques no. 7. Tervuren, Musée royal de l'Afrique centrale, 1985.

RIESZ János. *De la littérature coloniale à la littérature africaine. Prétextes-Contextes-Intertextes.* Paris, Karthala, 2007.

RUELLE Catherine (ed.), TAPSOBA Clément, SPECIALE Alessandra (collab.). *Afriques 50. Singularités d'un cinéma pluriel.* Paris, L'Harmattan, coll. "Images plurielles," 2005.

SALEH HAROUN Mahamat. *Bulletin de la Guilde africaine des réalisateurs et producteurs,* no. 1, March 2000.

SAUL Mahir, AUSTEN Ralph H. (eds.). *Viewing African Cinema in the Twenty-First Century: Art*

Films and the Nollywood Video Revolution. Athens, Ohio University Press, 2010.

SAWADOGO Boukary. *Les Cinémas francophones ouest-africains.* Paris, L'Harmattan, 2013.

SHAKA Femi Okiremuete. *Modernity and the African Cinema.* Trenton (NJ), Africa World Press, 2004.

SPAAS Lieve. *The Francophone Film: A Struggle for Identity.* New York, Manchester University Press, 2000.

SPECIALE Alessandra (ed.). *La nascita del cinema in Africa nera 1963–1987.* Milan, Fabbri Editori, 1987.

THACKWAY Melissa. *Africa Shoots Back: Alternative Perspectives in Sub-Saharan Francophone African Film.* Bloomington, Indiana University Press, 2003.

TCHEUYAP Alexie. *Postnationalist African Cinemas.* New York, Manchester University Press, 2011.

THIERS-THIAM Valérie. À chacun son griot. Le mythe du griot narrateurs dans la littérature et le cinéma de l'Afrique de l'Ouest. Paris, L'Harmattan, coll. "La bibliothèque d'Africultures," 2004.

UKADIKE Nwachukwu Frank. *Black African Cinema.* Berkeley, University of California Press, 1994.

———. *Questioning African Cinema: Conversations with Filmmakers.* Minneapolis, University of Minnesota Press, 2002.

VAN BEVER L. *Le Cinéma pour Africains.* Brussels, G. Van Campenhout, 1952.

VIEYRA SOUMANOU Paulin. *Le Cinéma africain. Des origines à 1973.* Paris, Présence Africaine, 1975.

———. *Réflexions d'un cinéaste africain.* Brussels, OCIC, 1990.

Postcolonial, Transnational, Diasporic, and Black Cinema

AMARGER Michel. *Djibril Diop Mambéty ou l'ivresse irrépressible de l'image.* Paris, ATM-MTM, 2000.

BERRY Torriano, BERRY Venise. *The 50 Most Influential Black Films.* Kensington, Citadel Press, 2001.

CAMERON Kenneth M. *Africa on Film: Beyond Black and White.* New York, Continuum, 1994.

CHALAYE Sylvie. *Nègres en images.* Paris, L'Harmattan, 2002.

CHAM Mbye, ANDRADE-WATKINS Claire (eds.). *Black Frames: Critical Perspectives on Black Independent Cinema.* Cambridge (MA), MIT Press, 1988.

CHAM Mbye. *Ex-iles: Essay on Caribbean Cinema.* Trenton (NJ), African World Press, 1992.

CHAVEZ Andres, CHAVEZ Denise, MARTINEZ Gerald. *What It Is . . . What It Was! The Black*

Film Explosion of the '70s in Words and Pictures. New York, Miramax Books, 1998.

CRÉMIEUX Anne. *Les Cinémas noirs américains et le rêve hollywoodien.* Paris, L'Harmattan, coll. "Images plurielles," 2004.

DE FRANCESCHI Leonardo (ed.). *L'Africa in Italia. Per una storia postcoloniale del cinema italiano.* Rome, Aracne Editrice, 2013.

DOWNING John D. H. (ed.). *Film and Politics in the Third World.* New York, Automedia, 1987.

ĎUROVIČOVA Nataša, NEWMAN Kathleen (eds.). *World Cinemas, Transnational Perspectives.* New York, Routledge, 2010.

EZRA Elizabeth, ROWDEN Terry. *Transnational Cinema: The Film Reader.* New York, Routledge, 2005.

FLORY Dan. *Philosophy, Black Film, Film Noir.* University Park, Pennsylvania State University Press, 2008.

FUSCO Coco. *Young, British and Black: The Work of Sankofa and Black Audio Film Collective.* Buffalo (NY), Hallwalls, 1988.

GABRIEL Teshome. *Third Cinema and the Third World: The Aesthetics of Liberation.* Ann Arbor, UMI Research Press, 1982.

GUNERATNE Antony R., DISSANAYAKE Wimal (eds.). *Rethinking Third Cinema.* New York, Routledge, 2003.

JAMES Darius. *That's Blaxploitation.* New York, Payback Press, 1995.

JONES William G. *Black Cinema Treasures: Lost and Found.* Preface by Ossie Davis. Denton, University of North Texas Press, 1991.

KILBOURN Russell J. A. *Cinema, Memory, Modernity: The Representation of Memory from the Art Film to Transnational Cinema.* New York, Routledge, 2010.

HOWARD Josiah. *Blaxploitation Cinema: The Essential Reference Guide.* London, FAB Press Ltd, 2008.

KOVEN Mikel J. *Blaxploitation Films.* Harpenden, Oldcastle Books, 2010.

LEDRU Julie. *Djibril Diop Mambéty: un autre cinéaste d'Afrique Noire.* Mémoire de maitrise d'études cinématographiques, Université de Paris III, Paris, 1999.

MARKS Laura U. *The Skin of the Film: Intercultural Cinema, Embodiment, and the Senses.* Durham (NC), Duke University Press, 2000.

MARTIN Michel T. (ed.). *Cinemas of the Black Diaspora: Diversity, Dependence, and Oppositionality.* Detroit, Wayne State University Press, 1995.

MASSOOD Paula J. *Black City Cinema.* Philadelphia, Temple University Press, 2003.

NAFICY Hamid. *An Accented Cinema: Exilic and Diasporic Filmmaking.* Princeton (NJ), Princeton University Press, 2001.

PETTY Sheila J. *Contact Zones: Memory, Origin and Discourse in Black Diasporic Cinema.*

Detroit, Wayne State University Press, 2008.

PINES Jim, WILLEMEN Paul (eds.). *Questions of Third Cinema.* London, British Films Institute, 1989.

REID Mark A. (ed.). *Black Lenses, Black Voices: African American Film Now.* Lanham (MD), Rowman & Littlefield Publishers, 2005.

RHINES Jesse Algeron. *Black Film, White Money.* New Brunswick (NJ), Rutgers University Press, 1996.

ROGIN Michael. *Blackface, White Noise: Jewish Immigrants in the Hollywood Melting Pot.* Berkeley, University of California Press, 1996.

SADA Niang. *Djibril Diop Mambéty: un cinéaste à contre-courant.* Paris, L'Harmattan, 2002.

SENE Nar. *Djibril Diop Mambéty. La caméra au bout . . . du nez.* Paris, L'Harmattan, coll. "La bibliothèque d'Africultures," 2001.

SHERZER Dina. *Cinema, Colonialism, Postcolonialism.* Austin, University of Texas, 1995.

SMITH Valerie (ed.). *Representing Blackness: Issues in Film and Video.* New Brunswick (NJ), Rutgers University Press, 2000.

STEWART Jacqueline Najuma. Migrating to the Movies: Cinema and Black Urban Modernity. Berkeley, *University of California Press, 2005.*

WAYNE Mike. *Political Film: The Dialectic of Third Cinema.* London, Pluto Press, 2001.

WALKER David, RAUSH Andrew, WATSON Chris. *Reflections on Blaxploitation: Actors and Directors Speak.* Lanham (MD), Scarecrow Press, 2009.

WYNCHANK Anny. *Djibril Diop Mambéty, ou le voyage du voyant.* Ivry-sur-Seine, Éditions A3, 2003.

Diaspora, Black Studies, and the Question of Representation

ADOTEVI Stanislav Spero. *Négritude et négrologues.* Pantin, Le Castor Astral Éditeur, coll. "*Les Pourfendeurs,*" 1998 [1972].

ANTA DIOP Cheick. *Nations nègres et cultures.* Paris, Présence Africaine, 1954.

APPIAH Kwame Anthony. *In My Father's House.* Oxford, Oxford University Press, 1993.

ASANTE Molefi Kete. *Afrocentricity.* Trenton (NJ), Afrika World Press, 2003.

———. *An Afrocentric Manifesto: Toward an African Renaissance.* Oxford, Polity Press, 2008.

BERTHOMIÈRE William, CHIVALLON Christine. *Les Diasporas dans le monde contemporain.* Paris, Karthala, 2006.

BOKIBA André Patient. *Écriture et identité dans la littérature africaine.* Paris, L'Harmattan, 1998.

BOUYAIN Sarah. *Métisse Façon.* Paris, La chambre d'échos, 2003.

BOYCE DAVIES Carole. *Black Women, Writing and Identity: Migrations of the Subject.* New York, Routledge, 1994.

BRAH Avtar. *Cartographies of Diaspora: Contesting Identities.* New York, Routledge, 1996.

BRAH Avtar, COOMBES Annie E. (eds.). *Hybridity and Its Discontents: Politics, Science, Culture.* New York, Routledge, 2000.

CHALAYE Sylvie. *Nègres en images.* Paris, L'Harmattan, 2002.

COQUERY-VIDROVITCH Catherine. *Afrique noire: permanences et ruptures.* Paris, L'Harmattan, 1992.

DUBOIS Régis. *L'Image du noir dans le cinéma américain blanc.* L'Harmattan, coll. "Champs Visuels," 1997.

DEPESTRE René. *Bonjour et adieu à la négritude.* Paris, Éditions Robert Laffont, 1988.

GARVEY Marcus. *Philosophy and Opinions of Marcus Garvey.* New York, Arno Press/New York Times, 1968.

GILROY Paul. *Small Acts: Thoughts on the Politics of Black Diaspora.* New York, Serpent's Tail, 1993.

GOMEZ-PENA Guillermo. *The New World Border.* San Francisco, City Lights Publishers, 2001.

HAMPÂTÉ BÂ Amadou. *Aspects de la civilisation africaine. Personne, culture, religion.* Paris, Présence Africaine, 2000 [1972].

LIAUZU Claude. *Race et civilisation. L'Autre dans la culture occidentale (Anthologie critique).* Paris, Syros, 1992.

LIONNET Françoise. *Autobiographical Voices: Race, Gender, Self-Portraiture.* Ithaca (NY), Cornell University Press, 1989.

MERCER Kobena. *Welcome to the Jungle: New Positions in Black Cultural Studies.* New York, Routledge, 1996.

MINH-HA Trinh T. *Woman, Native, Other.* Bloomington, Indiana University Press, 1989.

NDIAYE Pap. *La Condition noire. Essai sur une minorité française.* Paris, Gallimard, coll. "Folio actuel," 2009 [Calmann-Lévy, 2008].

PRATT Mary Louise. *Imperial Eyes: Travel Writing and Transculturation.* London, Routledge, 1992.

RAHIER Jean. *Representation of Blackness and the Performance of Identities.* Westport (CT), Bergin & Garvey, 1999.

ROBERTSON George, MASH Melinda, TICKNER Lisa, BIRD Jon, CURTIS Barry, PUTNAM Tim (eds.). *Traveller's Tales: Narratives of Home and Displacement.* New York, Routledge, 1994.

SAGOT-DUVAUROUX Jean-Louis. *On ne naît pas Noir, on le devient.* Paris, Éditions Albin Michel, 2004.

SENGHOR Léopold Sédar. *Anthologie de la nouvelle poésie nègre et malgache de langue française.* Paris, PUF, 1948.

SOYINKA Wole. *Myth, Literature and the African World.* Cambridge, Cambridge University Press, 1992 [1976].

THOMAS Dominic. *Black France: Colonialism, Immigration, and Transnationalism.* Bloomington, Indiana University Press, 2006.

WALCOTT Rinaldo. *Black Like Who?* Toronto, Insomniac Press, 1997.

WIREDU Kwasi. *Cultural Universals and Particulars: An African Perspective.* Bloomington, Indiana University Press, 1996.

Postcolonial Studies, Cultural Studies

APPADURAI Arjun. *Après le colonialisme. Les conséquences culturelles de la globalisation.* Paris, Payot, coll. "Petite Bibliothèque Payot," 2005.

ASHCROFT Bill, GRIFFITHS Gareth, TIFFIN Helen. *The Empire Writes Back: Theory and Practice in Post-Colonial Literature.* New York, Routledge, 1989.

BANCEL Nicolas, BLANCHARD Pascal. "De l'indigène à l'immigré: images, messages et réalités." Paris, Gallimard, coll. "Découverte Gallimard," no. 345, 1998.

BANCEL Nicolas, BLANCHARD Pascal, BOETSCH Gilles, DEROO Éric, LEMAIRE Sandrine (eds.). *Zoos humains. De la Vénus hottentote aux reality shows.* Paris, La Découverte, 2002.

BANCEL Nicolas, BLANCHARD Pascal, LEMAIRE Sandrine (eds.). *La Fracture coloniale. La société française au prisme de l'héritage colonial.* Paris, La Découverte, 2006.

BERNABÉ Jean, CHAMOISEAU Patrick, CONFIANT Raphaël. Éloge de la créolité. Paris, Gallimard, coll. "Hors série Littérature," 1993.

BHABHA K. Homi. *The Location of Culture.* New York, Routledge, 1994.

BLANCHARD Pascal. *La France Noire. Trois siècles de présence.* Paris, La Découverte, 2011.

BLANCHARD Pascal, DEROO Éric, MANCERON Gilles. *Paris Noir.* Paris, Hazan, 2001.

CÉSAIRE Aimé. *Cahier d'un retour au pays natal.* Paris, Présence Africaine, 1956.

———. *Discours sur le colonialisme.* Paris, Présence Africaine, 1956.

CHAMBERS Iain, CURTI Lidia (eds.). *The Post-Colonial Question: Common Skies, Divided Horizons.* New York, Routledge, 1996.

CHATTERJEE Partha. *Nationalist Thought and the Colonial World: A Derivative Discourse.* Minneapolis, University of Minnesota Press, 1986.

DIOP Samba. *Fictions africaines et postcolonialisme.* Paris, L'Harmattan, 2002.

DOYLE Arthur Conan. *The Crime of the Congo (Collected Works of Sir Arthur Conan Doyle).* Cambridge, Cambridge Scholars Publishing, 2009 [1909].

FANON Frantz. *Peau noire, masques blancs.* Paris, Seuil, 1952. (*Black Skin, White Masks,* trans.

Charles Lam Markmann, London, Pluto Press, 2008).

GASSAMA Makhily (ed.). *L'Afrique répond à Sarkozy. Contre le discours de Dakar.* Paris, Philippe Rey, 2008.

GILROY Paul. *The Black Atlantic: Modernity and Double-Consciousness.* London, Verso, 1993.

————. *There Ain't No Black in the Union Jack.* New York, Routledge, 1987.

GLISSANT Édouard. *Discours antillais.* Paris, Gallimard, coll. "Folio Essais," 1997 (*Caribbean Discourse,* trans. J. Michael Dash, Charlottesville, Caraf Books, University Press of Virginia, 1989.

————. *Introduction à une poétique du divers.* Paris, Gallimard, 1996 [1995].

————. *Traité du Tout-monde* (Poétique IV). Paris, Gallimard, 1997.

HALL Stuart, DU GAY Paul (eds.). *Questions of Cultural Identity.* London, Sage, 1996.

HALL Stuart, JEFFERSON Tony (eds.). *Resistance through Rituals: Youth Subcultures in Post-War Britain.* New York, Routledge, 1990.

HOCHSCHILD Adam. *King Leopold's Ghost.* Boston (MA), Mariner Books, 1998.

LAZARUS Neil (ed.). *Penser le postcolonial. Une introduction critique.* Paris, Éditions Amsterdam, 2006.

LECLERC Gérard. *Anthropologie et colonialisme. Essai sur l'histoire de l'africanisme.* Paris, Fayard, 1972.

LEMAIRE Sandrine, BLANCHARD Pascal. *Culture coloniale 1871–1931.* Paris, Autrement, coll. "Mémoires/Histoire," 2003.

LOUVEL Roland. *L'Afrique noire et la différence culturelle.* Paris, L'Harmattan, 1996.

MENIL René. *Tracées: identité, négritude, esthétique aux Antilles.* Paris, Robert Laffont, 1992 [1981].

MBEMBE Achille. *De la Postcolonie. Essai sur l'imagination politique dans l'Afrique contemporaine.* Paris, Karthala, 2000.

MBONIMPA Melchior. *Idéologies de l'Indépendance africaine.* Paris, L'Harmattan, 1987.

MEMMI Albert. *Portrait du colonisateur. Portrait du colonisé.* Preface by Jean-Paul Sartre. Paris, Payot, coll. "Petite Bibliothèque Payot," 1973 [1957].

MOURA Jean Marc. *Littératures francophones et théories post-coloniales.* Paris, PUF, 1999.

MUDIMBE V. Y. *The Invention of Africa: Philosophy and the Order of Knowledge.* Bloomington, Indiana University Press, 1988.

SAID W. Edward. *Orientalism.* New York, Pantheon Books, 1978.

SHOHAT Ella, STAM Robert. *Unthinking Eurocentrism: Multiculturalism and the Media.* New York, Routledge, 1994.

SHOHAT Ella, STAM Robert (eds.). *Multiculturalism, Postcoloniality, and Transnational Media.* New Brunswick (NJ), Rutgers University Press, 2003.

SPIVAK Gayatri Chakravorty. *Can the Subaltern Speak? In* Cary Nelson and Lawrence Grossberg
(eds.), *Marxism and the Interpretation of Culture*, pp. 24–28. London, Macmillan, 1988.

———. *A Critique of Postcolonial Reason: Toward a History of a Vanishing Present.* Cambridge
(MA), Harvard University Press, 1999.

TAGUIEFF Pierre-André. *La Force du préjugé: essai sur le racisme et ses doubles.* Paris, La
Découverte, 1987.

YOUNG Robert. *Colonial Desire: Hybridity in Theory, Culture and Race.* New York, Routledge,
1990.

Sociology and Identity

AIME Marco. *Eccessi di culture.* Turin, Einaudi, 2004.

AMSELLE Jean-Loup. *Logiques métisses. Anthropologie de l'identité en Afrique et ailleurs.* Paris,
Payot & Rivage, 1990.

ANDERSON Benedict. *Imagined Communities: Reflections on the Origin and Rise of
Nationalism.* London, Verso, 1983.

BAAZ Maria Eriksson, PALMBERG Mai (eds.). *Same and Other: Negotiating African Identity in
Cultural Production.* Stockholm, Elanders Gotab for the Nordiska Afrikainstitutet, 2001.

BAYART Jean-François. *L'Illusion identitaire.* Paris, Fayard, 1997.

BAUMAN Zygmunt. *Identité.* Paris, L'Herne, 2010.

———. *La Vie liquide.* Rodez, Rouergue, 2006.

———. *Vies perdues: La modernité et ses exclus.* Paris, Payot, 2006.

BAUMANN Gerd. *Contesting Culture: Discourses of Identity in Multiethnic London.* Cambridge,
Cambridge University Press, 1996.

———. *L'enigma multiculturale. Stati, etnie, religioni.* Bologne, Il Mulino, coll.
"Contemporanea," 2003.

BOUMARD Patrick, LAPASSADE Georges, LOBROT Michel. *Le Mythe de l'identité. Apologie de
la dissociation.* Paris, Economica, 2006.

BOURDIEU Pierre. *Langage et pouvoir symbolique.* Paris, Seuil, coll. "Points," 2001.

BOURDIEU Pierre, PASSERON Jean-Claude. *La Reproduction. Eléments pour une théorie du
système d'enseignement.* Paris, Les Éditions de Minuit, 1970.

BUTLER Judith. *Gender Trouble: Feminism and the Subversion of Identity.* London, Routledge,
1990.

CHAMBERS Iain. *Migrancy, Culture, Identity.* London, Routledge, 1994.

COLOMBO Enzo, SEMI Giovanni. *Multiculturalismo quotidiano. Le pratiche della differenza.*
Milan, Franco Angeli editore, 2007.

DELEUZE Gilles, GUATTARI Félix. *L'Anti-Œdipe. Capitalisme et schizophrénie 1.* Paris, Les
    Éditions de Minuit, 1972.

————. *Mille plateaux. Capitalisme et schizophrénie 2.* Paris, Les Éditions de Minuit, 1980.

DU BOIS William Edward Burghardt. *The Souls of Black Folk.* New York, Gramercy Books, 1994
    [1903].

ELIAS Norbert, *Che cos'è la sociologia?* Turin, Rosemberg e Sellier, 1990 [1970].

————. *La Société des individus.* Translated from German by Jeanne Etoré. Paris, Fayard, 1991
    (written in 1939).

ELIAS Norbert, SCOTSON John L. *Logiques de l'exclusion.* Paris, Fayard, 1965.

GARCIA CANCLINI Néstor. *Culturas híbridas. Estrategias para entrar y salir de la modernidad.*
    Mexico, Grijalbo, 1989.

GEERTZ Clifford. *The Interpretation of Cultures.* New York, Basic Books, 1973.

GRUZINSKI Serge. *La Pensée métisse.* Paris, Fayard, 1999.

HABERMAS Jürgen. *L'Espace public.* Paris, Payot, 1978.

HABERMAS Jürgen, TAYLOR Charles. *Multiculturalismo. Lotte per il riconoscimento.* Milan,
    Feltrinelli, 1998.

HOFFMANN Léon-François. *Le Nègre romantique.* Paris, Payot, 1973.

HONNETH Axel. *Lotta per il riconoscimento. Proposte per un'etica del conflitto.* Milan, Il
    saggiatore, 2002.

HUNTINGTON P. Samuel. *The Clash of Civilizations and the Remaking of World Order.* New
    York, Touchstone, 1996.

KAUFMANN Jean-Claude. *L'Invention de soi: une théorie de l'identité.* Paris, Armand Colin,
    2004.

KRISTEVA Julia. *Étrangers à nous-mêmes.* Paris, Fayard, 1988.

LAHIRE Bernard. *L'Homme pluriel. Les ressorts de l'action.* Paris, Nathan, 1998.

LAI Giampaolo. *Disidentità.* Milan, Feltrinelli, 1988.

LAPANTINE François. *Je, nous et les autres. Être humain au-delà des appartenances.* Paris, Le
    Pommier, 1999.

NICHOLSON Linda J., SEIDMAN Steven. *Social Postmodernism: Beyond Identity Politics.*
    Cambridge, Cambridge University Press, 1995.

PAPASTERGIADIS Nikos. *The Turbulence of Migration.* Cambridge, Polity Press, 2000.

REMOTTI Francesco. *Contro l'identità.* Rome, Editori Laterza, 2008 [Gius, Laterza e Figli, 1996].

————. *L'ossessione identitaria.* Bari, Anticorpi Laterza, 2010.

RICŒUR Paul. *Parcours de la reconnaissance.* Paris, Stock, 2004.

————. *Soi-même comme un autre.* Paris, Seuil, 1990.

SARTRE Jean-Paul. *L'Être et le néant.* Paris, Gallimard, 1976 [1943].

SARUP Madan. *Identity, Culture and the Postmodern World.* Edinburgh, Edinburgh University Press, 1996.

SEN Amartya. *Identità e violenza.* Bari, Laterza, 2006.

TAYLOR Charles. *Multiculturalism and the Politics of Recognition.* Princeton (NJ), Princeton University Press, 1992.

———. *Sources of the Self: The Making of the Modern Identity.* Cambridge (MA), Harvard University Press, 1989.

General Works

ALEMANNO Roberto. *Itinerari della violenza.* Bari, Edizioni Dedalo, 1982.

DARDENNE Luc. *Au dos de nos images, 1991–2005.* Paris, Editions du Seuil, 2005.

DIOP Boris Boubacar. *L'Afrique au-delà du miroir.* Paris, Philippe Rey, 2007.

KANE Cheick Hamidou. *L'Aventure ambiguë.* Paris, Julliard, 1961.

KI-ZERBO Joseph. *À quand l'Afrique? Entretien avec René Holenstein.* La Tour d'Aigues, Éditions de l'Aube, 2003.

LEIRIS Michel. *L'Afrique fantôme.* Paris, Gallimard, 1996 [1934].

LEVI-STRAUSS Claude. *Anthropologie structurale.* Paris, Plon, 1958.

———. *La Pensée sauvage.* Paris, Pocket, 1990.

MAALOUF Amin. *Les Identités meurtrières.* Paris, Éditions Grasset & Fasquelle, 1998 (*In the Name of Identity: Violence and the Need to Belong,* trans. Barbara Bray, London, Penguin Books, 2000).

MABANCKOU Alain. *Le Sanglot de l'homme noir.* Paris, Fayard, 2012.

———. *Verre cassé.* Paris, Seuil, 2006.

PARKS Gordon. *A Choice of Weapons.* Saint Paul, Minnesota Historical Society Press, 1965.

SÉDAR SENGHOR Léopold. "Ce que l'homme noir apporte." *In* Jean Verdier (ed.), *L'Homme de couleur.* Paris, Librairie Plon, 1939.

SIBONY Daniel. *Entre deux, l'origine en partage.* Paris, Seuil, 1991.

THURAM Lilian. *Mes étoiles noires. De Lucy à Barack Obama.* Paris, Philippe Rey, 2010.

Articles and Chapters

AKUDINOBI Jude. "Nationalism, African Cinema, and the Frames of Scrutiny." *Research in African Literature,* no. 32, 2001, pp. 123–142.

ANDRADE-WATKINS Claire. "Portuguese African Cinema: Historical and Contemporary Perspectives, 1969–1993." *In* Michel T. Martin (ed.), *Cinemas of the Black Diaspora:*

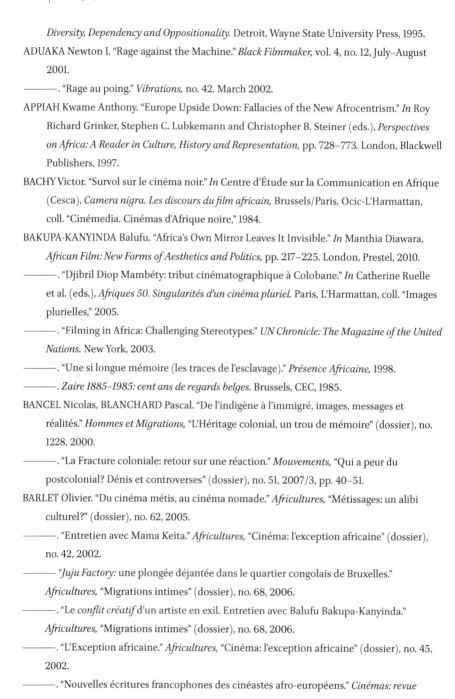

Diversity, Dependency and Oppositionality. Detroit, Wayne State University Press, 1995.

ADUAKA Newton I. "Rage against the Machine." *Black Filmmaker,* vol. 4, no. 12, July–August 2001.

———. "Rage au poing." *Vibrations,* no. 42, March 2002.

APPIAH Kwame Anthony. "Europe Upside Down: Fallacies of the New Afrocentrism." *In* Roy Richard Grinker, Stephen C. Lubkemann and Christopher B. Steiner (eds.), *Perspectives on Africa: A Reader in Culture, History and Representation,* pp. 728–773. London, Blackwell Publishers, 1997.

BACHY Victor. "Survol sur le cinéma noir." *In* Centre d'Étude sur la Communication en Afrique (Cesca), *Camera nigra. Les discours du film africain,* Brussels/Paris, Ocic-L'Harmattan, coll. "Cinémedia. Cinémas d'Afrique noire," 1984.

BAKUPA-KANYINDA Balufu. "Africa's Own Mirror Leaves It Invisible." *In* Manthia Diawara, *African Film: New Forms of Aesthetics and Politics,* pp. 217–225. London, Prestel, 2010.

———. "Djibril Diop Mambéty: tribut cinématographique à Colobane." *In* Catherine Ruelle et al. (eds.), *Afriques 50. Singularités d'un cinéma pluriel.* Paris, L'Harmattan, coll. "Images plurielles," 2005.

———. "Filming in Africa: Challenging Stereotypes." *UN Chronicle: The Magazine of the United Nations.* New York, 2003.

———. "Une si longue mémoire (les traces de l'esclavage)." *Présence Africaine,* 1998.

———. *Zaire 1885–1985: cent ans de regards belges.* Brussels, CEC, 1985.

BANCEL Nicolas, BLANCHARD Pascal. "De l'indigène à l'immigré, images, messages et réalités." *Hommes et Migrations,* "L'Héritage colonial, un trou de mémoire" (dossier), no. 1228, 2000.

———. "La Fracture coloniale: retour sur une réaction." *Mouvements,* "Qui a peur du postcolonial? Dénis et controverses" (dossier), no. 51, 2007/3, pp. 40–51.

BARLET Olivier. "Du cinéma métis, au cinéma nomade." *Africultures,* "Métissages: un alibi culturel?" (dossier), no. 62, 2005.

———. "Entretien avec Mama Keita." *Africultures,* "Cinéma: l'exception africaine" (dossier), no. 42, 2002.

——— "*Juju Factory:* une plongée déjantée dans le quartier congolais de Bruxelles." *Africultures,* "Migrations intimes" (dossier), no. 68, 2006.

———. "Le *conflit créatif* d'un artiste en exil. Entretien avec Balufu Bakupa-Kanyinda." *Africultures,* "Migrations intimes" (dossier), no. 68, 2006.

———. "L'Exception africaine." *Africultures,* "Cinéma: l'exception africaine" (dossier), no. 45, 2002.

———. "Nouvelles écritures francophones des cinéastes afro-européens." *Cinémas: revue d'études cinématographiques,* vol. 11, no. 1, 2000, pp. 113–132.

BAZZOLI Maria Silvia. "Spaesementi della storia. Odisee per un puzzle del cinema arabo-mediorientale." *In* Mohamed Challouf, Giuseppe Gariazzo, and Alessandra Speciale (eds.), *Un posto sulla terra. Cinema per (r)esistere.* Milan, Editrice Il Castoro, 2002.

BHABHA Homi K., RUTHERFORD Jonathan. "The Third Space: Interview with Homi K. Bhabha." *In* Ders. (Hg), *Identity: Community, Culture, Difference,* pp. 207–221. London, Lawrence and Wishart, 1990.

BLANCHARD Pascal. "Les Zoos humains, une longue tradition française." *Hommes et migrations,* "L'héritage colonial, un trou de mémoire" (dossier), no. 1228, 2000.

BASSAN Raphaël. "Haïlé Gerima, l'Afro-américain." *Le Cinéma noir américain.* Paris, Corlet, coll. "CinémAction," no. 46, 1988.

BLOOM Peter. "Beur Cinema and the Politics of Location: French Immigration Politics and the Naming of a Film Movement." *In* Marcia Landy, *The Historical Film: History and Memory in Media,* pp. 44–62. New Brunswick (NJ), Rutgers University Press, 2001.

BONI-CLAVERIE Isabelle. "L'Avenir fantôme." *In* Catherine Ruelle et al. (eds.), *Afriques 50. Singularités d'un cinéma pluriel.* Paris, L'Harmattan, coll. "Images plurielles," 2005.

BOUGHEDIR Férid. "Cinémas nationaux et politiques cinématographiques en Afrique noire: Du rêve Sud-Sud à la défense de la diversité culturelle." *In* Catherine Ruelle et al. (eds.), *Afriques 50. Singularités d'un cinéma pluriel.* Paris, L'Harmattan, coll. "Images plurielles," 2005.

BOULANGER Pierre. *Le Cinéma colonial. De "l'Atlantide" à "Lawrence d'Arabie."* Preface by Guy Hennebelle. Paris, Seghers, coll. "Cinéma 2000," 1975.

———. "Le Cinéma colonial ou la réalité coloniale travestie." *Cinéma,* no. 72, 1972, pp. 56–60.

BOUYAIN Sarah. "Quel avenir pour mon Afrique passée. Du fantasme à la réalité, de la pensée à l'action . . ." *Africultures,* dossier "Penser l'Afrique: des objets de pensée aux sujets pensants," no. 82, August 2010, pp. 145–151.

BRANIGAN Edward. "Quand y a-t-il caméra?" *In* Jean-Pierre Esquenazi et Bruno Pequignot (eds.), *Penser, cadrer: le projet du cadre,* pp. 19–31. Paris, L'Harmattan, coll. "Champs Visuels," no. 12–13, 1999.

———. "Qu'est ce qu'une caméra?" *In* Jean-Pierre Esquenazi and Bruno Pequignot (eds.), *Penser, cadrer: le projet du cadre,* pp. 33–55. Paris, L'Harmattan, coll. "Champs Visuels," no. 12–13, 1999.

CHANAN Michael. "Le Troisième Cinéma de Solanas et Getino." Paris, Corlet, coll. "CinémAction," no. 60, 1991, pp. 214–223.

CHINIEN Savrina. "Le cinematografies della diaspora africana: un'arte impegnata?" *In* Vanessa Lanari (ed.), Fabrizio Colombo, and Stefano Gaiga (collab.), *Camera Africa. Classici, noir, nollywood e la nuova generazione del cinema delle Afriche.* Verona, Cierre Edizioni, Sequenze, 2011.

CASSAVETES John. "Derrière la caméra." *Cahiers du cinéma,* no. 119, May 1961.

CHAM Mbye. "Le Passé, le présent, l'avenir." Écrans d'Afrique, no. 4, 1993.

————. "Le Cinéma africain: continuité et rupture." *In* Catherine Ruelle et al. (eds.), *Afriques 50. Singularités d'un cinéma pluriel.* Paris, L'Harmattan, coll. "Images plurielles," 2005.

CHIVALLON Christine. "La Notion de diaspora appliquée au monde noir des Amériques: l'historicité d'un concept." *Africultures,* dossier "Diaspora: identité plurielle," no. 72, Paris, February 2008, pp. 18–35.

CISSÉ Souleymane. "L'Afrique dans la lumière." *Cahiers du cinéma,* no. 402, 1987, pp. 28–30.

CLIFFORD James. "Diaspora." *Cultural Anthropology,* vol. 9, no. 3, August 1994, pp. 302–328.

————. "Travelling Cultures." *In* Lawrence Grossberg, Cary Nelson, and Paula Treichler (eds.), *Cultural Studies.* New York, Routledge, 1992.

COLETTI Maria. "Fantasmi d'Africa, dal muto al sonoro. Facce, faccette e *blackface." In* Leonardo de Francesci (ed.), *L'Africa in Italia. Per una controstoria postcoloniale del cinema italiano.* Rome, Aracne, 2013.

COQUERY-VIDROVITCH Catherine. "Le Postulat de la supériorité blanche et de l'infériorité noire." *In* Marc Ferro (ed.), *Le Livre noir du colonialisme.* Paris, Robert Laffont, 2002.

CRENSHAW Kimberlé. "Mapping the Margins: Intersectionality, Identity Politics, and Violence against Women of Color." *Stanford Law Review,* vol. 43, no. 6, 1991, pp. 1241–1299.

DANTO Arthur. "La Littérature comme philosophie." *In* Arthur Danto (ed.), *L'Assujettissement philosophique de l'art,* pp. 205–232. Paris, Seuil, 1993.

DEBRIX Jean René. "Dix ans de coopération franco-africaine ont permis la naissance du jeune cinéma d'Afrique noire." *Sentiers,* no. 1, 1973.

DELEUZE Gilles. "Philosophie et minorité." *Critique,* no. 369, 1978, pp. 154–155.

DIA Ibrahima Thierno, RICCI Daniela. "Identités et choc des représentations dans les cinémas africains de l'exil." *In* Patricia-Laure Thivat (ed.), *Voyages et exils au cinéma, transferts et/ou "chocs" culturels.* Lille: Presses Universitaires du Septentrion, coll. "Arts du spectacle. Images et sons," 2017.

DIAWARA Manthia. "Sub-Saharan African Film Production: Technological Paternalism." *Jump Cut,* no. 32, 1987, pp. 61–65.

DIOP Boris Boubacar. "Identité africaine et mondialisation." *Africultures,* no. 41, 2001.

DU BOIS William Edward Burghardt. "Strivings of the Negro People." *Atlantic Monthly,* 1897.

DUDLEY Andrew. "The Roots of the Nomadic: Gilles Deleuze and the Cinema of West Africa." *In* Gregory Flaxman (ed.), *The Brain Is the Screen: Deleuze and the Philosophy of Cinema,* pp. 215–249. Minneapolis, University of Minnesota Press, 2000.

EL FTOUH Youssef, PINTO Manuel. "L'Afrique dans les images coloniales." *In* Catherine Ruelle et al. (eds.), *Afriques 50. Singularités d'un cinéma pluriel.* Paris, L'Harmattan, coll. "Images plurielles," 2005.

ESQUENAZI Jean-Pierre. "Éléments de sociologie du film." *Cinémas,* vol. 17, no. 2–3, 2007, pp. 117–141.

GABRIEL Teshome H. "Thoughts on Nomadic Aesthetics and Black Independent Cinema: Traces of a Journey." *In* Russell Ferguson (ed.), *Out There: Marginalization and Contemporary Cultures,* pp. 395–410. Cambridge (MA), MIT Press, 1990.

GANGULY Keya. "Migrant Identities, Personal Memory and the Construction of Selfhood." *Cultural Studies,* vol. 6, no. 1, 1992.

GAUTHIER Guy, ESNAULT Philippe. "Le Cinéma colonial." *Revue du cinéma,* no. 394, May 1984.

GERIMA Haile. "Breaking Toys: The Demystification of Imaginary Lines." *In* Jim Pines and Paul Willemen (eds.), *Questions of Third Cinema.* London, British Films Institute, 1989.

GIKANDI Simon. "Introduction: Africa, Diaspora and Discourse of Modernity." *Research in African Literatures,* no. 27, no. 4, 1996.

GIVANNI June. "Cinémas et liberté: divergence ou dichotomie, entretien avec John Akomfrah." Écrans d'Afrique, no. 7, 1994.

———. "Haile Gerima : L'homme de 3 000 ans." Écrans d'Afrique, no. 12, 2001, pp. 31–33.

HAFFNER Pierre. "Entretien avec le père Alexandre Van den Heuvel, pionnier d'un 'cinéma missionnaire' au Congo." *In* Catherine Ruelle et al. (eds.), *Afriques 50. Singularités d'un cinéma pluriel.* Paris, L'Harmattan, coll. "Images plurielles," 2005.

———. "Jean Rouch jugé par six cinéastes d'Afrique noire." Paris, Corlet, coll. "CinémAction," no. 17, 1982.

HALL Stuart. "Cultural Identity and Diaspora. *In* Patrick Williams and Laura Chrisman (eds.), *Colonial Discourse and Post-Colonial Theory: A Reader,* pp. 227–237. London, Harvester-Wheatsheaf, 1994.

———. "Minimal Selves." *In* Lisa Appignanesi (ed.), *Identity: The Real Me: Post-Modernism and the Question of Identity,* document 6. London, Institute of Contemporary Art, 1987.

HAMPÂTÉ BÂ Amadou. *Le Dit du cinéma africain. Premier catalogue sélectif.* Paris, Unesco, 1967.

HONDO Med. "Cinémas africains, écrans colonisés." *Le Monde,* 21 January 1982.

IVANGA Imunga. "Au Sud, des cinémas." *In* Catherine Ruelle et al. (eds.), *Afriques 50. Singularités d'un cinéma pluriel.* Paris, L'Harmattan, coll. "Images plurielles," 2005.

KABORÉ Gaston. "L'Image de soi, un besoin vital." *In* Fédération panafricaine des cinéastes (Fepaci), *L'Afrique et le centenaire du cinéma.* Paris, Présence Africaine, 1995.

KANDE Sylvie. "Look Homeward, Angel: Maroons and Mulattos in Haile Gerima's Sankofa."

Research in Africa Literature, vol. 29, no. 2, 1998.

MERCER Kobena. "Black Art and the Burden of Representation." *Third Text,* vol. 4, no. 10, 1990.

MCCLUSKEY Audrey T. "South African Filmmaker Zola Maseko: We Are in the Process of Making a Tradition." *Black Camera* (Bloomington, Indiana University Press), vol. 19, no. 2, 2004, p. 2.

MURPHY David. "Africans Filming Africa: Questioning Theories of an Authentic African Cinema." *In* Elizabeth Ezra and Terry Rowden (eds.), *Transnational Cinema and the Film Reader,* pp. 27–38. New York, Routledge, 2006.

KORLEY LARYEA Nii. "Le Boom des vidéos." *Écrans d'Afrique,* no. 7, 1994.

LARDEAU Yann. "Cinémas des racines, histoires du ghetto." *Cahiers du cinéma,* no. 340, October 1982.

———. "Haile Gerima: pour un mouvement de libération culturelle." *Le Monde diplomatique,* no. 364, 1984.

LEFÈVRE Raymond. "Le Cinéma colonial." *Images et Colonies,* exhibition catalog and conference minutes. Paris, Association Connaissance de l'histoire de l'Afrique contemporaine (ACHAC)/Bibliothèque de documentation internationale contemporaine (BDIC), 1993.

LELIÈVRE Samuel. "Histoire, mémoire, et légitimation politique dans les cinémas africains." *Revue de l'Université de Moncton,* vol. 40, no. 1, 2009, pp. 5–31.

MALANDRIN Stéphane. "Les Cinémas africains en résistance." *Cahiers du cinéma,* no. 492, June 1995.

MAMBÉTY Djibril Diop. "Djibril, prince et poète du cinéma africain." *Écrans d'Afrique,* no. 24, 1998.

MARCORELLES Louis. "Haile Gerima: J'appartiens à la fois à l'Éthiopie et à l'Amérique noire." *Le Monde,* 7 July 1984.

MBEMBE Achille. "À propos des écritures africaines de soi." *Politique africaine,* no. 77, 2000, pp. 16–43.

MEDA YRZOALA Jean-Claude, "Le Cinéma colonial: les conditions de son développement," *Écrans d'Afrique,* no. 9–10, 1994.

NAFICY Hamid. "Phobic Spaces and Liminal Panics: Independent Transnational Film Genre." *In* Ella Shohat and Robert Stam (eds.), *Multiculturalism, Postcoloniality, and Transnational Media.* New Brunswick (NJ), Rutgers University Press, 2003.

NGANGURA Mweze. *In* Mahen Bonetti and Prerana Reddy (eds.), "Through African Eyes: Dialogues with Directors." New York, New York African Film Festival Edition, 2003.

PARDO Carlos. "Du cinéma africain à son dernier 'Cri du coeur,' entretien d'Ouedraogo: 'La force de continuer.'" *Libération,* 8 April 1995.

PATTERSON Tiffany Rubi, KELLEY Robin. "Unfinished Migrations: Reflections on the African Diaspora and the Marketing of the Modern World." *African Studies Review,* vol. 43, no. 1, 2000, pp. 11–45.

PETLEY Julian. "Testament." *Monthly Film Bulletin,* no. 56, 1989.

PETTY Sheila J. "Africa and the Middle Passage: Recoupment of Origin in *Sankofa.*" *In* Sheila J. Petty, *Contact Zones: Memory, Origin and Discourse in Black Diasporic Cinema.* Detroit, Wayne State University Press, 2008.

PERNET Thierry. "Pluies d'images sur les écrans africains." *Le Monde diplomatique,* no. 505, April 1996.

PFAFF Françoise. "Africa from Within: The Films of Gaston Kaboré and Idrissa Ouédraogo as Anthropological Source." *Society for Visual Anthropology,* vol. 6, no. 1, Spring 1990.

———. "From Africa to the Americas: Interviews with Haile Gerima (1976–2001)." *In* Françoise Pfaff (ed.), *Focus on African Films.* Bloomington, Indiana University Press, 2004.

PRATT Mary Louise. "Arts of the Contact Zone." *Profession,* no. 91, 1991, pp. 33–40.

REID Mark A. "Black Independent Film: Haile Gerima's *Sankofa.*" *In* Mark A. Reid (ed.), *Black Lenses, Black Voices: African American Film Now.* Lanham (MD), Rowman & Littlefield Publishers, 2005.

RICCI Daniela. "Ancora su Teza." *Lo straniero* 13, no. 108, 2009.

———. "Black African Diasporic Cinemas: Identities and the Challenge of Complexity." *In* Winston Mano (ed.), *Racism, Ethnicity and the Media in Africa: Mediating Conflict in the Twenty-First Century.* London, I.B. Tauris, 2015.

———. "Review of Dyana Gaye, "Under the Starry Sky." *African Studies Review,* vol. 58, no. 2, pp. 281–283.

———. "Subjectivités en mouvement et déplacements identitaires dans les cinémas africains contemporains." *Cahier Louis-Lumière,* no. 8, 2011.

———. "Migrations and Representations: the cinema of Griot Dani Kouyaté." *In* Cajetan Iheka and Jack Taylor (ed.), *African Migration Narratives. Politics, Race and Space.* Rochester, NY, University of Rochester Press, 2018.

———. "Nuovi modi di rappresentazione nelle cinematografie d'Africa e delle sue diaspore." *La Valle dell'Eden,* n. 32, 2018.

RICOEUR Paul. "L'Identité narrative." *Revue des sciences humaines,* vol. 95, no. 221, 1991, pp. 35–47.

ROUCH Jean. *Situations et tendances actuelles du cinéma africain.* Report written for UNESCO, Paris, 23 August 1961.

ROHTER Larry. "For Filmmaker, Ethiopia's Struggle Is His Own." *New York Times,* 29 March

2010.

ROOF María. "African and Latin American Cinemas: Contexts and Contacts." *In* Françoise Pfaff (ed.), *Focus on African Films,* pp. 241–270. Bloomington, Indiana University Press, 2004.

SAID Edward. "Reflections on Exile." *In* Russell Ferguson, Martha Gever, Trinh T. Minh-ha, Cornel West, *Out There: Marginalization and Contemporary Cultures,* pp. 357–363. Cambridge (MA), MIT Press, 1990.

SAMA Emmanuel. "Le Film africain étranger sur son propre territoire." Écrans d'Afrique, no. 4, 1993.

SÁMA Metta, THOMAS Greg. "Close-up Gallery: *Teza.*" *Black Camera: An International Film Journal,* vol. 4, 2013, pp. 106–133.

SEMBÈNE Ousmane. "Continuons à travailler sans relâche . . ." *In* Catherine Ruelle et al. (eds.), *Afriques 50. Singularités d'un cinéma pluriel.* Paris, L'Harmattan, coll. "Images plurielles," 2005.

SERCEAU Michel. "Le Cinéma d'Afrique noire francophone face au modèle occidental: la rançon du refus." *Nouveau discours du cinéma africain,* no. 18, 1995.

SERVANT Jean-Christophe. "Boom de la vidéo domestique au Nigeria." *Le Monde diplomatique,* 2001.

SMYTH Rosallen. "The Development of British Colonial Film Policy, 1927–1939." *Journal of African History,* vol. 20, no. 3, 1979.

SPECIALE Alessandra. "Abderrahmane Sissako: Pour l'amour du hasard il faut partir." Écrans d'Afrique, no. 23, 1998.

SPECIALE Alessandra. "Le Rêve africain du cinéma italien." *Écrans d'Afrique,* no. 9–10, 1994.

SPIVAK Gayatri Chakravorty. "Love, Cruelty and Cultural Talks in the Hot Peace." *Parallax: A Journal of Metadiscursive Theory and Cultural Practices,* no. 1, 1995, pp. 1–31.

———. *The Post-Colonial Critic: Interviews, Strategies, Dialogues.* New York, Routledge, 1990.

STAM Robert, SHOHAT Ella. "Film Theory and Spectatorship in the Age of the 'Post.'" *In* Christine Gledhill and Linda Williams (eds.), *Reinventing Film Studies,* pp. 381–401. London, Arnold, 2000.

STONEMAN Rod. "Axe Sud-Sud . . . pour un cinéma fait par, avec et pour les Africains." Écrans d'Afrique, no. 5–6, 1993.

TACKELS Bruno. "Où va le métis. Essai sur le cinéma africain." Iris, no. 18, 1995, pp. 47–69.

TAYLOR Charles. "Multiculturalism and the Politics of Recognition." *In* Enzo Colombo and Giovanni Semi (eds.), *Multiculturalismo quotidiano. Le pratiche della differenza.* Milan, Franco Angeli editore, 2007.

TAYLOR Clyde. "Film Reborn in Mozambique: Interview with Pedro Pimenta." *Jump Cut,* no. 28, 1983.

THOMAS Greg. "Close-up: Dragons! George Jackson in the Cinema with Haile Gerima—from Watts Films to *Teza*." *Black Camera: An International Film Journal,* vol. 4, no. 2, 2013, pp. 55–83.

———. "On *Teza,* Cinema, and American Empire: An Interview with Haile Gerima." *Black Camera,* vol. 4, no. 2, 2013.

UKADIKE Nwachukwu Frank. "Nouveau discours du cinéma africain." *Iris,* no. 18, 1995.

ZACKS Stephen A. "The Theoretical Construction of African Cinema." *Research in African Literatures,* vol. 26, no. 3, 1995.

ZEPPENFELD Axel. "Extase." *Les Cahiers du cinéma,* no. 632, 2008.

Africultures and *Black Camera* Dossiers

Africultures, "Cinéma: l'exception africaine" (dossier), no. 45, 2002.

Africultures, "Diaspora: identité plurielle" (dossier), no. 72, 2008.

Africultures, "Métissages: un alibi culturel?" (dossier), no. 62, 2005.

Africultures, "Migrations intimes" (dossier), no. 68, 2006.

Africultures, "Penser l'Afrique: des objets de pensée aux sujets pensants" (dossier), no. 82, 2006.

Africultures, "Postcolonialisme: inventaire et débats" (dossier), no. 28, 2000.

Africultures, "Sembène Ousmane (1923–2007)" (dossier), no. 76, 2008.

Black Camera: An International Film Journal, "Close-up: *Teza*" (dossier), vol. 4, no. 2, 2013.

Electronic Publications

AMARGER Michel. "Entretien avec Sarah Bouyain" [online]. *Sarahbouyain.fr,* 2 February 2011, http://www.sarahbouyain.fr/sarahbouyain/entretien.html.

ASANTE Molefi Kete. "A Quick Reading of Rhetorical Jingoism: Anthony Appiah and His Fallacies" [online]. *Asante.net,* 5 November 2009, http://www.asante.net/articles.

BARLET Olivier. "*Amistad* de Steven Spielberg. Toujours la vieille rengaine!" [online]. *Africultures,* 1 March 1998, http://www.africultures.com/php/?nav=article&no=320.

———. "Entretien avec Balufu Bakupa-Kanyinda. Berlin, février 2000" [online]. *Africultures,* 30 August 2002, http://www.africultures.com/php/index.php?nav=article&no=2476.

———. "Entretien avec Balufu Bakupa-Kanyinda. Paris, avril 1997" [online]. *Africultures,* 30 August 2002, http://www.africultures.com/php/index.php?nav=article&no=2475.

———. "Entretien avec Jean-Pierre Bekolo à propos du *Complot d'Aristote*" [online]. *Africultures,* 30 August 2002, http://www.africultures.com/php/index.php?nav=article&no=2477.

———. "Entretien avec Jean-Pierre Bekolo à propos de *Les Saignantes*. Être à la fois africain et contemporain. Paris, juillet 2005" [online]. *Africultures*, 8 August 2005, http://www.africultures.com/php/?nav=article&no=3944.

———. "Entretien avec Jose [Zeka] Laplaine" [online]. *Africultures*, 30 August 2002, http://africultures.com/entretien-dolivier-barlet-avec-jose-laplaine-2487.

———. "'Je voulais que la peau parle.' Entretien avec Zeka Laplaine" [online]. *Africultures*, 10 October 2003, http://www.africultures.com/php/?nav=article&no=3071.

———. "Le Développement est une diplomatie qui n'a rien à voir avec la qualité. Entretien avec Balufu Bakupa-Kanyinda à propos de *Juju Factory*" [online]. *Africultures*, 14 August 2006, http://www.africultures.com/php/?nav=article&no=4558.

———. "Les Nouvelles Stratégies des cinéastes africains" [online]. *Africultures*, 1 October 2001, http://africultures.com/les-nouvelles-strategies-des-cineastes-africains-1851 / "African Filmmakers' New Strategies" [online], *Africultures*, 30 September 2001, http://africultures.com/african-filmmakers-new-strategies-5505.

———. "*Notre étrangère*, de Sarah Bouyain" [online]. *Africultures*, 2 February 2011, http://www.africultures.com/php/?nav=article&no=9928.

———. "*Petite lumière* d'Alain Gomis (review)" [online]. *Africultures*, 7 March 2003, http://www.africultures.com/php/?nav=article&no=2799.

———. "*Teza* de Haïlé Gerima" [online]. *Africultures*, 26 February 2009, http://www.africultures.com/php/index.php?nav=article&no=8417.

———. "Universel comme le conte. Entretien avec Dani Kouyaté" [online]. *Africultures*, 1 June 2006, http://africultures.com/universel-comme-le-conte-2293.

BOCANDÉ Anne. "Afri' Festival: Belleville Citoyenne Gaël Faye rappe l'exil et le métissage. Entretien avec Gaël Faye" [online]. *Africultures*, 8 June 2012, http://www.africultures.com/php/?nav=article&no=10813.

CADASSE David. "Je suis béninois mais je fais des films français. Entretien avec Jean Odoutan" [online]. *Afrik.com*, 26 August 2004, http://www.afrik.com/article7584.html.

CHALAYE Sylvie. "Acteurs noirs" [online]. *Africultures*, 1 April 2000, http://www.africultures.com/php/?nav=article&no=1310.

Clap Noir, "*L'Afrance* d'Alain Gomis" (film file) [online]. *Clap Noir*, 2006, http://www.clapnoir.org/spip.php?article106.

DIAO Claire. "Entretien avec Sarah Bouyain" [online]. *Afrik.com*, 1 February 2011, https://www.afrik.com/notre-etrangere-eloge-de-la-femme-et-de-l-acculturation.

———. "Le 32ᵉ Festival du Film de Femmes de Créteil rend hommage à Safi Faye" [online]. *Africultures*, 7 April 2010, http://www.africultures.com/php/?nav=article&no=9413.

DIOP Boris Boubacar. "Identité africaine et mondialisation" [online]. *Afrik.com*, 1 October

2007, https://www.afrik.com/identite-africaine-et-mondialisation.

DUBUISSON François-Xavier. "'Je me sens redevable de mes poètes.' Entretien avec Balufu Bakupa-Kanyinda" [online]. *Africultures*, 12 December 2009, http://www.africultures. com/php/?nav=article&no=9073.

ELLERSON Beti. "Interview with Claude Haffner" [online]. *African Women in Cinema Blog*, http://africanwomenincinema.blogspot.fr/2012/03/claude-haffner-black-here-white-there.html.

HONNETH Axel. "Reconnaissance et justice" [online]. *Le passant*, no. 38, January–February 2002, http://www.passant-ordinaire.org/revue/38–349.asp#.

KABORÉ Gaston. "Masterclass de Gaston Kaboré au festival de Cannes 2007" [online]. *Africultures*, 20 June 2007, http://www.africultures.com/php/?nav=article&no=6627.

MANSOURI Hassouna. "Haile Gerima: Cinema of Disillusion. Interview with Haile Gerima" [online]. *Africine.org*, http://www.africine.org/?menu=art&no=8492.

MBEKA PHOBA Monique. "'Les Nouvelles Générations de cinéastes ont moins de lien avec la Fepaci que la nôtre.' Entretien avec Charles Mensah, président de la Fepaci." *Africultures*, 8 July 2009, http://www.africultures.com/php/index.php?nav=article&no=8746.

MBEMBE Achille. "Afropolitanisme" [online]. *Africultures*, 26 December 2005, http://www.africultures.com/php/?nav=article&no=4248.

MOLLO OLINGA Jean-Marie. "Nous ne sommes pas allés dans les guichets traditionnels. Entretien de Jean-Marie Mollo Olinga avec Balufu Bakupa-Kanyinda, cinéaste" [online]. *Africine.org*, 30 August 2008, http://www.africine.org/?menu=art&no=8049.

PHILIPPOT Vital. "Entretien avec Dani Kouyaté à propos de *Sia, le rêve du python*" [online]. *Sialefilm*, January 2002, http://www.sialefilm.com/presse/007-fr.html.

RICCI Daniela. "Les Cinémas contemporains d'Afrique et de la diaspora: films transnationaux et mise en scène de l'entre deux.' Le cas de Rage." *Têtes Chercheuses*, 25 March 2013, http://teteschercheuses.hypotheses.org/823.

SAMA Emmanuel. "*Notre étrangère* de Sarah Bouyain (France/Burkina Faso). Les déchirures du métissage" [online]. *Africine.org*, 23 April 2011, http://www.africine. org/?menu=art&no=10083.

SELASI Taiye. "Bye-Bye Babar" [online]. *LIP Magazine*, 3 March 2005, http://thelip. robertsharp.co.uk/?p=76.

SITCHET Christine. "'La Structure narrative est à la base de tout.' Entretien avec Balufu Bakupa-Kanyinda" [online]. *Africultures*, 12 May 2001, http://www.africultures.com/ php/?nav=article&no=8951.

THÉOBALD Fréderic. "Abderrahmane Sissako, réalisateur de 'Timbuktu': 'L'être humain est capable de remords.'" *La Vie*, no. 3201, 9 December 2014, http://www.lavie.fr/culture/

cinema.

TROIS COULEURS. "Interview avec Xavier Dolan" [online], 28 September 2010, http://www.mk2.com/troiscouleurs.

VAN PEEBLES Melvin, BEAUCHEZ Jérôme. "La Fierté noire en images: une infra-politique du film" [online]. *Cultures & Conflits,* no. 89, Spring 2013, http://conflits.revues.org/18674#quotation.

Video and Documentary Film Resources

BEKOLO Jean-Pierre. *Les Origines de la Françafrique.* Cameroon, 2010.

BENQUET Patrick. *Françafrique.* France, 2010, 68 min.

BOUGHEDIR Férid. *Caméra d'Afrique.* Tunisia, 1983, 99 min.

CHALLOUF Mohmed. *Tahar Cheriaa, à l'ombre du baobab.* Tunisia, 2011, 26 min.

CHIMAMANDA Adichie. "The Danger of a Single Story: Chimamanda Adichie on TED.com" [online]. Technology, Entertainment and Design (TED) Annual Conference, July 2009, http://www.ted.com/talks/chimamanda_adichie_the_danger_of_a_single_story.html.

DIAWARA Manthia. Édouard Glissant, un monde en relation. United States, 2009, 52 min.

KOTLARSKI François, MÜNCH Eric. *Les Fespakistes.* France/Burkina Faso, 2001, 52 min.

KOUYATÉ Dani. *Joseph Ki-Zerbo. Identités/Identité pour l'Afrique.* Burkina Faso, 2005, 52 min.

LEFAIT Philippe. "Mahamat Saleh Haroun sur son film 'Abouna.'" *Des mots de minuit,* 9 October 2002, http://www.ina.fr/video/I04215696.

Films Cited

Adwa, an African Victory (Haile Gerima; Negod Gwad Productions/Mypheduh Films; Ethiopia/United States, 1999, 97 min.).

À nous deux, France (Désiré Ecaré; France/Ivory Coast, 1970, 61 min.).

Absence (L') (Mama Keita; Kinterfin; France/Senegal/Guinea, 2009, 84 min.).

Afrance, (L') (Alain Formose Gomis; Mille et Une Productions; France/Senegal, 2001, 90 min.).

Afrique, je te plumerai . . . (Jean-Marie Teno; Les Films du Raphia; France/Cameroon, 1992, 88 min., doc.).

Afrique Mon Afrique (Idrissa Ouédraogo; La Sept Arte/Noé Productions Int./Polygram Audiovisuel; France, 1994, 52 min.).

Afrique sur Seine (Robert Caristan, Jacques Mélo Kane, Mamadou Sarr, Paulin Soumanou Vieyra; Groupe Africain du cinéma; France, 1955, 21 min.).

Afrique vue par (L') (Balufu Bakupa-Kanyinda, Rachid Bouchareb, Nouri Bouzid, Sol de Carvalho, Zézé Gamboa, Flora Gomes, Gaston Kaboré, Mama Keïta, Teddy Mattera, Abderrahmane Sissako; Laith Média; Algeria, 2009).

Afr@digital (Balufu Bakupa-Kanyinda; Akangbé Productions/Dipanda Yo!; France/DRC, 2002, 52 min., doc.).

After Winter: Sterling Brown (Haile Gerima; Ethiopia, 1985, 60 min.).

Ahmed (Alain Formose Gomis; Gindou Cinéma; France, 2006, 24 min.).

Allah Tantou (David Achkar; Guinea, 1990, 52 min.).

Alpha (Ola Balogun; Nigeria, 1972, 90 min.).

Amadi (Ola Balogun; Nigeria, 1975, 103 min.).

Amistad (Steven Spielberg; DreamWorks SKG/HBO Films; United States, 1997, 152 min.).

Andalucia (Alain Formose Gomis; Mallerich Films Paco Poch/Mille et Une Productions/MLK Producciones; Spain/France, 2007, 90 min.).

Anywhere Else (Asmara Beraki; Czech Republic/United States, 2012, 45 min.).

Article 15 bis (Balufu Bakupa-Kanyinda; Akangbé Productions/Dipanda Yo!; France/DRC, 1999, 15 min.).

Ashes and Embers (Haile Gerima; Mypheduh Films; Ethiopia/United States, 1982, 129 min.).

Aventure en France (Jean Paul N'Gassa; Cameroon, 1962, 26 min.).

Badou Boy (Djibril Diop Mambéty; Studio Kankourama; Senegal, 1970, 65 min. [1965, 20 min.].

Balufu Bakupa-Kanyinda (Issaka Compaoré; Sahel Films Productions; Burkina Faso, 2011, 26 min., doc.).

Bamako (Abderrahmane Sissako; Archipel 33/Arte France/Chinguitty Films (ex Duo Films)/ Louverture Film; France/Mali/United States, 2006, 118 min.).

Bamboozled (Spike Lee; 40 Acres & a Mule Filmworks; United States, 2000, 135 min.).

Bongo Libre (Balufu Bakupa-Kanyinda; Akangbé Productions/Dipanda Yo!; France/DRC, 1999, 26 min., doc.).

Borom Sarret (Sembène Ousmane; Senegal, 1963, 20 min.).

Boubou-cravate (Daniel Kamwa; France/Cameroon, 1972, 29 min.).

Burning an Illusion (Menelik Shabazz; BFI; UK, 1981, 105 min.).

Bush Mama (Haile Gerima; United States, 1976, 98 min.).

Bye bye Africa (Mahamat Saleh Haroun; Les Histoires Weba/Les Productions de la Lanterne; France/Chad, 1998, 86 min.).

C'est dimanche! (Samir Guesmi; Kaléo Films; France, 2007, 30 min.).

Chez les cannibales (Martin and Osa Johnson; France, 192–).

Chez les buveurs de sang: le vrai visage de l'Afrique (Baron Gourgaud; France, 1931, 57 min.).

Chez les chasseurs de têtes des mers du Sud (Martin and Osa Johnson; France, 1923).

Chez les mangeurs d'hommes (André-Paul Antoine and Robert Lugeon; France, 1928, 74 min. or 60 min.).

Chien andalou (Un) (*Un perro andaluz*) (Luis Buñuel; France, 1929, 16 min.).

Child of Resistance (Haile Gerima; United States, 1972, 36 min.).

Chronique d'une disparition (*Segell Ikhtifà*) (Elia Suleiman; Dhat production/Elia Suleiman; Palestine, 1996, 84 min.).

Cinematografías de Africa. Un encuentro con sus protagonistas (Gabriel Rosenthal; Casa Africa;

Spain, 2010, 58 min., doc.).

Coffee Colored Children (Ngozi Onwurah; UK, 1988, 15 min.).

Comédie exotique (Kitia Touré; Ivory Coast, 1984, 92 min.).

Complot d'Aristote (Le) (Jean-Pierre Bekolo; BFI/ Framework International/JBA Production; France/UK/Zimbabwe, 1996, 72 min.).

Concerto pour un exil (Désiré Ecaré; France/Ivory Coast, 1968, 42 min.).

Contras City (Djibril Diop Mambéty; Kankourama; Senegal, 1968, 21 min.).

Couleur café (Une) (Henri Duparc; Centre Cinématographique Marocain/Focale 13/Les Films Henri Duparc; Morocco/Ivory Coast, 1997, 95 min.).

Cri du cœur (Le) (Les Films de l'Avenir/Les Films de la Plaine; France/Burkina Faso, 1994, 86 min.).

Cry Freedom (Richard Attenborough; Universal Pictures/Marble Arch Productions; UK, 1987, 157 min.).

Damier, Papa National oyé! (Le) (Balufu Bakupa-Kanyinda; Dipanda Yo!/Centrale Productions & Cenaci/Myriapodus; France/DRC/Gabon, 1996, 40 min.) .

Daratt (Mahamat Saleh Haroun; Arte France cinéma/Chinguitty Films (ex-Duo Films)/ Entre Chien et Loup/Goi-Goi Productions/Illuminations Films/Pyramide international; Belgium/France/UK/Chad, 2006, 95 min.).

Death of Tarzan (The) (Haile Gerima, 1966, 3 min.).

Delwendé (Pierre Yaméogo; Dunia Production/Les Films de l'Espoir; France, 2005, 90 min.).

Des Étoiles (Dyana Gaye; Andolfi Production/Centrale Electrique/Cinékap/Rouge International; France/Senegal, 2013, 88 min.).

Dez dias com os guerrilheiros de Moçambique (Franco Cigarini; Italy/Mozambique, 1967).

Dix mille ans de cinéma (Balufu Bakupa-Kanyinda; Dipanda Yo!/Scolopendra Productions; DRC/France, 1991, 13 min., doc.).

Djib (Jean Odoutan; 45rdlc/Tabou-Tabac Films; Benin/France, 2000, 80 min.).

Donoma (Djinn Carrenard; Donoma Guerilla Prod; France, 2010, 135 min.).

Do the Right Thing (Spike Lee; 40 Acres & a Mule Filmworks; United States, 1989, 120 min.).

Échappée belle (Emilei Cherpitel; ElianeAntoinette Prod; France, 2015, 76 min.).

Emitai (Sembène Ousmane; Filmi Doomireew; Senegal, 1971, 95 min.).

En attendant le bonheur (Heremakono) (Abderrahmane Sissako; Arizona Films/Arte France/ Chinguitty Films/Duo Films; United States/France, 2002, 95 min.).

Enfant (L') (Jean-Pierre and Luc Dardenne; Les Films du Fleuve; Belgium, 2005, 95 min.).

Enfants du Blanc (Les) (Sarah Bouyain; Athenaïse/Pyramide Films/Stalker Films; France/ Burkina Faso/Switzerland, 2000, 60 min., doc.).

Escadron blanc (L') (*Lo squadrone bianco*) (Augusto Genina; Italy, 1936, 100 min.).

Et la neige n'était plus (Ababacar Samb Makharam; Baobab Films; Senegal, 1965, 22 min.).

Exilé (L') (Oumarou Ganda; Cabas-Films; Niger, 1980, 78 min.).

Ezra (Aduaka I. Newton; Arte France cinéma/Cinéfacto, Granite Filmworks/Sunday Morning Productions; France/UK, 2006, 110 min.).

Faat Kine (Sembène Ousmane; Filmi Doomireew; Senegal, 1999, 120 min.).

Femme sous influence (Une) (*A Woman under the Influence*) (John Cassavetes; Faces; United States, 1976, 155 min.).

Fleuve (Le) (Mama Keita; Renaissance Films/Renaissance Productions; United States/France, 2003, 90 min.).

Funeral (Newton I. Aduaka; Chaya Films; France, 2003, 12 min.).

Grigris (Mahamat Saleh Haroun; France 3 Cinéma/Goi-Goi Productions/Pili Films; France/ Chad, 2013, 101 min.).

Haine (La) (Mathieu Kassovitz; Lazennec Productions/La Sept Cinéma/Studio Canal/Kasso Inc. Productions; France, 1995, 96 min.).

Handsworth Songs (John Akomfrah; Black Audio Film Collective; UK, 1987, 60 min., doc.).

Harvest: 3000 Years (*Mirt Sost Shi*) (Haile Gerima; Ethiopia, 1976, 150 min.).

Heritage Africa! (Kwah Ansah; Film Africa LTD; Ghana, 1989, 125 min.).

Homme du Niger (L') (Jacques de Baroncelli; France, 1940, 102 min.).

Homme qui crie (Un) (Mahamat Saleh Haroun; Entre Chien et Loup/Goi-Goi Productions/Pili Films; Belgium/France/Chad, 2010, 100 min.).

Hour Glass (Haile Gerima; United States, 1972, 13 min.).

Husbands (John Cassavetes; Faces; United States, 1970, 154 min.).

Il va pleuvoir sur Conakry (Cheick Fantamady Camara; COP-Films/Djoliba Production; France, 2006, 115 min.).

Identité (Pierre-Marie Dong; Gabon, 1972, 90 min.).

Identité malsaine (Amog Lemra; France, 2010, 70 min.).

Imaginaires en exil. Cinq cinéastes d'Afrique se racontent (Daniela Ricci; France, 2013, 52 min., doc.).

Immatriculation Temporaire (Gahité Fofana; Bafila Films/Leo & Cie; Guinea, 2001, 77 min.).

Imperfect Journey (Haile Gerima; First Run/Icarus Films (FRIF); Ethiopia, 1994, 88 min.).

Jardin de papa (Le) (Zeka Laplaine; Les Histoires Weba; France/DRC, 2004, 75 min.).

Joseph Ki-Zerbo. Identités, Identité pour l'Afrique (Dani Kouyaté; Centre d'Études et de Développement Africain [CEDA]; Burkina Faso, 2005, 52 min., doc.).

Juju Factory (Balufu Bakupa-Kanyinda; Akangbé Productions/BlackStarLine/Canal+ Horizons/ Dipanda Yo!; France/Belgium/DRC, 2007, 97 min.).

Keïta! L'héritage du griot (Dani Kouyaté; Les films de la Lanterne/Sahélis Production; France/

Burkina Faso, 1995, 94 min.).

Kinshasa Palace (Zeka Laplaine; Bakia Films/Les Histoires Weba; France/DRC, 2006, 75 min.).

Lebess (Hedy Krissane; Associazione Culturale Art Studio; Italy, 2003, 15 min.).

Leçon du cinéma (La) (Albert Mongita; Congo, 1951).

Léon (Luc Besson; Les Films du Dauphin/Gaumont; France, 1994, 110 min.).

Lettre paysanne (Kaddu Beykat) (Safi Faye; Production Safi Faye; Senegal, 1975, 98 min.).

Lieux saints (Jean-Marie Teno; Les Films du Raphia/Raphia Films; France/Cameroon, 2009, 70 min.).

Lincoln (Steven Spielberg; DreamWorks SKG/Reliance Entertainment/Participant Media/ Amblin Entertainment/Parkes-MacDonald Productions/Touchstone Pictures; United States, 2012, 150 min.).

Little Senegal (Rachid Bouchareb; 3B Productions/Canal+/France 2 Cinéma; France, 2001, 98 min.).

Living in Bondage (Chris Obi-Rapu; production Kenneth Nnebue; Nigeria, 1992, 120 min.).

Love Brewed in the African Pot (Kwaw Ansah; Film Africa LTD; Ghana, 1981, 125 min.).

Luta continua (A) (Robert Van Lierop; Mozambique, 1972, 32 min.).

Mama Aloko (Jean Odoutan; 45rdlc/Tabou-Tabac Films; France/Benin, 2001, 90 min.).

Mandat (Le) (Mandabi) (Sembène Ousmane; Comptoir Français du Film Production (CFFP)/ Filmi Doomireew; France/Senegal, 1968, 105 min.).

Mean Streets (Martin Scorsese; Warner Bros/Taplin-Perry-Scorsese Productions; United States, 1973, 110 min.).

Medan vi Lever (While We Live) (Dany Kouyaté; DFM/Film i Skåne/Way Creative Films; Sweden/Gambia, 2016, 91 min.).

Mémoires d'immigrés (Yamina Benguigui; Bandits Productions; France, 1997, 160 min., doc.).

Mississippi Burning (Alan Parker; Orion Pictures/Production Frederick Zollo & Robert F. Colesberry; United States, 1988, 128 min.).

Monangambé (Sarah Maldoror; Angola/Algeria, 1969, 19 min.).

Moolaadé (Sembène Ousmane; Centre Cinématographique Marocain (CCM)/Cinétéléfilms/ Direction de la Cinématographie Nationale du Burkina Faso (DCN)/Filmi Doomireew/ Les Films Terre Africaine; Burkina Faso/Cameroon/Morocco/Senegal/Tunisia, 2004, 124 min.).

Morbayassa, le serment de Koumba (Cheick Fantamady Camara; COP-films/Djoliba Production; France, 2015, 120 min.).

Mort de style colonial, (Une): l'assassinat de Patrice Lumumba (Thomas Giefer; ICTV Solférino/ Quartier Latin Media; France/DRC, 2008, 52 min., doc.).

Mortu nega (Flora Gomes; Instituto Nacional do Cinema e Audiovisual; Guinea-Bissau, 1987,

85 min.).

Mouramani (Mamadou Touré; France, 1953, 23 min.).

Musulman rigolo (Le) (Georges Méliès; France, 1897).

Nationalité immigré (Sidney Sokhona; Comité du Film Ethnographique/Groupe de Recherches et d'Essais Cinématographiques (GREC)/SERDDAV; France, 1975, 90 min.).

N'gunu N'gunu Kan (Rumeurs de guerre) (Soussaba Cissé; Mali, 2013, 114 min.).

Niaye (Sembène Ousmane; Filmi Doomireew; Senegal, 1964, 35 min.).

Nikki de Saint Phalle (Peter Schamoni; Germany, 1995, 95 min., doc.).

Nine Muses (John Akomfrah; Smoking Dog Films/UK Film Council; UK, 2011, 94 min., doc.).

Noire de . . . (La) (Sembène Ousmane; Filmi Doomireew; Senegal, 1966, 60 min.).

Noire ici, blanche là-bas (Claude Haffner; Natives at Large/Néon Rouge Production; South Africa/Belgium, 2012, 52 min., doc.).

Notre étrangère (The Place in Between) (Sarah Bouyain; Athenaïse/Abissia Productions; France/Burkina Faso, 2010, 82 min.).

Nous aussi avons marché sur la lune (Balufu Bakupa-Kanyinda; Dipanda Yo!/Laith Media; DRC/Algeria, 2009, 16 min. Part of the *L'Afrique vu par . . .* collection).

On the Edge (Newton I. Aduaka; Granite Filmworks; UK, 1998, 28 min.).

One Man's Show (Newton I. Aduaka; Granit films; France, 2013, 75 min.).

One More Vote for Obama (Mama Keita; Laith Media/OverEasy Productions-Soho; Algeria/United States, 2009, 13 min. Part of the *L'Afrique vu par . . .* collection).

Onzième commandement (Le) (Choisis-toi un ami) (Mama Keita; Phenix Production; France, 1997, 80 min.).

Otomo (Frieder Schlaich; Filmgalerie 451/ZDF; Germany, 1999, 84 min.).

Oubliés (Les) (Los olvidados) (Luis Buñuel; France, 1950, 80 min.).

Paris selon Moussa (Cheick Doukouré; Bako Prod./Films de l'Alliance; France/Guinea, 2003, 97 min.).

Paris XY (Zeka Laplaine; Bakia Films/Les Histoires Weba; France/DRC, 2001, 80 min.).

Passage du milieu (Le) (Guy Deslauriers; Les Films du Dorlis/Les Films du Raphia/France Ô/Kreol Productions; France/Martinique, 1999, 85 min.).

Passante (La) (Safi Faye; Senegal, 1972, 10 min.).

Pays des sorciers et de la mort (Au) (Marquis de Wavrin; Belgium, 1933, doc.).

Petite Lumière (Alain Gomis; Mille et Une Productions; France, 2003, 15 min.).

Pièces d'identités (Mweze Dieudonné Ngangura; Films Sud/Sol'œil Films; Belgium/DRC, 1998, 93 min.).

Pim-pim tché: toast de vie (Jean Odoutan; Tabou-Tabac Film/45rdlc; 2010, 84 min.).

Pneus gonflés (Les) (Emmanuel Lubalu; Congo, 1953).

Point de vue du lion (*Le*) (Didier Awadi; Studio Sankara; Senegal, 2011, 72 min., doc.).

Pour la nuit (Isabelle Boni-Claverie; Neon Productions; France, 2004, 27 min.).

Princes noirs de Saint-Germain-des-Prés (*Les*) (Ben Diogaye Bèye; France/Senegal, 1975, 14 min.).

Pressure (Horace Ové; BFI; UK, 1975, 136 min.).

Promesse (*La*) (Jean-Pierre and Luc Dardenne; Les Films du fleuve/Touza Production/Samsa Films/Touza films/RTBF; Belgium/France/Luxembourg, 1996, 94 min.).

Quartier Mozart (Jean-Pierre Bekolo Obama; IDE-Akvideo; France, 1992, 79 min.).

Qui a peur de Ngugi Wa Thiong'o (*Who's Afraid of Ngugi?*) (Manthia Diawara; Mali, 2006, 86 min., doc.).

Radio (*La*) (Armand Brice Tchikamen and Fidèle Koffi; Predartor Studio; Ivory Coast, 2012, 15 min.).

Ragazzi (Mama Keita; Performance Company; France, 1991, 85 min.).

Rage (Newton I. Aduaka; Granite Filmworks Ltd; UK, 1999, 93 min.).

Rasalama maritiora (*La mort de Rasalama*) (Raberojo Philippe; Madagascar, 1937).

Réalisateur nègre (*Le*) (Jean Odoutan; 45 rdlc; France, 1997, 7 min.).

Rengaine (Rachid Djaïdani; Or Production/Les Films des Tournelles; France, 2012, 75 min.).

Retour d'un aventurier (*Le*) (Moustapha Alassane; Argos Films; France/Niger, 1996, 34 min.).

Roger Milla, le lion des lions (Balufu Bakupa-Kanyinda; Dipanda Yo!; DRC, 2006, doc.).

Roma (Federico Fellini; Ultra Film/Les Artistes Associés; Italy/France, 1972, 113 min.).

Saignantes (*Les*) (Jean-Pierre Bekolo; Jean-Pierre Bekolo SARL; Cameroon, 2004, 92 min.).

Sambizanga (Sarah Maldoror; Angola, 1972, 104 min.).

Sankofa (Haile Gerima; Negod Gwad Productions/WDR/NDR/National Commission of Culture (Ghana)/DiProDi; Germany/Burkina Faso/Ethiopia/United States, 1993, 124 min.).

Saaraba (Amadou Saalum Seck [dir. and prod.]; Senegal, 1988, 86 min.).

Sarraounia (Med Hondo; Direction de la Cinématographie Nationale du Burkina Faso/Les Films Soleil Ô; Burkina Faso/France/Mauritania, 1986, 120 min.).

Scipion l'Africain (*Scipione l'africano*) (Carmine Gallone, Italy, 1937, 107 min.).

Sexe, gombo et beurre salé (Mahamet-Saleh Haroun; film TV/Agat Films & Cie; France, 2007, 81 min.).

Shadows (John Cassavetes; Lion International; United States, 1959 [second version], 81, 84, or 87 min.).

Slam (Marc Levin; Off Line; United States, 1998, 100 min.).

Souvenirs encombrants d'une femme de ménage (Dani Kouyaté; Les Productions de la Lanterne; France/Guadeloupe, 2008, 52 min., doc.).

Sous la croix du Sud (*Sotto la Croce del Sud*) (Guido Brignone; Italy, 1938, 81 min.).

Statues meurent aussi (Les) (Chris Marker and Alain Resnais; Présence Africaine; France, 1953, 30 min., doc.).

Taafe Fanga (Adama Drabo; Centre National de la Production Cinématographique du Mali/ Projet Eine Welt/Taare Films/ZDF; Mali/Germany, 1997, 98 min.).

Tam-tam à Paris (Thérèse Sita Bella; Cameroon, 1963, 30 min.).

Testament (John Akomfrah; Black Audio Film Collective; Ghana/UK, 1988, 76 min.).

Tey (Aujourd'hui) (Alain Formose Gomis; Granit Films/Maia Cinema/Agora Film/Cinekap; France/Senegal, 2011, 86 min.).

Teza (Haile Gerima; Pandora Film Produktion/GmbH/Negod-Gwad Production/Unlimited; Germany/United States/France/Ethiopia, 2008, 140 min.).

Thomas Sankara (Balufu Bakupa-Kanyinda; Channel Four/Dipanda Yo!/Myriapodus; UK/DRC/ France, 1991, 26 min., doc.).

Through the Door of No Return (Shirikiana Aina; Mypheduh Films; United States, 1997, 80 min.).

Tilai (Idrissa Ouédraogo; Les Films de l'Avenir/Waka Films/Rhea Films; Burkina Faso/France, 1990, 81 min.).

Timbuktu (Abderrahmane Sissako; Les Films du Worso/Dune Vision/Arches Film/Arte France Cinéma/Orange Studio; France, 2014, 100 min.).

Touki Bouki (Djibril Diop Mambéty; Cinegrit; Senegal, 1973, 87 min.).

Trop Noire pour être Française? (Isabelle Boni-Claverie; Quark Productions; France, 2015, 53 min., doc.).

Tourbillons (Alain Formose Gomis; Movimento Production; France, 1999, 13 min.).

Twelve Years a Slave (Steve McQueen; Fox Searchlight Pictures; United States, 2013, 133 min.).

Vacances au pays (Jean-Marie Teno; Arte Deutschland (ZDF/ARD)/Les Films du Raphia/ Zweites Deutsches Fernsehen; 2000).

Valse des gros derrières (La) (Jean Odoutan; 45rdlc/Tabou-Tabac Films; France/Benin, 2004, 72 min.).

Venceremos (Dragutin Popovic; Mozambique, 1966, doc.).

Viva Frelimo! (Leonid Maksimov and Yuri Yegorov; Mozambique, 1971, 13 min., doc.).

Vie sur terre (La) (Abderrahmane Sissako; La Sept Arte/Haut et Court; France/Mali, 1998, 61 min.).

Watt (Balufu Bakupa-Kanyinda; Dipanda Yo!/Akangbé Productions; DRC/France, 1999, 19 min.).

Wilmington 10–USA 10,000 (Haile Gerima; United States, 1978, 120 min., doc.).

Xala (Sembène Ousmane; Société nationale de cinématographie/Les Films Doomireew; Senegal, 1974, 128 min.).

Yaaba (Idrissa Ouédraogo; Arcadia Films/Thelma Film/Les Films de l'Avenir/Télévision Suisse
Romande/Zweites Deutsches Fernsehen/La Sept; France/Switzerland/Burkina Faso, 1989,
90 min.).

Yeelen (Souleymane Cissé; Les Films Cissé/Atriascop/Midas; Mali/Burkina Faso/France/
Germany, 1987, 104 min.).

Young Soul Rebels (Isaac Julien; BFI/Film Four International; UK, 1991, 102 min.).

Index